Becomi...

His First Two Lives

*John,
Thank you for your kindness.
I appreciate the way you have
helped and encouraged me.
     Kraig "Cameron"*

As told to
Tammy Vaughn by Joshua

outskirts press

Becoming Joshua
His First Two Lives
All Rights Reserved.
Copyright © 2022 Tammy Vaughn & Joshua
v4.0

The opinions expressed in this manuscript are solely the opinions of the author and do not represent the opinions or thoughts of the publisher. The author has represented and warranted full ownership and/or legal right to publish all the materials in this book.

This book may not be reproduced, transmitted, or stored in whole or in part by any means, including graphic, electronic, or mechanical without the express written consent of the publisher except in the case of brief quotations embodied in critical articles and reviews.

Outskirts Press, Inc.
http://www.outskirtspress.com

ISBN: 978-1-9772-5329-3

Cover Photo © 2022 Joshua Illustrations - Joshua.
All rights reserved - used with permission.

Outskirts Press and the "OP" logo are trademarks belonging to Outskirts Press, Inc.

PRINTED IN THE UNITED STATES OF AMERICA

Use Your QR App
To Learn More Today
www.becomingjoshua.org

*For those who have been rejected by their
family, friends, and communities.
May they find acceptance and love.*

Author's Note

I HAD BEEN working at Lansing Community College in the Learning Commons for a little more than ten years when I first met Joshua. He was introduced as a new Supplemental Instruction leader, and that was all I knew until he began to see me for Mathematics tutoring in the spring of 2019. When we stepped away from graphing and equations for a few minutes, we began to get to know each other. In addition to his conversion to Christianity in Iran, he shared he enjoyed writing and was working on a book about his life. I shared that I was working on a novel and sent him a few chapters.

We worked together again during the summer when he took his next math course, and he asked if I would like to read his book and give an opinion. I was hesitant at first. I don't think of myself as being associated with any religious group and I had no knowledge of Iran or what it might be like to be a refugee. I didn't know what I could contribute.

As the summer progressed, I began to read, and Joshua told me about his search for a ghostwriter. The further I went, the more I wanted to know. I began to write down questions that arose while I was reading. By the end of the summer, I had pages of questions. I wanted to know more about people and places. I wanted to know more about what was behind the events that I read about and the events that were only hinted at. Even though I didn't think of it as 'my kind of book' I was hooked. On the last day of the semester, I handed Joshua my twenty pages of questions and said if he wanted my help as a writer I would be honored to help.

I never expected that he would take me up on it. When he did, I wasn't sure that I could do it because it was such a departure from anything I'd written before. Through the whole process, Joshua trusted and encouraged me. He believed in my ability to do it, sometimes more than I did and for that I will always be grateful.

This book is Joshua's story as he told it to me over the course of hundreds of hours of interviews over a year and a half. The names of people and places have been changed to protect the lives those who are still in Iran, and to protect the anonymity of those who now reside elsewhere in the world.

Table of Contents

Chapter One.. 3
Chapter Two 12
Chapter Three 26
Chapter Four.. 38
Chapter Five 47
Chapter Six... 55
Chapter Seven 69
Chapter Eight 82
Chapter Nine 92
Chapter Ten 104
Chapter Eleven 114
Chapter Twelve.. 125
Chapter Thirteen 133
Chapter Fourteen 143
Chapter Fifteen 154
Chapter Sixteen 167
Chapter Seventeen.. 182
Chapter Eighteen 194
Chapter Nineteen 204
Chapter Twenty... 217
Chapter Twenty-One... 225
Chapter Twenty-Two... 236
Chapter Twenty-Three.. 245
Chapter Twenty-Four.. 256
Chapter Twenty-Five... 265
Chapter Twenty-Six... 274

Part I
Iran

Chapter One

IRAN IS MY home.

I was born in the city of Arima in Northern Iran in 1982, three years after the Islamic Republic overthrew the patriotic monarchy in the Iranian Revolution. I grew up in the shadow of Ayatollah Ruhollah Khomeini, knowing Iran only as a theocracy where the principles of Islamic Law were enforced by the full might of the state. I learned what that meant when I was seven years old.

On that August day, I set off for school from my family's home in one of the most desirable neighborhoods in the center of the city. My older brother left earlier, so I walked through the tree-lined streets alone in my school uniform, my backpack slung over my shoulders. Arima, like most of Iran, isn't in the desert, but arid heat still gathers and settles in the summer months. I lifted the bag away from my body in hopes a lazy breeze would tickle across my sweaty back as I hurried across the sunny patches and savored the cool pools of shade created by white mulberry and pomegranate trees. My mind was occupied with the most serious concern I had; what I would receive in trade for the lunch my mother had packed for me.

My school was across the street from a Shia mosque. As I got closer to my destination the bright, top note of laughter from arriving children was overshadowed by a base angry sound. Ahead there was a crowd of men in a close packed semicircle in front of the mosque shouting at someone or something that was hidden from me. Their words were studded with jagged edges, their shoulders tight, their fists clenched.

The other children, my friends among them, had gathered in groups outside the school to savor their last few minutes of freedom before the day began. They were oblivious to the anger that suffused the air only a short distance away. I turned away from them, crossed the street, and made my way around the edge of the incipient mob. There was no gap between the men, so I bent down and looked through their legs at a mound of dirt with a person trapped in the center of it. Only their white-shrouded head and shoulders were visible above the raw soil. Patches of vivid blood soaked through the cloth. The figure cried out, pleading for mercy. It was a woman.

The crowd of bearded men shouted words I didn't understand, but I recognized the harsh tone of insult. I was transfixed by the way she twisted and arched like a pale, bloodied worm inside the confines of the earth. The disconnected shouts united into a chant. She twisted left and right, her back arched and taut like a bowstring. A man picked up a broken brick from a pile next to the crowd. He stepped toward her, his words garbled by the venom they were laced with. Her desperate cries relegated to the spaces between the expressions of anger.

He hurled the brick with the full force of his outrage. It connected with her head with a sickening crack. There was a truncated cry and she went limp and still. Fresh blood bloomed from under the cloth.

I stood there, eyes wide. The stain spread and the breeze teased the loose folds of the shroud, but the woman didn't move. A chill rolled over me. I backed away, my eyes on the circle of men, but all I could see was that still shrouded figure. My heel hit the sidewalk. I turned and fled across the street, into school.

"Come on, you're going to be late," one of my classmates said as he trotted past me, heading for the school's outdoor courtyard for morning assembly.

I followed him, the sounds and sights of what I had just seen tangled together with the chattering children and teachers giving

CHAPTER ONE

directions to quiet down. I took my place in line with my classmates.

All around me, the other students had formed straight lines too, one behind the other, facing a raised platform and waiting for the school principal to come on the loudspeaker and make the day's announcements. This was the way we began every school day, but that day it just washed over me. Who had she been? Why had they been so angry at her? There were other questions too, questions I didn't have the words for. To kill someone, to murder them in the street, that was wrong. That much I knew.

The announcements finished as they always did. The principal stood up straight, took a deep breath, and shouted, "Death to America! Death to Israel!"

It was a ritual that was repeated each day at every school across Iran. If I didn't shout the words, I would be questioned about why I refused and what my family believed. Even at seven I knew the risk of staying quiet. I chanted the familiar words surrounded by a courtyard full of students who did the same.

A reading from the Qur'an followed in Arabic, a language I was only beginning to learn. That day I didn't even try to follow along. I just stood there and pretended to pay attention while, unbidden, my mind conjured the crack of brick on bone and bright red blood soaking through white cloth.

At the end of the reading we walked over American and Israeli flags that were painted on the floor to get to our classrooms. The words the men had been shouting still rang in my ears.

There was no way I would be able to concentrate on my lessons until I found out what the men were saying. When I got to my classroom, I asked my teacher, "What's 'whore'?"

Shock and fear passed over her face before she could hide it. She shook her head and tried to infuse her voice with firm authority. "Don't repeat that word. Take your seat so we can get started."

It wasn't an answer, but I couldn't press the point. My lessons were a blur. During a break between classes I went to find my older brother. I described the scene and asked what the word meant. He

5

told me it was a bad word as he and his friends ran toward the school gates. They wanted to see for themselves.

The way her body had twisted as she struggled. The impact of the brick. Those were the ghosts that haunted me during the quiet moments throughout the day.

When I got home, my mother was waiting. My story spilled out in a tangle of words as I tried to tell her everything at once. She told me to slow down, to take a deep breath, to start at the beginning, but I couldn't. Eventually she gave up and waited until I sputtered to silence. I expected shock or revulsion, but there was none of that. It was as though I hadn't just described a violent death.

"She must have done something very bad." My mother didn't meet my eyes. She thought the bound woman had deserved such a horrible fate. She was my mother, I couldn't imagine that she was wrong, but each time I closed my eyes, I saw the bright blood on the white cloth.

When my father got home that evening I stood and waited for his permission to speak. That was his rule and even for something like this I didn't dare break it. I shifted from foot to foot under the weight of the story until he acknowledged me. My story flooded out again in no better order than the first time.

"She probably betrayed her husband with other men. If she did such a thing, the law says she should be punished that way."

It was enough for him, and how could I argue with the law? That night, I sat down with the notebook I used as a diary. I loved to draw, so it was filled with as many pictures as words. Most of those pictures were crosses. I had always loved to draw the cross. They covered the margins of notebooks and pages of my diary. I even drew the cross on my skin. I don't know why I was so fascinated. Maybe it was because the only crosses I saw were at an Armenian church that was on the way to my family's vacation home, and that was only a fleeting glimpse from the wrong side of the high walls that surrounded the building and cemetery. Even then I knew that, as a Muslim, I wouldn't be allowed to see behind those walls. Maybe the prohibition added

CHAPTER ONE

to the fascination. Wherever the interest came from, I would jealously guard that flash of a moment when I could see the crosses on top of the graves. I always thought the people in that cemetery had something important that I was missing.

That night, I wondered if that missing piece could help me make sense of a begging woman, angry men, the crack of brick on bone, and blood on a limp, shrouded body. In pictures and the best words a seven-year-old could muster, I tried to transfer the images from my mind to the pages. It was an effort that would continue throughout my life.

That same year I found another passion; wrestling. Wrestling is one of the most popular sports in Iran, and many children participate, including one of my brothers. At first, I wanted to do it because he did. Whenever he went to training, I would beg to go along too. Once I started, I loved learning how to defend myself and others. It gave me confidence, and the more I trained, the better I got. But whether I was good or not didn't really matter to my family. For them my religious studies were more important.

My father had already decided that I would be a great mullah, a person who teaches Islam. For him, a Sunni Kurd from northwestern Iran, religion was at the center of his life. He had memorized two of the seven parts of the Qur'an and built and restored domes for mosques when he wasn't running his other business. I wanted to follow in his footsteps. To help me on this path, my family had me dedicated at a mosque. It was a proud day for my father. There were several mullahs on his side of the family, and they all attended. It was one of the rare times when his eyes weren't tight with anger.

Religion and wrestling became the focus of my life. I prayed five times a day. I was up before the sun for the first prayer and finished the last one after midnight. I read the Qur'an and committed many verses to memory. I attended religious studies classes at the mosque,

BECOMING JOSHUA

where I listened to stories about Islam and learned how to look for deeper meanings concealed in the verses. When Ramadan—the month devoted to repentance and renewed relationship with God—approached, I fasted from sunup to sundown for several days before and for a week after. It sharpened my mind and let me focus on my faith.

Three years after I began my studies, I earned the title of "Hafiz al Qur'an," meaning that I knew the Qur'an from memory. It is a respected title that is valued even more than a college degree.

When I wasn't studying or praying, I was training and competing in wrestling. I became good enough that my coaches wanted me to travel for competitions. My father was against it. He thought it would distract me from my religious studies. It took the combined effort of my mother's family and coaches to convince him that travel would be good experience for me. He relented and I could travel to meets all over the country. Each time I won, I wanted to compete again, to win a bigger title, to defeat a more skilled opponent. My father only watched me compete once. When I won, the arena erupted into a cheer, but my father remained silent. He sat with his arms folded and shook his head as if I had disappointed him with the victory.

When I had questions about the Qur'an, a conversation with the mullah helped me to better understand the words, the lessons, and the history behind the verses. As I grew older and my knowledge deepened, my questions grew increasingly complex.

In Islam, there are over one hundred names for God. The one that I struggled with the most was "Al-Makkar," which means "he who deceives." Why would God have to deceive? Satan deceives. If God is also deceitful, how is he different from Satan? That single name shaded the meaning of the verses I was studying until the theology was draped in an uncomfortable shadow.

I went to the mosque to speak with the mullah. He poured tea for

CHAPTER ONE

both of us from a stainless-steel samovar, and we sat across from each other in his comfortable office.

"You said you have a question," he began.

"How can we trust a god who, according to his name, deceives us?"

The small glass paused halfway to his lips, and he studied me. He tried to keep his expression neutral, but his eyes narrowed just a fraction. He set the glass down again. "Not all questions should be asked," he said.

"But—"

"Be careful. You don't want to gain the reputation of being too inquisitive." His brow smoothed and he took a sip of the tea. "Some things belong in the realm of faith."

For him, the matter was closed. His faith told him so. But I couldn't let it go. The shadows thickened and clung to all those things I had thought were so certain. I couldn't ignore them, but there might be a way to dispel them.

A few days later, my parents, my brother, Aria, and I were sitting in the living room after lunch. I turned to my father. "Have you ever read the holy books that were written before the Qur'an?"

As soon as I asked the question, my mother and brother looked from my father to me and back again. My father was not an approachable man, especially not about religion.

I watched his jaw tense and his eyes harden. "We don't need to read those books because the Qur'an is enough. The Qur'an answers all questions."

"But according to the Qur'an, we should read them. Surah Yunus 10:94 says, 'If you are in doubt as to what We have revealed unto thee, then ask those who have been reading the Book from before thee: the Truth hath indeed come to thee from thy Lord: so be in no wise of those in doubt.'"

I watched the muscle in my father's jaw flutter; then he took his copy of the Qur'an off the bookshelf next to his chair, and I waited while he looked up the verse. It was the first time he had ever checked a verse that I had quoted to him. His finger hovered over the page as he read, he sat up straight in the chair, and his eyebrows drew together. He stared at the page, his eyes darting from right to left. His shoulders tensed. Then, despite his obvious anger at me, he closed the book with careful respect. "I don't need to read another book. The Bible the Christians have today is a corrupted Bible."

"But how do you know the Bible is corrupt without reading it, without doing any research? Maybe the Christians believe the Qur'an is corrupt."

He looked away. He was always willing to show us his anger, but never his uncertainty. "We can't know the answer to every question." He returned the book to its place on the shelf. "But never forget: God created the world just for the prophet Mohammad."

That was it. As far as he was concerned, the conversation was finished.

I sat back in my chair and stared at him. How could we accept some parts of the Qur'an, but ignore other parts that couldn't be conveniently explained? I stopped asking those questions, but what my father said stayed with me and fueled my doubts about the other parts of the Qur'an.

The prophet Mohammad had around seventeen wives, and committed adultery with his son Yasser's wife. When he was fifty-seven years old, he married Aisha, a seven-year-old girl. This was the person God had created the world for? What about me, I wondered. I couldn't even imagine how our great prophet could do these things. I wondered how Muslim women could know all of this and the fact that men can have up to four wives and still want to follow Islam. I also questioned the verses that talked about how to kill and confiscate goods from people who were not Muslim. Not because they had done anything wrong, but because of what they believed.

I couldn't accept this any longer. If Allah couldn't show me the truth, then no one could.

I didn't want to be Muslim anymore.

But I had been born a Muslim, and I thought I must live and die as

CHAPTER ONE

a Muslim. All my studying, all my work and prayer and devotion had only driven me further away from God. Perhaps I couldn't change the fact that I was a Muslim, but I could choose not to practice my religion. I stopped reading the Qur'an. I stopped praying, and I stopped fasting during Ramadan.

I wasn't even sixteen yet, and I had nothing to believe in.

Chapter Two

WRESTLING FILLED THE place that religion had left.

I'd won competitions all over Iran, but now I was preparing for my first international competition. I spent seven to ten hours a day in the gym to prepare. I studied the way my prospective opponents approached matches. I trained harder than before and I grew more aggressive. When I wasn't training or working out for myself, I coached friends who wanted to learn more about wrestling and fighting. Mentally, I wasn't as focused as I could have been. Even though I had left my faith behind, I still prayed for my success, though it wasn't a prayer in the way I had known before. It was more of a wish sent to someone or something in the universe.

I lost the final match of the international competition in overtime. I changed the focus of my training for more endurance and I believed, arrogantly, that the next time I competed at that level, I would come in first. I made sure everyone knew that's what I thought.

When I wasn't in the gym, I drew. My pencil moved with more confidence now, and the images I produced were becoming more complex, but the cross was still my favorite thing to draw.

One day, my friend Reza and I were sitting in the shade of one of the pomegranate trees in my yard, perfecting indolence in the way that only teenagers can.

"Why do you do that?" Reza asked, breaking the silence that had settled between us.

My head had been resting back against the trunk of the tree. I

CHAPTER TWO

opened my eyes to look at him. "Do what?"

"That." He pointed at my arm.

I looked at the cross I had drawn on my forearm. No one had ever asked me why before. I traced the lines with my fingers. "I don't know. I just like how it looks."

"You should put it there permanently," he said. "Save you the trouble of drawing it every day."

I looked at him. "How would I do that? Even permanent marker washes off eventually."

He picked up a leaf and tore it along the veins to the central spine. "My uncle does tattoos. It's not that hard. I could show you how to do it."

I thought he was joking, but no nascent humor twitched the corners of his lips.

Getting a tattoo was against everything I'd been taught, everything I'd believed, for so many years. I looked down at my arm again and knew that none of that mattered. I wanted to be able to look down and see the cross I'd drawn. I wanted to know it was a part of me, even when I couldn't see it. I looked up at him again.

"When?" I asked.

I would have done it that day in the yard, but it was going to take more planning than that. At my house or at Reza's house, there was no privacy. Even if we managed to find a few minutes of quiet, we were sure to be interrupted before we were finished. I called my cousin Vahid.

"You want to do what?" he said.

I glanced around to see if I was still alone. "A tattoo. Reza learned how from his uncle—"

"Come here," he said. "I'll keep watch, but I have to see this for myself."

Over the next few days, I drew different versions of the design and tried them out on my arm. I refined the lines. I added flourishes and curves that scrolled in complex patterns. Each time, I imagined the new design as a permanent part of me. None of them was right.

13

BECOMING JOSHUA

I went back to the simpler version I'd been drawing for years and added a book to the base.

It had been several days since our conversation in the shady part of the yard, but as Reza and I set off for the older part of the city, I was more determined than ever to go through with it.

Arima had been occupied for more than a thousand years, creating places where a person could step back into history. Our neighborhood was laid out in neat blocks on a predictable grid. Only a few miles away, the city changed. The streets there were narrow and twisted at eccentric angles. Houses huddled closer together and eventually melded into covered alleys that were only wide enough to allow a single person on foot to pass. This patchwork of passageways was a remnant from a time when invaders were mounted on horseback, but the maze was still in use by those who didn't want to be observed or followed. A person who didn't know the way could become lost in that dim warren in a matter of minutes. The streets themselves weren't much better, but I'd visited often enough to walk with confidence through the laneways.

My grandmother's house had been standing for at least a century. It was built in the U-shaped *Hafti and Hashti* style around a central courtyard with a fountain sparkling in the sunshine and a wide balcony around the second level. It was still a home for the extended family on my mother's side. In generations past, the house would have been all bustle and gossip. It was still a busy place, but not as much as it had once been. My grandmother—I called her Nane—liked to spend her days on the balcony across from the central entrance gate. She saw who came, who went, who lingered, and who hurried on their way, all as she smoked hookah.

I often went to visit my cousins. Nane would have no reason to think this time was any different. When we got there, I saw Vahid working on his motorcycle in the courtyard and waved to him. He set his tools aside and joined Reza, Nane, and me for tea and dried fruit on the balcony. I introduced Reza to Nane, and she quizzed me about how the family was and how I was doing at school. As soon

CHAPTER TWO

as we could escape the interview, we went to Vahid's room as we usually did. His room had a good view of the rest of the courtyard. If anyone was coming, we'd have time to make it look like we weren't up to anything but hanging out together.

Vahid took up his position by the cracked open door while we put down a sheet of plastic and towels to protect Nane's carpets before we started. Reza made ink from burned elastic mixed with water, but I didn't really study what he was doing. I sat staring at my forearm, the pen poised over my skin. I had drawn similar images there for as long as I could remember, but this one was different. This one would always be with me. I changed my grip on the pen, took a deep breath, and drew the image of the cross and book on my forearm. I wouldn't be able to keep it secret for long, but this was where it belonged.

"You sure you want to put it there?" Vahid asked.

I didn't raise my eyes. "That's where I always put it. Besides, I want to be able to look down and see it whenever I want."

Voices from the courtyard filtered in and blended with the music we were playing. Reza dipped a sewing needle into the homemade ink and poked it into my skin at the top of the cross. I clenched my jaw against the pain, but Reza didn't notice. All his concentration focused on following the lines I'd drawn. It was a slow process, and Reza's uncertain skill meant that the needle often dug too deep. Blood dripped down my hand in warm trickles as he etched the raw lines into my flesh. Silence would have drawn attention, so we talked about Vahid's motorcycle, a topic that anyone who passed by would have heard us discuss most times we were together. It was a poor distraction from the burning pain, but all I could do was grit my teeth and think of the result. It took the rest of the afternoon for the cross to become a permanent part of my body.

When it was over, I stared at my swollen forearm. Pain throbbed in time with my heartbeat. I touched an angry-looking, raw line and then pulled my finger back. What had I done? With my forearm oozing blood, the cross and book emblazoned across it, it was too late to change my mind.

"You can't go around like that," Reza said, looking at my arm. He left and came back with bandages. I cleaned things up as best I could and wrapped it so that the fresh tattoo was hidden. What was I going to tell my family? I decided that I couldn't go home yet, so I stayed with Vahid's family as I had so many times before.

They probably noticed the bandage, but Vahid was a mechanic and was always getting hurt at work. Someone wearing a bandage likely didn't register anymore. They didn't say anything about it and neither did I.

A few days later, the swelling had come down. I wrapped an elastic bandage around my arm and went home. I hadn't been home for an hour before my mother noticed the bandage.

"What did you do to your arm?" my mother asked. I could see that she was concerned.

I just shrugged and tried to walk away. "I hurt it at the gym."

She followed me. "The gym? You've hurt your wrist or your elbow, but not the middle of your arm. What did you do?"

"Nothing." I did my best to look innocent.

"If it was nothing it wouldn't be bandaged. Let me see, or I'll tell your father."

I didn't want either of them to know, not yet, but with her standing there, looking at me like that, I didn't have a choice. I couldn't quite meet her eyes as I unwrapped the bandage.

As soon as the tattoo came into view, her eyes widened. She reached toward the scabbed-over lines and then pulled her hand back. Her hand covered her mouth instead. Shock and fear flashed through her eyes. "Your father will cut your arm off."

She wasn't exaggerating by much. For as long as I could remember, my father's anger and violence had haunted our comfortable house. My brothers, sisters, and I had all worn the evidence of it, going to school with purple-black bruises he had inflicted with a short length of hose he kept for the purpose on a shelf in his corner of the living room along with his keys and other things he liked to have within easy reach. We'd all done our best to shut our ears to the insults that

CHAPTER TWO

created wounds deeper and more lasting than bruises. We'd all suffered the embarrassment of being dragged from a family gathering because his anger couldn't wait to be satisfied. We'd all seen how my mother's family, the only relatives we had in the city, looked down at him and pitied us because we were his children.

I knew exactly what to expect. I couldn't rely on my mother to protect me from it either. If she'd tried, she would be beaten too. For the rest of the day I waited, feeling the hours slip away toward evening. There would be no use in trying to convince my father it wasn't as bad as it looked, no use in apologizing. All I could do was wait.

My arm was covered the whole time, but the rest of the family knew something was going on. The tension thickened as the sun went down.

I was in the living room with my brothers and sisters when we heard the front door open with a thump. My mother met my father in the small entry. I couldn't hear what she said. I didn't really need to. I could hear the pressured anxiety in her voice. I stood and walked around the sofa, wanting to be ready. He came in, radiating rage, grabbed his piece of hose, and began to swing. Argument or explanation would do no good. I pulled my newly tattooed arm tight against my body, to protect it until he decided I'd had enough. Pain exploded from the heavy blows, but I planted my feet and stood still.

"What's wrong with you? Not only do you get a tattoo, but you tattooed the cross? Who in our family is Christian? Your father's side or your mother's side?" he shouted as he swung. The anger and exertion frayed the edges of the words.

I stood there, my arm pulled against my chest, determined to stand still and take the beating while I tried to wall off the pain. My family stood around me, silent and watching.

At last my younger brother, Parsa, cried out. Tears streaked his face. "It's only drawing! He won't do it again, please stop!"

My father didn't stop.

Parsa was seven. He probably didn't even know what a tattoo was.

The longer it went on, the harder it was to be still. I raised my arm to protect myself. My father hesitated, then struck me again. I fended off that blow as well. His eyes locked with mine and he lowered his arm.

"Get in the car." He gestured toward the door with the hose.

I didn't know what he had in mind, but his anger hadn't abated. I didn't dare disobey or ask any questions. Fetid silence, heavy with the weight of unspoken insults, collected around us as he drove the familiar route to my grandmother's house. I had always been his favorite son. The son who had made him most proud. Now I was the one who had disappointed him the most.

When we got to Nane's house, he pulled me through the gate by my ear while demanding the key to her basement. I'm not sure what Nane thought had happened, but I could see the concern on her face as she gave him a brass key that looked like it belonged to another age.

He unlocked the door and dragged me through two rooms where Nane stored food and other things that the household needed. The third room was rarely opened and held things that were too old or too broken to be useful, but that couldn't be parted with. He shoved me inside and began to beat me again to drive me deeper into the dusty space.

"You'll stay here until you die." he said, stepped back, and slammed the door shut. The scrape of the key in the lock made me shiver.

The damp, deserted air around me settled into silence again. Moments later, cockroaches tapped and skittered as they emerged from hiding in the pile of broken furniture that crouched along one wall or from the torn and dusty carpets piled next to the opposite wall.

I was alone. Abandoned. Pain throbbed through my arms and legs from injuries too numerous to count. The fresh tattoo hadn't escaped. The deep black bruise was already well formed, and my forearm was twice the size it should have been. I was afraid I had a blood clot, but

CHAPTER TWO

I didn't call out or try the door. If he were waiting, that would only make him angrier.

I dragged one of the carpets out from the wall and lay down on it, the scent of the raw earth floor filtered up through the dusty wool. Pain accompanied each heartbeat. I had been alone with the dust and the cockroaches long enough to lose track of time when I heard the key in the lock again. I stood and tensed sore muscles to prepare for yet another beating. Instead of my father, it was Nane with a plate of bread and cheese and a red plastic jug of water. I sat down on the carpet. I wasn't going to be beaten, but she wouldn't risk my father's wrath to let me out.

I stared up at her for a moment, then took the plate she offered. "Thanks." It was a surly mumble.

"Well, I couldn't let my grandson starve to death. No matter what he's done." I don't know how she found out, but I can guess that she'd called my mother as soon as my father left her house.

"Suppose you agree with him," I said.

"What would you like me to say?" Nane asked. "You can't expect that I'd approve of what you did, or the fact that you used my house to do it."

I kept my eyes fixed on the plate of food. "Figured you'd think what he did was alright."

"Did I say that? You know what he's like. He can't sit with something that scares him; he has to lash out at it."

I looked up at her. "He didn't look scared to me."

"Are you sure? He thinks about that," she pointed at my arm, "and all he sees are things you've given up because you wanted to show what a man you were. Who's going to let you marry their daughter? Who's going to hire you? They'll see that and think that you've been to prison, or that you're in a gang. The fact that it's a cross just makes it worse. He's afraid that you're rejecting everything, and if you do that, what will you have left? How long do you think it'll take to get over that kind of fear?"

I shrugged and pushed the food around on my plate.

"Think about it and eat. I'm not feeding the roaches." She left me alone again.

Several times a day Nane brought me food and water and stayed with me while I ate. When she wasn't there, I stared at the lines I'd etched into my skin. She was right about how I'd be perceived, but there was a certainty in knowing that whenever I looked down, I would see my drawing of the cross. I liked how that felt.

Outside of that dusty space, life for the rest of the family at my grandmother's house went on as usual. People walked through the courtyard and along the balconies with either the intention of age or the blithe pace of youth. They laughed and gossiped, cooked and ate, slept and awakened to a new day. They knew I was there. If they hadn't witnessed my arrival, then they had certainly been told about it. None of them even came to the door to see if I was still alive. I couldn't help but think that if one of my cousins had been imprisoned in the basement, they wouldn't have been left alone and forgotten.

The shadows were growing longer on the third day when the door opened again. I expected to see Nane in the doorway. My father stood there instead.

"Go home," he said, and left me to find my own way there.

It took me half an hour. Each time I passed someone I tried to turn away and hide the vivid bruises. No one in the family said a word about where I had been. No one asked how I was, despite the evidence of violence painted across my skin. For weeks, I sat alone while my anger simmered and everyone else went about their lives as if I wasn't there. This was the isolation of being alone in a crowd, and it was just as punishing as being alone with the insects.

I had to heal before I could go back to the gym, and when I did, I would have to tell my coach about the tattoo. He would see it as soon as I started training. The first day I was able to go back, I found him in his cluttered office and unwrapped the bandage. He stood and looked from the cross to me. It was as if I had suddenly become a stranger to him.

"Are you stupid? You don't think?" he yelled, so much like my

CHAPTER TWO

father. "How do you expect to go into competition like that? And a cross? How are the gym directors going to explain to the officials that not only does one of their wrestlers have a tattoo, but he has a tattoo of the cross? Well?"

I couldn't look at him.

"Get out." He turned away from me and waved toward the door. "You're finished here."

There was nothing to say. I left.

Everything was gone now. I was alone and adrift. In the eyes of my family, I was an outsider. What my grandmother had said was true, tattoos were associated with gang members and people who had been to prison. Even though they knew I was neither of those, I was still looked upon with suspicion. I wasn't allowed to see Vahid anymore. I couldn't see my friends from the gym. I was ignored, alone. I spent hours in the park with pencils and my notebook. I still drew the cross in the same way I had drawn it for the tattoo, but I also took Farsi words and sculpted them into broken hearts and other figures. I was still alone, but I was alone among strangers.

Nearly three weeks later, the coach called me into a meeting.

"The directors wanted to replace you, but they thought the prospects of the team would suffer," he said. "In training or competition, you keep it covered."

I was glad to be wrestling again, but it wasn't the same. I wrapped my arm, but when it slipped, I could see the judgment on people's faces. I had been so close to my teammates, but now they wanted nothing to do with me outside of the gym. I spent time with other friends or by myself.

I grew to value my independence because now I couldn't rely on anyone else.

All while I was growing up, my father built or restored domes for mosques. It wasn't his main occupation, but once a year or so, he would take on one of these projects to give back to his religion. He kept his planning, calculations, and the way he began the foundations a secret. He did all that work himself and then turned the rest over to others to finish. He wanted all his sons to learn these techniques, both to earn money and to serve Islam.

When we were children, he'd let us see how the materials worked, how they felt and how they fit together. He talked about the mathematics of how the domes were formed. He turned it into a game and sharpened our curiosity to learn more. My brothers didn't have an aptitude for it, but I had always been interested in architecture. I could see the curves and slopes, the arches and the way the bricks fit together.

I don't think my father believed it at first. When I was sixteen, he contracted to build a small dome and challenged me to prove I could do it. He told me that if I couldn't, he would tear it down and start again. I think he expected me to fail. But this was my chance. I was sure that I could build a better dome than he designed on paper. As soon as I started, I could see that it was going to be more complex than I thought. I used what I had learned through the years and devoted more time to planning.

Once the six support columns were finished and I took my measurements, I knew that it was perfect.

As far I knew, my father never visited the job site while I was working on the dome. He might have gone when I wasn't there, but when it was finished, I think he was proud. In the next year, I built two domes for him, then a third on my own. When I was seventeen, my father helped me to set up my own construction company because he was concerned I wouldn't be able to find work. Even without the tattoo, he knew that my attitude would make it difficult for me to follow someone else's orders.

It was his influence that got me my first contract worth ten times what the average person makes in a year. Throughout the project, he worked with me to teach me more about construction and how to run a company and manage people. I remember being in his office one day when three of his employees came in to complain about several others. He listened and told them to go back to work. Once they were gone, he told his secretary that he wanted the three who complained fired. When I asked why, he said that instead of complaining about each other, they should be helping the others learn to do better. When the project finished successfully, he bought me my own house. It wasn't as large as my family's house, but it was more modern and spacious for just one person.

My father built domes as an expression of his faith. For me it was business. Where he built one or two a year, I employed twenty-five people and built six, both for mosques and as a status symbol in private homes. I standardized the design and mixed classic style and clean, modern lines. One of the first things I did with the money I earned was to buy an apartment in Tehran so I'd have a private place to have parties with friends. The house was comfortable, but my parents knew so many people in Arima that no matter what I did, it would get back to them.

At that time, I was also training for my third international competition. In the second one, the first match I drew had paired me with an opponent I should have met in the final. That first loss meant that, even if I won all the rest of my matches in that competition, the best I could hope for was third place. It shook my confidence. When we got back, my coach had threatened that I might not be able to go to another one. I trained even harder to stay on the team.

The business was thriving, but I wanted more. Wrestling and training every day kept me in good condition, so when I signed a client who owned a clothing company that produced casual wear and formal wear, I suggested he should use me as a model. He agreed and from that job I got others. Modeling was fun at first, and it brought me a certain amount of fame. I was featured in ads over the city, and when I went out, I was often recognized. At a time when dating was always a prelude to a marriage, I had many casual girlfriends. I never considered the consequences to either of us. If the girl's family had found out, either one or both of us could have been killed.

My arrogance and greed seduced me. I believed that nothing I did mattered.

Yet the cross was still a permanent part of me.

"Why did you tattoo the cross on your arm?" people would sometimes ask.

"I'm Christian," I would say. I wanted to shock them.

In those days, I had everything the world could give me. I had a comfortable living from the business, a little fame, time to enjoy life, and an international competition that I had spent months working toward. Even with all that, there was still an emptiness no ephemeral pleasure could fill. When I was much younger, that emptiness wasn't there. But that was when I still had faith.

I tried to push all that out of my mind. I didn't have room for it. I had to focus on my training and getting ready for the biggest competition that I'd been in so far. About two weeks before I left with my team, I was driving back to my apartment a little after two in the morning. The streets were nearly deserted, and I was alone on the overpass when my eye caught the cross on top of an Armenian church. I'd driven that way too many times to count, but this time the cross was bathed in a pink halo of light.

What about you? I thought. *You're supposed to be God. Can you give me a new heart? A new mind?*

The silence that followed felt like another loss. As I drove, the pink flare faded in my rearview mirror.

The memory of the pink flare on the cross in the quiet of the night was consumed by the excitement that buzzed through our arrival at the competition. There wasn't room for anything other than the planning and strategy that I would need to win, because winning felt like the most important thing I could imagine.

Soon enough, anticipation gave way to the thrill of the competition itself. I had worked for it for so long, focused on it, used it to distract myself, told myself that it was all I wanted. I had seven matches during that competition, the final one I won by points, but it didn't matter. I'd won. The crowd erupted into a cheer. For me. For my victory.

I rode that rush as I changed and waited for the medal ceremony. When it was my turn, I stepped onto the middle part of the podium. The highest part, the part reserved for the winner. This was what I had worked so hard for. The roar of the crowd filled the arena. I bent down to receive the gold medal from one of the competition organizers, a legendary wrestler in his own right, and the roar of the crowd shifted, as if they were retreating down a long tunnel until, at last, they were gone. The person who placed the medal around my neck was frozen in that moment. I had slipped into a fissure in eternity, but I wasn't alone there.

What's next? a calm voice asked.

The cheering swelled and shattered that bubble of silence as the medal came down around my neck. I stood up victorious, but I had never felt so empty.

Chapter Three

WHAT WAS NEXT? The question teased at the edges of the celebratory air on the flight home. It was still there when we were welcomed with flowers at the airport and chocolates and congratulations at the gym. At home, a place had been made in the center of our trophy wall for my medal. The only one who wasn't there to welcome me was my father. When he finally arrived, he didn't even smile. He just looked at the medal as if he didn't know what it was. After the celebrations were over, the question rose from the back of my mind to taunt me.

Because of wrestling's long history in Iran and the trust placed in wrestlers who were as successful as I was, friends and family began coming to me for help. I did help, but I used it as an opportunity to keep myself distracted. I used the aggression and skill I'd learned in wrestling to fight in the street when someone I cared about was threatened, sometimes with fists, sometimes with machetes. I told myself I was defending people who needed it, but I think I was using the risk and violence to silence the question. It worked so well that eventually I was able to deny that there had been a question at all.

My friend Abdolrahim was one of those who asked for help. He was a taxi driver and had to renew his permit. A drug test was part of the requirement, but he was a heroin addict. He wouldn't be able to pass, so he asked me to go to the appointment in his place. We'd grown up together and we resembled each other enough that I thought we could get away with it.

The permit was issued by the government. I had to go to a

CHAPTER THREE

laboratory that was under the administration of the local police. I arrived at eight in the morning, presented Abdolrahim's identification to the soldier at the desk, and told him why I was there. He found the name on the list and buzzed me into the building. Once inside, I handed the soldier at the reception desk all the paperwork.

He glanced through it to see that it was all in order and told me where I could wait to be called. There were no magazines or newspapers to read. I told myself to stay calm, that it was just a few tests. No one questioned me when I used his ID at the desk. All I had to do now was remember to answer to his name and everything would be fine. As the minutes stretched into hours, I did my best to convince myself that this would be easy, that I couldn't possibly get caught.

At first, it seemed like I was right. I went in and took the drug test and then went into another room for the eye exam. I handed the doctor the papers and sat down.

He glanced down at the papers and then up at me, his glasses perched halfway down his nose. "Abdolrahim?" the doctor asked.

"Yes," I said.

He turned toward me, and I thought he was going to start the test, but he stopped. His eyebrows drew together. "Why do you have a cross tattooed on your arm?"

I gave him my standard response. "I'm Christian."

He sat back in his chair and studied me. "How can that be? You have an Islamic name."

I wondered why he was asking so many questions about something that had nothing to do with an eye test. "I love Christianity and I'm Christian." My voice was firm. I hoped that would be the end of it.

"Is your family Christian?"

"Yes, we are."

He stared at me and tapped his pen against the papers in his hand, considering. "Wait here. I'll be back soon."

He walked out of the room and closed the door.

I stared at the clock, then started to pace, covering the tiny room in a few anxious strides in each direction. The twenty minutes that passed seemed to take hours as I turned over in my mind what I could say when the doctor came back. Should I admit that I wasn't Abdolrahim? Should I try to play it off? I heard the click of the door and I pivoted toward it.

Two unarmed city policemen in green uniforms filled the doorframe. "We need you to come with us," the taller one said. He stood aside and gestured toward the hall.

They must have figured out I was lying about who I was. I walked out into the hall with them, my mouth dry, heart pounding. "I'm not Abdolrahim. I know I shouldn't have tried to take his drug test."

"We'll talk about all of that when we get to the station." There was a police car parked just outside the front door.

How could I have done something so stupid? I had a successful company. I had enough money to enjoy my life and people to enjoy it with. Why throw it all away on something like this? I tilted my head away from the window, hoping no one would recognize me on the short ride to the small police station. The two officers led me into the quiet main room of the station and to a battered wooden desk occupied by an older police sergeant, his hair graying at the temples. He looked vaguely familiar. It took a minute, but I recognized him as someone who had given a career talk at my school.

"Sit down, please." He pointed at the chair in front of the desk without really looking at me. The phrase less of an invitation and more of an order. I sat.

He took a blank form from the top of the stack, his pen poised. "Do you know why you're here?"

I thought the doctor must have told them everything, and if I admitted what I'd done it'd make things easier. "My friend had to renew his taxi permit, but he was worried he couldn't pass the drug test. I knew I could, so I said I would take it for him."

I saw surprise cross his face, but he wrote down what I had said. "What's your friend's name?"

"Abdolrahim."

He nodded and the pen moved across the page again. "We'll take

CHAPTER THREE

care of this as well." The sergeant leaned back to study me and the chair protested with a loud squeak. It was the first time he looked at me since I arrived. "Now, how are you Christian?"

Why wasn't he asking about my crime? I gave him the same answer I gave the doctor.

He studied me, then picked up the pen and made a note on the page again. "All right." He waved over a couple of police officers without looking at me. "Take him down to interrogation."

They took me down a flight of stairs and put me in a small, bland yellow room with a table. Two chairs were on one side, and a small metal bench painted the same color as the walls was on the other. I was told to sit on the bench. Once I sat, they left me alone. The room was quiet, but every so often the muffled sounds of people drifted in from the hallway. Each time they did, I sat up straighter, my attention trained on the door. Each time the voices passed by, I slumped back down again. Each time, the tension in my body took longer to abate. Why was I being made to wait? I had already shown that I was willing to confess.

There was no clock in the room, so I don't know how long it was before two men in plain clothes came in and sat across from me. Both had beards, as did most of the police and government officials. Both wore long-sleeved shirts—the slimmer one in blue, the slightly heavier one in white—with the collar and cuffs buttoned. They didn't introduce themselves.

The one in blue dropped a folder onto the table and sat down. "So, we're trying to figure out how you became Christian. Who converted you?" His sharp eyes were at odds with the friendly tone in his voice.

The question took me by surprise. "I don't know what you mean." What little I knew about Christianity was interesting, but I believed what I had been taught, that it was impossible for a Muslim to convert to another religion.

He spread his thick-fingered hands. "You're the one who told Dr. Nazary at the laboratory that you were Christian. You told the sergeant that you're Christian. We know you weren't born a Christian, so you must have been converted. Who's your *Shaban*[1]?"

"Shaban?" I asked. "The person who goes out in the field with the sheep? How does that have anything to do with me?"

"You tell us." The younger one sat back in his chair. "You're the one making the claims."

I looked from one to the other. "I took a drug test for my friend," I said. "I know I shouldn't have, but that's all I did."

"We'll get to that." The older one gave a dismissive wave. "Where did you learn about Jesus?"

"The same place everyone else does, the Qur'an."

They didn't like that answer, but it was the truth and they knew it. The interrogation went on for hours. What house church did I go to? Where did I get the Bible? Was my family Christian? They varied the wording and the order, but the questions were all about Christianity. The longer it went on the more ridiculous it was. I was tired and hungry and just wanted to put an end to the whole thing.

"Look, I don't know anything about Christianity, and I don't know why I said I did. I'm Muslim. I just wanted to help my friend pass his drug test."

I could feel the weight of their scrutiny while the silence thickened. They stood up, the younger taking his cue from the elder and picked up the folder.

"We'll talk again soon," the older one said, then led the other one out of the room.

A soldier took me to a holding cell that was already occupied by two other people and gave me a tattered blanket that hadn't been washed in longer than I cared to imagine. The cell itself was a bare concrete space. The miasma of human waste, illness, and fear added weight and texture to the air.

In Iran, a person who is arrested has no rights. No right to legal representation, no right to silence, no right to know how long they will be held, no right to know why they're being arrested in the first

---

[1] There is no word in Farsi for "pastor." The word for shepherd is used instead.

CHAPTER THREE

place. The ability to contact family to let them know about the arrest is entirely at the discretion of the police. Wealth can buy the arrested person a bit more consideration, if the police know who he is. Most who are arrested are entirely at the mercy of the officers.

In court, it's not much better. The interpretation of the law and the kinds of sentences imposed are entirely subject to the discretion of the presiding mullah.

As I sat in that holding cell, I had no idea how long I would be there or even what I was really being held for. No one wanted to talk about the crime I had committed. I couldn't see how religion could even be a crime. All I could do was hope that the next day I would be released or sent to court.

The next day brought more questioning. At night, I was put into the holding cell to sleep on the concrete floor with my filthy blanket and whatever strangers were unlucky enough to be detained with me overnight. I lost track of names and what they'd done. There were others who stayed for an hour or two and made even less of an impression. Unpalatable food was brought in, but always at different times. Even that wasn't predictable.

I was exhausted and on edge. I hadn't been allowed to contact anyone. I have no idea what people thought had happened to me. The questions my interrogators asked me were always the same, and I gave them the same answers because I didn't know any other way to tell the truth. By the third day, the tone of the questioning had changed. The certainty that I knew the answers was fading.

On the morning of the sixth day, a uniformed officer appeared at the door of the holding cell and announced my name. "You're in court this afternoon." He held up handcuffs and shackles. "Come over to the door."

I hadn't been handcuffed when they brought me in, nor at any point when I was being interrogated or walked from one place to another within the police station. The idea of being chained like an animal awakened what little will I had left. "No," I said. I'd have to walk the block to the courthouse. The humiliation of having to shuffle through the streets while everyone stared was too much.

"Come over here and give me your hands." His voice was firm.

I moved to the back of the cell. "If you want to put those on me, you come in here and do it." The other men in the cell moved to the opposite corner and turned toward the wall. Within minutes I was facing five policemen armed with pepper spray and riot shields. I didn't care how many there were, I was ready to fight with all of them. They advanced in a half-circle, closing in. I braced myself.

Someone outside the cell called out, "Stop!"

A moment later, Hasan, a friend of my family's and a court official, edged into the cell. "What do you think you're going to accomplish with this?" he asked me.

I didn't know what to say. My eyes darted from Hasan back to the semicircle of police.

Hasan didn't wait for an answer. "If I can trust you to behave yourself, we'll go upstairs and talk about this."

I nodded and went with him upstairs into the main room of the police station. Hasan's position with the court meant that he wielded a great deal of influence. I waited by the door while Hasan talked with the sergeant.

"I appreciate that he doesn't want to be shackled and cuffed, but if we don't, anything could happen. He could get out the door and run." The sergeant gestured at me.

"Need I remind you that he hasn't been convicted of anything? You can't just parade him through the streets like a criminal when there's been no conviction," Hasan said.

The sergeant struggled to keep his voice even. "And what about the judge? Would he be happy to have an unrestrained prisoner in his courtroom?"

Hasan picked up the phone. "What courtroom is he going to?"

The sergeant told him.

Hasan dialed and had a short conversation in which he explained the situation. "I'll take personal responsibility for his behavior." He listened for a momet, then hung up. "You'll leave the shackles off,"

CHAPTER THREE

Hasan said to the sergeant.

The police weren't happy about that, but they cuffed my hands in front of me for the walk to the court. When it was time to leave, Hasan draped his jacket over my hands and walked alongside me and the police escort to the courthouse. I still felt like everyone was staring. I lowered my head and hid my face from the people we passed.

For an hour and a half, I waited in a bland hallway on an unyielding metal bench. Every few minutes, the courtroom door opened next to me. Each time I moved to the edge of the bench, ready to stand. Each time my name wasn't called, I slid back on the bench. What was left of my nerves had begun to fray.

When it was finally my turn, I stood in front of the judge at a small podium at the center of the empty room with a soldier behind me. I was in the same clothes I had worn for nearly a week. I was exhausted and humiliated and all I wanted was for the whole thing to be over.

I knew better than to expect a trial. There was no prosecutor to lay out the evidence against me, no defense attorney to refute it. The presiding mullah didn't question me or ask if I had anything to say for myself. He had determined my guilt and had decided what my sentence would be before I ever arrived in the courtroom.

I was anxious to get back to my life, so, when prompted, I swore to Allah that I knew nothing about Christianity and that I had lied when I said I did. The judge barely looked down at me from the bench. "By claiming to be Christian, you've insulted Islam and your fellow Muslims." He looked at me from beneath bushy gray eyebrows. "This is a serious offense for which you will spend ninety-one days in jail."

I couldn't breathe. If I had been sentenced to ninety days in jail, I could have been released after a relatively short time if I showed that I was reformed. The additional day meant I would have to serve the entire sentence. As they led me out of the court, I shambled along following wherever I was led. Someone must have made a mistake. They must have. Then two soldiers put me into a car and drove me to the jail where I would spend the next three months.

BECOMING JOSHUA

Throughout the centuries, Arima had stretched and expanded, consuming places that had once been far outside the centers of commerce and habitation. The jail I was taken to had been in use for five centuries. It had been built far outside the city but was now surrounded by it. The curving slopes of partial domes, the only part of the building that was visible, rose and intersected like opposing waves.

This wasn't my life. It couldn't be. I had a successful business, good friends, a good family. I couldn't end up in places like this.

Once I was inside, I learned that, even though the building looked small, tiers of cells were built down into the ground, leaving the center open. Light and air from the oculus at the center of each dome illuminated and ventilated even the lowest levels.

The next few hours passed in a tangled blur. There were forms to fill out and paperwork to process. I was given a jail uniform and some soap. I would be allowed to wear my own clothes most of the time, but I'd have to wear the uniform when speaking to jail officials. Then I was taken to a long, narrow cell on the second tier that was already occupied by twenty men. They stared at me with hard eyes and crossed arms, appraising what vulnerabilities I had and what new ones they could create in the service of their own needs. I noticed several were wearing *patul*, the traditional Kurdish pants cut in a wide-legged style, so I greeted them in Kurdish. Expressions changed immediately, and I was welcomed like a brother.

One of the first people I met was one of my cellmates, Ali. He was tall with the hardened physique of a laborer and the disposition of a fighter. I soon learned that he came from a family of shepherds and was in jail because he had stabbed someone during a robbery. The people in his area spoke a local dialect, so his Farsi was heavily accented, and he often put words in the wrong order. Unsophisticated as he was, he knew how to survive in prison and, as we got to know

CHAPTER THREE

each other, he taught me what he knew.

Each cell had a boss, and the boss of my cell was also the boss of the floor. The boss kept order and made sure that inmate codes were followed and enforced. I was lucky that the boss was also Kurdish and knew another of my brothers. I was given a bunk close to his, a most coveted location.

When I told my cellmates that I had been arrested for lying to the doctor about being Christian, they laughed at me. Today, it's well known that Christianity is a crime in Iran. At that time though, most Iranian citizens didn't know this. Access to the Internet was limited, so those who did know couldn't easily spread the word to others. That first night, as I lay there in the unfamiliar darkness, I began to wonder why the authorities thought Christianity was so powerful. I had bullied and insulted people, I had fought with people in the street, and an offhand comment about being Christian is what put me in a cell with men who had robbed and stabbed others? Why were they so afraid of Christianity?

There were no answers.

Another of my early lessons about life in jail was that there were as many criminals outside of the bars as inside. Most of the guards brought in drugs and sold them to the prisoners. If a person could pay, he could get just about any drug he wanted. For some of my cellmates, the temporary escape was worth the price.

In quiet moments, Ali would tell stories about his family and his flock of sheep. Through the bold strokes of his thick accent, he drew vivid pictures of life on the plains, the color of the sky in the morning, the sound of the conversation between the wind and the beasts, and the freedom of being alone in the middle of all of it. When we were both out, he invited me to come and stay with him. I told him that he was welcome to stay with me too, although I couldn't quite imagine him in the city.

I thought about his invitation and his bright description of his plain whenever I needed a momentary escape from the monotony of daily life behind bars. During the day, cells were opened, and inmates could socialize with each other. I quickly learned that, even though my fellow inmates were criminals, they all had an understanding of business. I'd had an apartment in Tehran for quite a while, but only used it as a place to visit. They were the ones who began to educate me about where the money was in the city and who the influential people were. Talking with them shaped my thoughts about what I would do after my release.

The other thing that my fellow inmates took seriously was chess. There were several sets made by the inmates, and the patina of constant use highlighted the intricate figures. The winner played until he lost and was replaced with the next man on the list. More than once I saw fights erupt over these games that drew in not only the players but all their friends as well.

Every Friday at noon the prisoners gathered in a recently built space next to the jail to have prayer. Compared to the dim light and concrete floors of the jail, the prayer building was a different world. The floors were carpeted and the lighting warm. Going to prayer wasn't mandatory, but it was an indication of reform. Sign-in sheets went to the prison director and could help the inmate gain early release. Everyone tried to attend, but most of the prisoners didn't care if the mullah spoke about Islamic traditions or law, reason or consensus. During the prayer, they just imitated him. They didn't really know how to pray.

When I was in jail, my friends came to see me, and a couple of my cousins too, but never my parents or my brothers and sisters. Through the thick, metal mesh we traded playful insults and made plans for when I was released. The visiting room was also the place where I found out why I had gotten such a long sentence. My cousin Vahid told me that my father had used his influence with the judge.

According to Vahid, my father had believed I had been out of control for quite some time. He didn't like my friends or the fact that I was fighting in the street, no matter what my reason was. It was bad for his reputation and could affect his business. When he heard that I had been arrested for claiming to be Christian, he seized the

CHAPTER THREE

opportunity to reassert his control. As soon as I heard that, my anger flared, but I knew that wouldn't help. I made plans instead. His influence could take months out of my life, but I could cultivate influence of my own. Influence that could surpass his.

I kept my plans to myself and kept listening to the conversations of my fellow inmates. Ali was the only one who knew the bones of my intentions. I wanted to get out, buy a house, and set up everything for myself.

Finally, the day came when I was to be released. My friends were waiting for me just outside the gate. They welcomed me as if I were a hero. We drove in a long procession of cars and motorcycles to my friend Hady's house. I stayed with him for a few weeks while I spent time with my girlfriend and made my plans.

My house was still in my father's name, and so was the business. They were his and if the last few months had taught me anything, it was that I needed to build something that he couldn't take away. I left Arima and everything that he owned and went to live in Tehran.

My apartment building had a pool and jacuzzi in the basement. I had agreements with my neighbors that gave each of us exclusive use of the pool for one day a week. I used my day to throw parties for the sons and daughters of the wealthy and influential. I provided the place, the music, the alcohol, and the drugs. They would dance and drink and then recommend my company to their fathers. It was a beautiful plan.

More than once I found myself standing amid all that illegal revelry—submerged in the throb of the music and the scents of perfume and cologne mingling with the sharp undertone of chlorine—certain that I had missed something. Something profound.

Surrounded by everything anyone could want, I was still empty.

Chapter Four

OVER THE NEXT three years I built my business in Tehran. My plan was to garner influence with the sons of the powerful, and that had worked as I had hoped it would. Before long I was negotiating contracts with individuals and corporations alike. Some I sold to other companies, keeping a tidy profit for myself. Those that interested me in some way, I had my own workers fulfill. I spent time with friends and girlfriends. I gave and attended parties and enjoyed everything the city could offer, both legal and illegal.

I still spent time with my family, though my relationship with my father was never the same. It was clear that I wasn't his favorite anymore, but I didn't need his approval. I was a success in my own right with my own influence. I was happier that way.

Around this time my former wrestling partner, Asghar, got married. The reception was held at a venue outside the city in a spacious room decorated in rich blue and vining gold. It was still too early to start the dancing, so I stood on the men's side of the room with several friends I hadn't seen in what felt like too long. Surrounded by the joy of the event, we found one of the fruit and flower decorated tables and sat down to our conversation. A few minutes later a friend of my uncle's, Farhan, asked if he could sit with us. He was much older than we were, and no one at the table thought of him as any more than a distant acquaintance at best, but it was a table for eight and there were only three of us. No one wanted to be impolite, so we agreed.

As the night went on, my friends got a little more drunk and the dance music started. They went to dance, and I was getting up to join them when Farhan spoke for the first time.

"How's your uncle Hosein? I thought he would be here tonight," he said.

I looked at the dancers and tried not to sigh. "He's doing fine, but the shop keeps him busy."

"So, he's doing well then. Does he still make regular trips to Dubai?"

"Yes." I started to stand. "If you'll—"

"It's good to see Asghar getting married. Marriage pleases God." I sat again, but didn't meet his eyes. I didn't want to be drawn into the conversation. He persisted. "Hosein said you were a very religious person, that you know the Qur'an very well." He took an apple from the bowl on the table and the knife from the place setting.

I looked at him and smiled. "You're right, I was very religious, but I'm not anymore." I shrugged. "All religions are the same and all religious people are the same."

He turned toward the dancers, but he watched me out of the corner of his eye. "You don't have to be religious to love God. God is universal, just like love is universal." He sliced carefully through the skin of the apple, creating a long, precise coil. "God doesn't need or want people to be religious."

This was the last conversation I wanted to have. I turned toward the revelers and started to get up, intending to forget I'd even seen Farhan.

The throbbing bass and strobing lights from the dance floor stretched and stuttered. I fell into the gaps between the beats as the moments slipped around me. *He's right*, a quiet voice said from just behind my right ear. *Listen to him.* The bubble of quiet burst and the heartbeat of the music pressed in.

Farhan took advantage of the slow return of my equilibrium. "That's why you went to jail for three months," he said.

I turned away from the dancers, my demand for an explanation written in my gaze.

"Your uncle told me," Farhan went on. "You went for no reason other than saying Jesus' name. Luke 21:12 says, 'But before all this, they will seize you and persecute you. They will hand you over to synagogues and put you in prison, and you will be brought before kings and governors, and all on account of my name. This will be your opportunity to serve as witnesses.'"

I glanced around the spacious room. Farhan and I were the only ones at our table, and most of the remaining guests were on the dance floor. The music pressed those still in conversation closer together.

"Who is Luke?" I asked.

He turned toward me. "If you read the Gospel, you'll know who he is, and you'll know who the true Love is."

That conversation with my father flashed into my mind, my desire to read the book that came before the Qur'an and his anger at such a suggestion. The words formed on my lips to ask him for the Gospel, but the memory of jail loomed larger in my mind. Those memories kept me silent and rearranged the words that were in my heart.

I turned away so I wouldn't have to look him in the eye. "There is no true Gospel."

"You might reach that conclusion, but don't you think you should read it for yourself first?" he asked. "It's very short. I can give it to you, if you like." He sliced through the apple and took a bite, chewing slowly as if we were talking about nothing more serious than the latest novel.

I wanted to say yes, but how could I trust a veritable stranger? I put my glass down and got up from the table.

"It was a pleasure meeting you, but I'm sure my friends are wondering where I am."

He smiled, but his eyes flickered with appraisal. "It was a pleasure to meet you too. Why don't we trade numbers? Just in case you want to talk again."

I agreed. I could easily ignore a text or phone call.

Over the next few days I tried to forget about Farhan, and about our discussion. I had wanted to read the Bible all those years ago.

CHAPTER FOUR

I had wanted to decide for myself. What if that had been my only chance? Those days when I wanted to make my own decision were before I'd lost my freedom over a comment. In the quiet moments over the next few days, I returned to that conversation and the stuttering bubble of quiet that made me listen in the first place. The edges of my worry dulled a bit, and I thought I should have taken him up on his offer.

A few days later I was in my office getting ready to have lunch when I received a text from Farhan.

Would it be convenient to meet tomorrow morning?

I was glad to see his message and didn't hesitate to respond. *Yes, what time?*

7:45am?

That was odd, but I knew he had a job to go to. That might be the only time he had. I agreed.

The next morning, he arrived at my house at precisely 7:45 with a folded newspaper under his arm. I offered him some tea, but he said he had to get to work. He unfolded the paper and left a single slim book with a red cover on the table and told me I could call him any time.

After I closed the door behind him, I leaned back against the counter, grabbed the book, and started to leaf through the delicate pages that were densely packed with text. When a verse caught my eye, I read it and moved on while I finished my tea. Nothing stood out to me until I read the first line of the Gospel of John: "In the beginning, there was the Word, and the Word was with God, and the Word was God." I'd had a conversation with my mother when I was no more than five years old. I asked why we speak and if we could create by our words alone. She hadn't known what to say, but the idea never left me. I would trace the question through the sinuous lines I drew in my notebooks as I sought the answer. Here, in this forbidden book, was a clue.

I stretched out on the living room sofa and read the first thirteen verses of John. That was as far as I could go at first. I reread them, turned over the implications, then went back to the beginning until I forced myself to move on and read the entire chapter.

After I read all of John, I read Matthew, Mark, and Luke. Eventually I called my office and told them I wouldn't be in. All day I went back and forth between the four Gospels, assembling pieces of the story from each one. From Matthew I saw the connection to Islam. The image of the Last Supper and the way the wine was changed into blood struck me as cannibalistic, but I saw the connection between that idea and the first miracle Jesus performed when he turned water into wine. Now wine was being turned into blood. As the hours ticked by, I read and reread. I parsed words and deconstructed phrases. I connected ideas and began to excavate meaning from the words. At close to midnight I closed the book with careful respect. For a long moment I sat there in the quiet and traced my fingers over the smooth cover. The simple movement gathered the threads of all I had learned throughout the day.

Jesus, I thought. *You were a great man and a great prophet. You suffered through a hard life and carried a lot of people's pain. I wish I could have been there to carry some of it for you. I love you, but I cannot believe that you're God.*

I sighed and put the book on the coffee table, though I let my hand linger on the cover as I stood, only lifting it when distance made it impossible to maintain contact. Once I was in bed, sleep didn't come as easily as it usually did. One of the verses from John tickled the edges of my thoughts just enough to keep me awake: "Then you will know the truth, and the truth will set you free."

But what was the truth?

I tossed and turned as late night crept toward early morning, the question and the verse tangling together in my mind until I fell into a restless sleep. Then, I wasn't asleep. I wasn't dreaming. I was alone amid a vast landscape.

The earth did not exist among the billowing clouds in which I stood. Neither did fear. Tendrils of vapor swept around me, the gray light coalescing into silvery peaks that shifted with the breeze. I could

CHAPTER FOUR

feel it against my skin, feel it tease locks of my hair.

In the distance, sparks of orange and yellow and pink surrounded something silvery. It dipped, twisted and turned, undulated and doubled back; the warm light that followed grew as it approached. At first, I just watched the curving shapes and graceful movement. As it grew closer, I was able to see that it was a sword, but the way the blade moved brought to mind the flow of mercury rather than the rigidity of steel. Its reflected colors deepened and purified as they caressed the edges of the blade and highlighted its keenness. I could hear it slice through the air, and the hiss grew louder and lasted longer the closer it got.

It was coming toward me, but standing there safely supported by the clouds, I felt no need to try to escape. It might as well have been forever until the blade turned; the tip pointed right at me. I didn't try to run. There was no need. In this safe place, fear didn't exist. In one precise stroke, it sliced deep into my throat, cleaved muscle, tendon, and tissue in an instant, and then disappeared in a burst of colored sparks. Pain followed behind that delicate motion and then the blood welled up. It pulsed forth from the wound in the same rhythm as my heartbeat and flowed down my chest in a thick, warm torrent. My life drained away in that crimson river until the flow slowed to a weak trickle.

I've died, I thought. There was no fear, only acknowledgment.

A hand moved toward me from the same direction the sword had come from. Suddenly it was right in front of me and it dwarfed me. It held a tiny piece of bread before my lips.

Eat. The word resonated through my mind. I knew the sensation of the voice. It had spoken to me when I received my medal and again at the wedding. It had always seemed so far away. Now I was surrounded by the presence of it.

I couldn't speak, but I knew what I thought and felt would be understood. "You've cut my throat and you ask me to eat bread?"

I know, but I tell you to eat.

The hand opened my mouth and fed me the bread, then moved

down to the front of my throat. Radiant warmth emanated from his touch. I felt the wound seal. Blood gurgled in my bisected windpipe as I began to breathe again.

I've changed your blood and I've given you my body. From now on, you won't live for yourself; you will live for me.

With a terrified gasp, I woke up.

My arm was crossed over my chest, and I could feel my heart pounding against my ribs. In the margin between sleep and full waking, I mistook the warm sweat covering me for the blood that had flowed from my throat in the dream. I felt for the wound but found nothing. The world came back. I felt the bed under me. The sheets were tangled around my legs. The silhouettes of familiar furniture, etched a deep, velvety black, surrounded me in the dark room. Real things. Solid things. The dream had been just as real, just as solid. I could still feel the bread in my mouth.

My hand trembled with fearful elation as I turned on the light, got out of bed, toweled the sweat off my chest, and began to pace. With every step I curled my toes into the carpet to reassure myself that I was in my house, that there was a solid floor beneath my feet. A fact that was easily forgotten amid the images and sensations that flooded back.

What was it? What did it mean? Could it really be a sign from God? What else made sense?

I turned that over in my mind as the sun rose. My hand drifted back to my throat. My fingers searched for traces of the wound that must still be there. When I found nothing they went back to my sides as I paced, only to find their way back to my throat a few minutes later to search for the wound that must be there.

It hadn't been a dream. I had been in that place. I had been in that powerful presence. My blood had been spilled, I had been healed, and I was different.

At eight in the morning I called Farhan and with a tremor in my voice told him I needed to see him.

"I'll be right over," he said.

CHAPTER FOUR

I began to make tea, but the water that cascaded over my hand when I filled the kettle reminded me of the flow of blood over my chest. The steam that rose from it a few minutes later took me back to the clouds that had billowed and surrounded me.

When he arrived, the water was still in the kettle, heated but unpoured.

I began to tell him about the dream as soon as he stepped inside. I went forward and backward in the span of the narrative, unable to get everything out fast enough or in the right order.

Farhan leaned forward and nodded. The corners of his lips lifted into a smile. He listened until I was finished; then he hugged me. "Remember what Jesus said in Luke 22:19-20. 'And he took bread, gave thanks and broke it, and gave it to them, saying, *This is my body, given for you; do this in remembrance of me*. In the same way, after the supper he took the cup, saying, *This is my blood, which is poured out for you*."

We were both crying, though maybe for different reasons.

"Jesus is my God," I said, "but I was born into Islam. I can't be a real Christian, even if I wish I could be."

He shook his head. "Muslims think they can't change, but I was born a Muslim as well. Romans tells us, 'Everyone who calls on the name of the Lord will be saved.' When I accepted Jesus, I was so happy and proud. God chose me, he saw me, he heard me, and I know that God loves me. But, keep in mind you cannot just give one small part of yourself. He wants everything from his followers, and he gives us the secrets of his words in the Bible."

For so long I had believed that the happenstance of my birth meant that I was trapped within a religion, that the tenets of that faith imprisoned me as surely as the bars and walls of the jail had. Now the doors were opened, and the walls crumbled. I was born again, with a new life and a new purpose. It was the happiest moment of my life.

"What should I do?" I asked Farhan. "I want to tell everyone that Jesus is God, but who will believe me?"

He smiled. "God will walk and talk before you. The only thing you need to do is live in your faith and be strong in it. Remember what Zechariah teaches us, 'Not by might nor by power, but by my Spirit.' Before anything else though, you must consider your safety. They put you in jail for three months just because of His name, and you weren't even Christian then. Be careful, because you have a lot to do."

Chapter Five

I HAD ALWAYS had the sense that everything I had in this life could be taken away. My father taught me that. Power and influence could fade. Fortunes could be lost as well as won. Relationships waxed and waned with time and circumstance. I'd been seeking something that would last for eternity, and now I had it.

My whole way of life changed. I didn't go out with friends anymore. I stopped throwing parties. At first my friends thought that something had happened to me. They thought it was grief or some struggle that I couldn't share with them. For a while they didn't question my desire to isolate myself. As time went on though, my acquaintances began to realize that this change in me was permanent. Most drifted away and I began to lose some of the contracts I acquired through those connections. The quality of my work still spoke for itself, however, and I acquired contracts through other sources. Every night I read the Bible and got lost in the words for hours on end.

I wanted an image of Jesus in my house, but a drawing or painting wasn't enough. I had been experimenting with sculpture, so I had one of my workers mount three inches of plaster onto the wall of my living room. When it was ready, I began to carve Jesus in relief.

As I worked on the image, I realized that learning the Bible wasn't enough. My father had always told me that if I made a mistake, I should be brave enough to apologize. He had never apologized for the hurt he had caused, and I didn't want to be like that. I had to try to repair some of the damage I had done to others out of my selfishness

BECOMING JOSHUA

and vanity, and I had to start with Mona.

I'd met Mona when I first moved to Tehran. Her father owned a real estate agency, and she worked with him. She taught me about the property markets in the city, and we began seeing each other. As far as she and her family were concerned, we were heading toward marriage. She had a good head for business, but I thought she was too plain. As soon as I met other women I thought were more attractive, I wanted to end it with Mona. I got my chance one day when we were shopping. Everything she did had begun to annoy me, and that day was no different. We began to argue in the store. People had stopped to stare, so we left. As soon as we got outside, I decided to end it.

I told her it was over as soon as we were on the sidewalk. She reached into her bag and pulled out the straight razor she always carried for protection. She opened it and held it poised over her wrist.

"It's over?" Her voice was heavy with threat.

I gave a wary look to the people passing us. "Don't be stupid."

Mona brought the blade down in a certain arc and incised a deep wound in her wrist. The blood fell in thick, heavy drops down her arm to splash onto the pavement. She made two more shallow wounds in rapid succession, staring at me the whole time. Maybe she wanted me to change my mind, or maybe she just wanted to show me what she thought I'd done to her, but I didn't feel either one. I could only wonder how she could do that to me. Anyone passing could think I had attacked her. They could have called the police and held me until they arrived, and that meant I'd end up back in jail. I couldn't take that chance. I left her standing there, a razor in one hand, blood trickling down the fingers of the other. Someone would take care of her.

Back then, how she felt, what she was going through didn't matter as long as I got what I wanted.

I'd changed. I didn't know what I was going to say, but I knew I had to say something.

I parked across from her father's offices and waited for her to leave for the evening. I wondered how she would react when she saw me. Maybe it would be better if I just let it go.

CHAPTER FIVE

While I was debating with myself, I saw her walk out into the afternoon sunshine. She paused and looked directly at my car. She still remembered. It was too late to leave. I went over to her.

"Can we talk for a minute?" I asked. She nodded and we went to sit in her car. "I just wanted to apologize for what I did, the way I ended things, and I wish you nothing but the best."

Calm evaporated and anger flashed in her eyes. "Do you have any idea what you did to me? You ruined my life! I told everyone—my family, my friends—everyone that you were the one and then I had to tell them that you weren't. I didn't know how to tell them I'd been taken in by you. I lay there in that hospital listening to everyone being so kind and reassuring and I felt like a complete fool." Tears streaked her cheeks. "And now, after all this time you just show up with your apologies and 'I wish you well.'"

I opened my mouth to say something, but she went on.

"You only want me to forgive you so that you'll feel better. Get out."

"That's not—"

"Get out!" She turned in her seat and kicked me.

"Sorry," I said and got out.

I walked back to my car and wondered if she'd been right. Maybe I was still being selfish. Maybe she hadn't accepted my apology today, but it might mean something to her later.

I sought out the people I had wronged to ask for their forgiveness. I apologized to people I had fought with, those I had injured, and those I had insulted. They didn't forgive me. I explained to the girls I had been seeing that I had never intended to marry any of them. I apologized for leading them on. I was as honest and sincere as I could be. Like Mona, none of them forgave me.

Slowly, steadily, the image of Jesus emerged from the plaster. I stood eye to eye with him daily as I discovered his features. I knelt before him to create the folds of his robe. I had to be honest with myself. The way I had been living had injured others more deeply than I had ever realized. I looked up at the figure emerging from the sculpted clouds, his hands spread in silent benediction, and dedicated myself to following wherever his path led me.

As a constant reminder of that commitment, I lettered a sign to hang over it.

> *Forget safety.*
> *Live where you fear to live.*
> *~Rumi*

I had no doubt that Jesus was my Shepherd. But what did that really mean? Like everyone else, I could define the word shepherd. I had seen pictures of men watching over flocks of sheep and goats, but what did a shepherd do? I immersed myself in the verses about the Good Shepherd, but the more I turned that question over in my mind, the more I came to believe that I had to understand the life of a shepherd.

So, I called Ali, my former cellmate.

While we were still in prison, I'd invited him to stay with me in Tehran after his release. I will never forget my first sight of him. His presence filled the doorframe and hesitated there. His eyes widened in what could have been wonder or panic as they slid over the comfortable, modern rooms and smooth surfaces.

"What's wrong?" I asked. "Come in. Make yourself comfortable."

"It's so clean." He placed his foot over the threshold as if the tiles would crack under his weight. Once inside, he treated everything in my home as if his presence would somehow mar it. He took off his shoes as soon as he entered, but he worried that his socks weren't clean enough to walk on the carpets. He wouldn't sit on the furniture. He chose the floor instead. Often, he would walk around with a tissue and wipe surfaces as soon as he'd touched them.

The way he moved through the city of Tehran was something else entirely. If he perceived a challenge in a gesture or a glance, he was ready to fight. A parking space became a confrontation; attractive women drew shouts and obvious stares. I'd done my best to smooth his rough edges, but the rough edges made him who he was. In the

CHAPTER FIVE

end, he became more accustomed to life in the city, but he never really adapted to it.

He stayed with me for nearly a month. When he finally had his fill of the city, he went back to his family and his flocks. We still talked every day. I knew I could trust him.

That day, the conversation had wandered as it usually did. Then, I asked him, "Do you remember when you invited me to come and visit your plain?"

"Of course!" he said. "So, when do you want to come?"

"I was thinking sometime in the next month or so, if that's convenient."

"Something in there should work. What makes you so interested in sheep all of a sudden?"

I hesitated for a moment. "I've become Christian. I want to learn more about what a shepherd does, how he lives."

He didn't hesitate. "That's as good a reason as any."

I'd been right. Ali didn't care about religion. He was just happy at the thought of seeing me again. We worked out the details and set a firm date.

The day-long journey brought me from the bright lights and smooth roads of Tehran to wind, dust and shallow wheel ruts in the desert soil. There were no signs and few landmarks. A wrong turn would have taken me into an uninhabited landscape full of scrub and wind-scored earth. If that happened, I'd have little chance of finding my way back.

Ali's family had owned this part of the plain for five hundred years, drawing their livelihood from the wool and meat of countless sheep that had grazed there. The first thing that struck me was the sound. The sibilance of the wind danced with the sounds of the animals gathered in the shallow valley below. The constant movement in the air around me was at odds with the quiet landscape painted in neutral tones. Here rain was scarce and when it did fall, it was taken almost immediately by the dry air, making surface water precious. Water flows deep underground and sustains vegetation that matches

51

the earthy beige of the rolling hills and the wool of the sheep.

The animals moved across the landscape in a close herd as if they were one living creature. Browns, stony grays, and the sandy golden tones all shifted together under a sky the color of light-blue slate.

It was the most beautiful place I had ever seen.

That night, Ali killed one of the sheep and prepared a meal to welcome me. There were three other men who worked with him, and as we ate, I got to know a bit more about them and what they did. When the sun went down, the dry heat of the day gave way to a clear, cold night. The constant light of the city was nothing but a distant memory, and soon the Milky Way arched above us and described infinity in shades of subtle pinks, warm purples, and blue-whites accented with bright, celestial diamonds.

I spent five days with Ali and his flock. Since I didn't know how to be a shepherd, during the day I would sit by the fire to keep it going and make sure there was tea ready for Ali and the others when they wanted it. Sometimes, I walked the low hills and sat above the flock. There, surrounded by the conversation of the wind and the animals, I read the Gospel. By the time I went back to camp, the wind had erased the footprints I'd made on the way there. At night I slept with the others in the small hut that was draped with strong desert garlic, a natural barrier to the deadly snakes and scorpions that live in that region. My mind had only begun to quiet when it was time to go back home.

Five days wasn't nearly enough. I couldn't just abandon the business though. I employed good people, so it only took a couple of weeks to make arrangements so that I could be gone for two months. I was so anxious to get back to those quiet plains that it felt like it took forever.

During the second visit I was able to really learn what a shepherd does. Everything is focused on the protection of the flock, even the way the shepherd eats. The day starts before the sun comes up when a fire is prepared in a pit. Tea and a quick breakfast of fresh sheep's milk, and bread cooked on a hot, vertical stone are prepared and eaten. The coals of the fire are then ready to make *digi*; a pot of meat,

CHAPTER FIVE

rice, potatoes, and sheep's butter, cooked by burying it in the pit all morning. This frees the shepherds to follow the flock. They walk for miles each day, moving the animals from grazing land to water and back again. Even when they sleep, they're alert to the sounds of their dogs barking at marauding wolves.

If this was all, I would have thought that the shepherd acts out of love for his sheep. The idea would have been a simple one.

But there was more to it than that. Every four or five days, Ali slaughtered one of the sheep to feed us. The rest of the flock was fed and cared for so that they could be taken to market and butchered. For months the shepherds lived without the comforts most of us take for granted, not out of love for their animals, but because of the benefit this hardship would eventually bring them.

The idea of the shepherd, an idea that was so beautiful to me, now became challenging. Did Jesus protect us for his own benefit? I began to feel as if I'd been deceived. I still sat by the fire and made tea for the shepherds, still walked to the tops of the hills and tried to discern the secrets the wind was whispering to me, still watched the mysteries of the universe unfold overhead every night, but none of it was quite the same. I fell into a deep, tangled silence that held me fast. Ali noticed how my attitude had changed. We still talked, but he couldn't help me sort through it. There was nowhere I could turn except the Gospel.

John the Baptist gave me the answer. He called Jesus the Lamb of God.

Now it made sense. The one who has only been a shepherd would protect his flock, but also use them for his own benefit. They would be no more than a means to an end. But the person who has been the lamb and becomes the shepherd protects his flock because he loves them, as Jesus loved us on the cross. If a pastor hasn't suffered for his people, hasn't been one of them himself, he cannot truly be a good shepherd. I felt the tendrils of uncertainty that had bound me slip away.

As my time with Ali began to draw to a close, I wanted to thank

BECOMING JOSHUA

him for all he had done for me. Being a shepherd was a difficult life, but it was made harder by the fact that Ali didn't have a vehicle. He and the other shepherds used donkeys to carry water and supplies. Before I left, I bought him a Jeep. Ali was thrilled. I watched him drive over the rolling hills, a thick plume of dust following him.

    I went back to the city with a renewed sense of confidence in my purpose.

Chapter Six

ONCE I GOT back from Ali's plain, Farhan spent several hours a day with me to teach me about the Bible and about Yale, the UK organization that supported several underground churches in Iran. I was eager to learn, and I believe he could see that, but now I think he was especially attentive because I had money and was more able than some to support the church. At the time I simply gave myself over completely to what I was being taught.

During these months I spent time with my family every week. I wanted to find a way to share my faith with them, but I could never find the right words or the right moment.

On September 17, 2003, the whole family was together for dinner and I seized the moment I was given. My father sat at the head of the laden table and said a brief prayer of thanks for food. It was the opposite of Muslim tradition, but it was the way he always did it. We bowed our heads in silence and said our own thanks.

"Amen," everyone responded when he finished.

"To the one true God," I added.

No one said anything. My older sister Zary—who was sitting between my father and me—rolled her eyes.

Now that I had started, I wasn't going to be deterred. I broke a piece of bread off the flat loaf in the middle of the table. "It's important to know the true God."

"Oh, please," Zary said. "Can't we just have dinner?"

"And by the true God, I mean Jesus," I said.

The whole family looked from me to my father and back again. His eyes narrowed and I could see the tension gather in his hands and his shoulders. My younger brother Parsa, who was thirteen at the time, turned to my father.

"Maybe you should listen to him. He's changed a lot in the last few months, he doesn't hit me at all anymore, and he's a lot nicer."

The anger that had been simmering in my father's eyes ignited. He picked up a large bowl of autumn orange *khoresht* stew and threw it at me. I dodged. Zary tried to. The food caught my side and left a trail of burn and blisters along my ribs. Zary caught the worst of it on her shoulder and upper chest. She screamed. The *khoresht* splattered over the wall and the light wood cabinets, dripping down to the white tile floor. My father tossed another dish toward my mother, but she moved just in time. The bowl flew off the table and shattered next to her. The whole family fled. My younger siblings took shelter from my father's rage behind the breakfast bar.

Zary was still screaming. She pulled her clothing away from it to take that minimal pressure off her blistered skin. My mother ran to her side. My father grabbed the largest carving knife from the block on the counter and ran toward me. I believe he wanted to kill me, but my brothers and sisters got between us. They begged him not to hurt me and stayed between us until finally he threw the knife at me out of frustration. It hit the wall with a dull thud and clattered to the floor.

"You never listen to anyone! You just get angry!" My body was tense, poised for the next attack but unwilling to back down.

"Listen? Listen to what? Lies?" The room wasn't large enough to contain his anger. It vibrated through the air like a physical force.

"What are you afraid of? You don't care who you hurt as long as you don't have to admit that you're wrong about something?"

"Get out!" he shouted. "Get out of my house and stay away from my family until you give up this Jesus delusion. I won't have your madness infecting my children." To consider that I might be right shook the very foundations of his world. He couldn't stand the uncertainty.

I backed toward the door. The stew dripped off my clothes and left

CHAPTER SIX

orange stains on the carpet. "That's it, it's done," I said. "I will never call you 'father' again. Jesus taught me not to call anyone father!" I slammed the door as I left. Once the break was complete, the spike of adrenaline began to fade, and the pain of the burn intensified. I peeled the shirt off and ran for my car. I pulled out of the driveway fast enough to make the tires squeal.

My departure from the house had been so chaotic, I had no way of knowing if my brothers and sisters agreed with my father. Even though there was a significant age gap between Parsa and me, we had always been close. If anyone would speak to me, he would. The burn still itched when I went to see him. He liked to go to the park near his school. We hadn't been able to contact each other, but I went to the park anyway. I knew I'd find him there. I hadn't been there long when I saw him coming along the path. I fell into step beside him.

"They're all mad at you," he said as we walked along the path in the warm afternoon sun.

"For being Christian?" I asked.

"No, they're mad because you upset Mom and Dad so much. They're getting old. What if something happens to them?"

"That's not my fault. All he had to do was listen for a few minutes. I never said he had to agree."

"He's never listened before," he said and looked down for a moment. "He's still mad. He wants to take everything from you."

"Let him try," I scoffed.

He looked up at me again. "No. You know he has a lot of friends. Don't come back here for a while. If you want to fix things, maybe Nane can help."

I shook my head. "I'm not wrong and I'm not going to say that I am just so he'll allow me back in his house."

Worry creased his forehead. "Be careful," he said.

Parsa had been right. My father would try to take everything from me. The house and company in Arima were still in his name. His name was on the accounts associated with that business. He thought if he owned everything that he would own me. The company in Tehran, my home there, the success I had built, those things were mine. He didn't know about them, and I can only imagine how angry he was when he realized that he didn't have the kind of power he thought he had.

My pastor invited me to spend weekends with other new believers at an underground church where we could worship and pray in relative safety. This small group became more important to me than before because they were all I had. Our meeting place became a different kind of home, one where we could share our joys and our struggles and help each other grow in our faith.

In my free hours, I studied the Bible. I was so eager to know Jesus that I learned the Bible more quickly than most. To study on my own was one thing, but I wanted a deeper understanding. Intensive classes in Bible study took place in neighboring countries and lasted anywhere from a few days to a few weeks. Even outside of Iran there was still danger.

To cross borders required the proper paperwork, and that meant the government was able to track where a person went and how frequently. Too many trips to the same place would raise questions and draw closer scrutiny. Flying would draw the closest questioning. Driving would bring less, but different countries had different traffic laws. I drove to the border and took a bus for the actual crossing. It was convenient and no one questioned me.

The first time I wasn't sure what to expect. The classes were taught mainly by pastors from Europe, and time was at a premium. To make the most of it, those days began at seven in the morning and ran until ten in the evening. I spent December and January splitting my time as best I could between study and the business.

CHAPTER SIX

One of the most difficult times that first year was Nowruz, the celebration of the New Year. The tradition of that celebration on the vernal equinox traces back 3,000 years. It is a two-week-long event that brings families together to mark a new beginning. Many businesses close for those two weeks, mine included. After my staff left that last evening I lingered in my office. I straightened papers that didn't need it and organized files that were already in order and wondered what I was going to do without my family.

While the rest of the country enjoyed the company of those they were closest to, I spent days alone in my workshop. Tigers had been my favorite animal when I was younger because I saw them as powerful. As I grew older, I began to respect the eagle's wider view of the world. While families celebrated, I watched an eagle emerge from a block of white stone.

A week into the new year, Ali called and invited me to visit him on *Sizdah Bedar*, the thirteenth day after the new year. New lambs had been born and he had thought of me. Traditionally, this is a day when everyone goes out to enjoy nature. Spending time with Ali's flock seemed the perfect way to celebrate.

"How was your Nowruz?" he asked as we walked toward the pens.

I was silent for a long moment. "I tried to tell them about Christianity. There was a huge argument, and my father told me not to come back. I spent the holiday in my workshop." I couldn't meet his eyes as I said it.

He didn't say anything. Didn't ask for details. He just stopped and hugged me. For all his faults and flaws, Ali was my best friend. I trusted him with my life and I still do.

For the rest of the time I was there, we watched the new lambs as they danced and wobbled through the grass on their too-long legs.

Their fleece shone brighter white against the golden shades of the grass and the dusty flanks of their mothers. As I was getting ready to leave, I saw one of the other shepherds strike the leg of one of the new lambs with his staff.

The crack of bone was unmistakable, as were the sounds of pain that came afterward. I was horrified. "What's he doing? He just broke that one's leg on purpose."

"That's the best way to keep it safe," Ali said.

"But—"

"That one likes to jump. If it jumps over the fence at night, it'll get lost or be killed. We break the leg and then carry it when the flock moves for the next two months. It'll heal and by the time it does, the lamb won't jump anymore."

It was a brutal form of protection, but it was effective. This added to my picture of the shepherd. Not only does he protect his flock from the wolves and the dangers outside, but he also protects his sheep from the dangers they create themselves.

At first, I wanted to know the Bible better for myself, but as I moved through the initial levels to more in-depth study, I could teach new believers. It wasn't something I wanted to do at first, but I came to understand that it was something Jesus wanted us to do, to learn and then help others understand. I worked hard to be able to answer the questions posed by Muslims and to use my knowledge of the Qur'an and the Bible to help them better understand who Jesus is.

In meeting with new believers, there were often times I wanted to give them a Bible. I knew that Bibles were illegal, but I had no idea how rare they were. The first time I asked Farhan for a Bible, I was told that there might be two or three available in the next month, or, if that didn't work out, we might be able to make a few photocopies. I thought about the first day I spent reading and rereading the Gospels, how I had drawn meaning and connection in my own way and in my

CHAPTER SIX

own time. I couldn't deny that to someone else.

I had Kurdish relatives in the border region of Iran, Iraq, and Turkey, so I called my uncle Ako and asked if he knew anyone who could help. Less than an hour later, he called me back with numbers and introductions to smugglers.

The treacherous mountains that mark the border between Iran, Iraq, and Turkey are riddled with illicit highways. Unmarked, unmapped trails travelled by men desperate to provide for their families in a time when the Shia government has moved factories and other means of employment from the border regions to marginalize the Sunni Kurds. If people from that region attempt to find work elsewhere, they are usually turned away because they are Kurdish. By strictly controlling the importation of goods, the Iranian government has contributed to the creation of these networks. Electronics and designer clothing come into the country in the same way as alcohol and Bibles—packed onto the backs of men and boys who know that when they set out, they might never return home.

For them, the walk through the mountains takes between six and eight hours. The trails are narrow and rocky and, in places, nearly vertical. A wrong step could send a man and his heavy burden tumbling down onto jagged rocks. In some places a wrong step could trigger one of the mines planted along the known trails by Iranian border patrol agents.

During the summer, the long columns of men are easily visible against mountainsides. This makes them easy targets for border patrol agents who shoot to kill. They spare no one, not even the pack animals. In the fall, snow blankets the mountains. This makes it more difficult for the border agents to reach the more remote areas, but the men trudge through snow that's several feet deep. Frostbite and hypothermia are added to the list of dangers they must contend with.

The trek through the mountains is only the first part of the journey. Once goods reach the Iranian side of the border, they must be driven to their final destination through multiple police checkpoints between the border and Tehran. The men who make this leg of the journey drive as fast as they can, and they do not stop for the police. If they do, there won't be an arrest and a trial. They will be shot.

To the government, these men are less than human. Their lives mean nothing, and the fewer of them there are, the better.

In this border region there is no family that hasn't lost a father, a brother, a husband, or a son. They know the risks, but they have no other choice.

The financial cost to bring in Bibles was high, but the cost in blood and lives far exceeded mere money. I had no choice. No matter where we got Bibles from, they would have been smuggled into the country.

Once our supply line had been secured, I rented a garage just inside the Iranian border to store the Bibles until they could be transported to Tehran. In the city it was far too dangerous for anyone to store them in their homes. Possession of a Bible is considered a more serious crime than possession of a gun. I couldn't ask anyone to take that kind of risk. I rented another garage to use for storage.

The Bibles had to come in as contraband, but I couldn't just use these men like mules. When I hired new workers, I made certain that most of them were from the Kurdish area and Afghanistan, groups that had the most difficult time finding employment.

Sharing Christ with others is one of the most important and most dangerous things we could do as Christians. When we spoke to strangers about Christ, we never knew how those ideas would be received. It was possible that the people would be indifferent, or that they would want to know more. It was just as likely that the person might work for the government or may have a hatred of Christians and would turn us in to the police.

As terrible as it would be for a Christian to be arrested, anyone associated with that person would also suffer. The government is so threatened by Christianity that when a person is arrested for being

CHAPTER SIX

a Christian, they are questioned or tortured to secure the names of other Christians and the locations of underground churches. After one arrest, an entire community could be at risk.

When we spoke to someone, we followed a strict protocol. The first step was to strike up a friendship. We'd ride around in a taxi for an hour and chat with the driver. We'd ride the bus or the metro and have a friendly conversation with a fellow passenger. If that conversation went well, we'd try to meet again. In a city the size of Tehran, finding the same person was nearly impossible. Even if we could find them, it took days or weeks to build a friendly connection first. During those early contacts we always gave false names. When we found someone who expressed interest, we met with them in neutral locations, like parks or cafés. Then we'd meet at the person's home. Throughout this entire process the person knew only one member of our group. Once it was certain that the person was serious about Christianity, they would be invited to an underground church. It was a slow and uncertain process that was inefficient at best and a complete waste of time at worst.

Another way to share the Gospel with people was to leave a Bible in the back of a taxi when we left the vehicle. I strongly disagreed with that tactic. Our Bibles had been paid for in sweat and uncertainty, blood and lives. I thought that the Bibles should be kept safe until we found a person who was eager for the word of God. Leaving them behind to be discarded trivialized and disrespected everyone who had sacrificed so much to bring them to the city in the first place.

I wanted to increase the number of new believers and I wanted to do it in a more effective way with less risk. The Gospel gave me the answer. Jesus was a carpenter. He took material that was raw or broken and created objects that were beautiful and useful. I decided to do the same thing.

The upper levels of Iranian society benefited from the structure of the government and would not be inclined to do anything that would jeopardize their own position. The middle levels of society had the most police presence because they didn't see any direct benefit, but they had disposable income and free time. This was a combination that could lead to the pursuit of illicit ideas and activities. Addicted to drugs or mentally ill, the homeless were thought of as worthless and were largely ignored by the police. If a homeless person was arrested and tried to gain favor with the police by telling stories of the Christians they know, the police would consider anything they said to be lies or drug-fueled ravings.

To me, it was the perfect opportunity to spread God's word in a safer, more efficient way. I was excited to share my idea with Farhan.

Farhan often stopped by my office after business hours. My company's offices had a modern design with office and meeting spaces defined by glass walls. It was airy and bright, but privacy was at a premium. Above my office was a private conference room, and we often went up there to relax with tea while we chatted.

"I want to reach out to the homeless," I said once the tea was poured.

He reached for the glass and then stopped. "In what way?"

"To bring them God's message," I said.

He sat back and clasped his hands in his lap. The silence that settled in the room told me what he thought of the idea even before he spoke.

"As always, God will guide us," he said.

I can't say I was surprised by his reaction. The pastors knew I didn't stop learning at the end of a lesson. I dug deep into the Bible for answers, and some didn't like it. I knew it was a good idea though, even if it was more an idea than a plan. Each time Farhan and I met, I talked about it and tried to convince him. Most of the time he changed the subject and hoped that I would forget about it.

It took a couple of months for Farhan to realize how serious I was. Once he accepted that I wasn't going to let go of the idea, I'm sure he thought I would do it on my own, with or without his approval.

At our next meeting he arrived at my office with six other pastors. Bringing so many together at the same time was unusual. One of the

CHAPTER SIX

ways to maintain the safety of the group was to keep the leadership separate.

I greeted them and directed them to my conference room; then I asked the office manager to make some tea for all of us. They'd left the chair at the head of the table empty, but I sat between Roya and Mahi on the left side of the table. While we waited for the tea, the greetings and small talk held tense undertones.

Khale, the pastor with the most senior position in the organization, said less than the others. She took a notebook and a pen out of her bag. She twirled it and tapped it against the pages. As soon as the office manager brought the tea and closed the door, Farhan asked me to describe my plan. Some didn't quite meet my eyes; the others did their best to give the impression of attention. I'd seen clients do that. They were going to reject anything I had to say. Before I could say anything, Cyrus, another pastor and a good friend of mine, arrived. Grateful for the delay to organize my thoughts, I waited until he had tea and greetings were exchanged.

Farhan looked at me. "So, we're all here to listen to your idea."

I leaned forward. "I think we should be spreading the message to the homeless."

"This is not how we do things," Khale said, her pen poised over the paper.

"Maybe it should be," I said. "We waste weeks trying to get to know someone, trying to gauge if they can be trusted and, if they go to the police, they will be listened to and taken seriously. The homeless won't go to the police, and even if they did, the police won't listen."

"What makes you think they'll even understand the message?" Farhan asked.

"What makes you think they won't?" I countered. "Do they not deserve to know Jesus because they don't have homes or because they're addicts?"

"Of course, we're all the same in God's eyes," Mohsen said. "But we have to think of our safety first."

"I don't see how it's any more dangerous than what we do now," I replied.

"He's right." Cyrus turned the steel bracelet around on his wrist in slow circles, as if the motion drew his thoughts into sharper focus. "Working with the addicted would be safer because they don't trust the police, or anyone they perceive to be in authority. It's one of the rules they live by. They wouldn't break that rule for something they'd see as trivial."

I caught the look of disapproval in Khale's eyes, but if Cyrus did, he ignored it.

"Maybe you're right," Eli said. "Maybe this is the way to share the message, but what makes you think that you're the right person to do it?"

Before I could answer, Khale spoke. "We've listened, but I think that this is simply too dangerous." She put away her notebook. "We will continue to teach you and help you, but we have to consider the safety of our underground churches. It might be better if we parted ways."

Cyrus sat forward, turning to Khale. "I think we should continue to pray about this."

"No one is saying he can't do it if he wants to." Khale gestured at me as if I were a piece of furniture. "This simply isn't right for Yale."

After that there was no more to say. Before I could even say goodbye, Khale had picked up her things and left. I could see the embarrassment on the faces of the others as we said goodbye. They agreed with her position, but not with how abrupt she'd been about it. I walked them downstairs and out to their cars, wishing them a safe trip home. After the last one had left, Cyrus and I went back upstairs.

"She was looking for a reason to get rid of me," I said.

"She's not comfortable with new ideas, but I don't know why she just left like that." He was silent for a moment. "So how are you going to do it?"

"I have no idea," I said. I knew what I wanted to accomplish, and I was certain I was right, but I knew nothing about the world

CHAPTER SIX

I was about to walk into. Cyrus did, though. I'd met him through Farhan and for a while I had no idea that he was a pastor. Farhan was the one who usually spoke, but when Cyrus did speak it was with authority. When I got to know him a little better, I learned that Cyrus had spent years as a heroin addict before his conversion. If anyone would know how to make this work, he would. "Will you help me?"

He was silent for a moment. Then he nodded. "Yes."

For the next few weeks, no one contacted me. Then Farhan called. He didn't say he'd changed his mind, but I agreed to see him.

He arrived at my house the next evening with a small towel under his arm. He told me they had decided that I should be baptized. This was something I had wanted for a long time but didn't think it would happen. In Iran, baptism with water is rare because it is so dangerous. When it happens at all, it is without all the ceremony and community celebration that should be associated with such an event. If the government finds out what is happening, the person giving the baptism will be killed because only those with a high position in the church are allowed to baptize others. People who convert in this kind of environment receive a baptism of fire with the Holy Spirit first, then, sometimes many years later, a baptism of water.

I will never forget the spiritual moment when Farhan knelt before me and washed my feet. We were both crying.

He looked into my eyes. "Servants are not greater than the Master."

The next night, February 2, 2005, at around eight in the evening, Farhan arrived at my house with three others. Two of them I had never met and would likely never see again, probably because they were higher up in the organization. He introduced me to everyone by what I knew were false names. This was always done to protect the safety of the one who gives the sacrament. I didn't care. I was just so happy to be baptized. They baptized me in my bathtub, and all left immediately afterward. It didn't matter. I was so happy.

I'd only been a Christian for three years, and now it was time to serve God in a new way.

Chapter Seven

MY JOURNEY INTO Christianity began with a dream. Cyrus's began with a miraculous release from years of addiction. He drew on his memories of those dark times to educate me about the community I planned to walk into.

This was a world completely different than any I'd known. We dealt with the practicalities first. So many things would make me seem suspicious, not the least of which was my accent and the way I spoke. It was decided that I would say as little as possible until I was accepted.

I looked far too healthy to have a serious drug problem. I decided I would tell them that I'd been kicked out of my family's home because I failed an exam. The part about being separated from my family was the truth.

Addicts and the homeless were sometimes targets for violence, and they didn't have much to defend themselves with, only the needles they used to inject their drugs. Those needles could carry HIV and other bloodborne pathogens. I was physically strong, but that wouldn't help me if someone felt threatened and attacked me. I decided to dress in heavy layers as a precaution.

Those things would allow us to do what was most important: spread the message. We chose specific verses about love and forgiveness that could be used in response to stories shared by people we met. None of the verses mentioned Jesus by name. It was up to me to remember the right verse at the right moment.

When the day arrived, Cyrus and I made our way to the south side of Tehran. The north side of the city is home to the affluent. If any of the homeless appeared there, the residents wouldn't hesitate to summon the police. Here, unless a wealthy person complained of a homeless person committing petty crimes, the police ignored them. The poor of the south side couldn't offer anything in bribes.

We parked at a small lot a couple of blocks from our intended destination and walked the rest of the way. Even before we got there, I could see the shell of a building with no windows or doors sitting on the edge of a dry riverbed. The rough structure was one of the places the homeless would find shelter. The bridge over the riverbed was used for shelter too, but by a different group. We went down the steep slope and headed toward a makeshift encampment huddled in the shade.

The distance and the deep shadows concealed most of the camp and the people who survived there. As we moved closer, I could see shelters built of jumbled scraps of wood and plastic. Small fires illuminated rail-thin men and women sitting on the ground, some slumped forward, others rested back against the bridge abutment. All were immersed in whatever drug held them prisoner. The stench of human waste and filth wove together with the deeper smell of lurking death. It stole out of the darkness and surrounded us as we drew closer.

I had never seen anything like this before. I had never imagined such a place existed anywhere let alone in the city I called home. Everywhere I looked was a heartbreaking and frightening new reality, and it was simply too much to take in. Human beings couldn't live like this, could they? Yet here they were. People who hadn't bathed in weeks or even months, people who slept and ate surrounded by the same thick miasma that surrounded Cyrus and me like fetid water. Maybe they weren't human. Maybe drugs and desperation had leached all humanity out of them in stealthy degrees. No one would care if they died. I don't think they would have cared either. Everywhere I looked, desperation was sketched in bold lines.

I thought there couldn't be anything worse when a man lurched out from one of the shelters. His skin was caked with dirt, and the piece of yellow rubber tubing he was using as a tourniquet stood out around his neck. A syringe dangled from the vein just below it. My eyes went wide. What planet was I on? How could I imagine that I could do anything here?

"You're staring. Stop it," Cyrus hissed at me.

"I can't help it," I said, my eyes still fixed on the man as he made a meandering trip to one of the fires. The tube and syringe quivered in different rhythms as he lurched along.

Some of the others looked our way, their gazes laced with suspicion.

"Come on," Cyrus said when more took notice. "You're not ready yet. We'll try again another day."

Questions crowded into my mind while we drove back. How could human beings live that way? Had Cyrus lived that way? I hadn't known him when he was in the grip of his addiction. Maybe that's why he chose that place; it was familiar to him. The part that bothered me the most was the fact that I had been blind to it. If I had lived in the city for years and been blind to their suffering, I wondered if God was blind to it too.

I couldn't eat or sleep that night. How could I when people in my own city didn't even have the most basic comforts. The sights and the smells merged with the stark questions from the other pastors. Maybe they had known what I would be walking into. Maybe they were right. Maybe what I wanted to do was impossible. How could I know? I had been so caught up in my own shock and revulsion that I hadn't even spoken to anyone about it. How could I say that they were right, that this wouldn't work, if I didn't try?

The next day at work I didn't want to see anyone. I needed to think, to try to understand everything I'd seen. Everything I thought and felt was still too big to put into words, but I knew what I had to do. I called Cyrus and asked when we could go back.

Two days later Cyrus showed me how to get into the building. It looked to me as though the contractor had run out of money halfway through the build and the incomplete shell had been abandoned. There were boards over the empty doors and downstairs windows. But for those who needed shelter, there was always a way in. As soon as we entered, we were stopped and told that, because we were strangers, we had to pay to stay there. It wasn't much. No one who needed to stay there would have much to give. We paid.

The difference between the way of life inside the building and the camp was obvious. The people who lived there were addicted and homeless. As with those outside, they were unwashed and dressed in ragged clothes. But I could hear a lively discussion about philosophy and politics going on. There was shared laughter. Someone else was reading. There was addiction and deprivation, but these people hadn't given up on life.

Cyrus had told me that the best way to begin to connect with the people we met was to provide drugs. I wasn't happy about doing it, but we had arrived prepared. Cyrus pretended to use with them. After that they regarded us with less suspicion.

Despite our tenuous acceptance, this was like no community I had ever been a part of. I had to learn a completely different set of rules. Drugs were more important than food. Any money they came by would be used first to supply their habit. If I wanted to share a meal with my newfound friends, I couldn't simply bring it with me or have others deliver it. No one goes into a camp with a desire to help. Such a gesture would be viewed with suspicion and refused.

When we shared food, Cyrus and I made it look like it had been partially eaten. We mixed it together in bags, as if a restaurant had gotten rid of leftovers. Then we would mix the bags in with the trash in the dumpsters close to the building for others to discover.

I didn't speak much at first. They had their own slang, and their own accent. When I spoke, they laughed and asked when I was going to go home to my family.

One of the first people we met was Behram.

The first time I saw him, he sat with his back against the wall, away from the loose groups of others who were gathered. Most were

CHAPTER SEVEN

thin, but I could almost see the space between the bones in his forearm. The next thing I noticed was the small black bag he had with him. Possessions were limited to things that were immediately useful and easily carried. In that black bag, Behram had a towel and books.

The more time we spent there, the more we learned. The community inside the building shifted from day to day, but Behram was the one everyone went to when problems arose. At first, he watched the way we interacted with others, paid attention to the questions we asked and the answers that we gave. He was addicted and had been for many years, but he took his role as a leader seriously. As we got to know him, we could tell that he was educated and often talked about philosophy. I wondered what had led him to addiction and then to this abandoned building.

Cyrus was the one who chose who we spent time with. He looked for people who weren't so lost to the drug that they wanted to talk about other things. To begin, we listened to them talk about their lives, their losses, their thoughts and ideas. We couldn't know which of the verses would resonate with them unless we got to know them first.

The first time we used one of our planned verses, we had only been in the building for a few days. It was getting late and conversation had slowed and quieted. Most people were beginning to settle down to sleep or silence. One of the young men sitting with Cyrus rocked, his arms crossed over his stomach. His thin frame had all but sunk into the layers of grimy clothing he wore; his eyes were fixed on a curved scar on the floor. "You don't know what it's really like out here," he said to me.

I moved closer to him. "Tell me."

"It's like fading away, becoming invisible. They must see me because they walk around me. They turn away, but not before I see their disgust. If they do look at me, they insult me, tell me I'm no better than garbage and that I would be doing the world a favor if I died. Sometimes I think they're right, but I insult them back, call them names, anything I can think of to make them feel some of what I feel."

"When they hurled their insults at him, he did not retaliate; when he suffered, he made no threats. Instead, he entrusted himself to him who judges justly."

The motion of his body stopped. His eyes searched mine; then he moved away for the night.

The idea was foreign to him and the others who occupied the building. In that community, if a person is hurt or insulted, the expectation is that they will retaliate. We would have to see if the idea made any impression.

The next day, as we were leaving, Cyrus asked, "What was that verse?"

"First Peter 2:23," I said.

"It was perfect."

After several weeks the filth and the drug use faded into the background, and I began to see that these people were no different than anyone else. Every day they worked at the business of survival in circumstances that had been unimaginable to me only a short time before. For most, drug addiction had stripped away families, jobs, homes, and dignity in painful layers until it left hearts and souls raw and bleeding. So many told us that they wanted their lives back, but each felt powerless against the strength of their addiction.

Cyrus and I spent several nights a week getting to know each small group within the building. We believed that with the extra time they would remember us. When we saw someone we knew, we'd sit with them for an hour or so to remind them of who we were, because often they forgot. Everything about them seemed slower, but I learned that the people we spoke with remembered the verses we'd used and other things we'd said in conversation. They would repeat the verses in the context they had heard them while they spoke to each other or would come back and ask questions hours or days later.

The person I spoke to more than anyone else was Behram. We

CHAPTER SEVEN

talked and argued about philosophy for hours. Those discussions would have been more at home in a café than an encampment of the homeless and addicted, but no matter where we were, I felt well out of my depth in those discussions. Even though he had been using different kinds of drugs for twenty years, he still retained his love of poetry and his ability to be logical. I wondered what he had been like before addiction had dug its claws into him.

We also spent time in the encampment under the bridge, and I began to see the difference between the two groups. The people in the building had regarded us with suspicion in the beginning, but they'd become friendlier and even welcoming. In the encampment we were treated as objects of curiosity at best, or prey at worst. The people who lived there listened to us and analyzed our words only to determine if we were a threat. They had lost as much as those who lived in the building, but they were so far removed from themselves that they no longer had a memory of what they had been. They lived in a half-remembered dream that tormented them daily and left them waiting impatiently for death to finally arrive.

Cyrus and I spent half the week for three months with the homeless, mostly in the abandoned building. Society had rejected them, but there was still power and potential there. They were resourceful and always found a way to get what they needed, whether it was drugs or food. They knew about life, death, and survival. And they were still important to God. He didn't want them to die, no matter how sick or addicted they were.

We had spent time where they were, seen how they lived, and listened as they shared their desire for a way out of their addictions. Now we had to find a way to help them on that journey.

From the beginning Cyrus and I had talked about how many people we thought might accept our offer of help. We'd been selective about who we spent time with, gauged their reactions to the verses, and analyzed the questions they asked. We thought that perhaps ten or twenty would decide to try, but we would have felt successful with six. We had secured a small lot in the city to use as a gathering point.

It was time to make the offer and see if our unorthodox approach would bear the kind of fruit we had hoped for.

―∞―

On the last night we filled Cyrus's car with several hundred meals from a take-out restaurant, wrote the address of the gathering point on the packages, and drove to the building. People were shocked when we pulled up in the stuffed vehicle. The few who had seen us had called to the others inside the building, and before long a crowd was gathered around Cyrus's car. Questions floated in the air above them. Where did we get so much food? Whose car was it? Had it all been a trick from the beginning? I started to hand out the food. Once everyone was mostly silent, Cyrus began to speak.

"We've talked to you for almost three months. We've eaten together, smoked together, cried together, and laughed together. We heard you when you said that you want to change, but you don't have the chance. Everything we've talked about, all the verses we've shared have been about Jesus. 'Come to me, all you who are weary and burdened, and I will give you rest.' That's what we're offering you. A chance for rest. A chance to put down the burden of your addiction. If you want this chance, truly want it, come to the address written on the box tomorrow."

As soon as Cyrus fell silent, the speculation started again. Some finished the food and tossed the package away. Others searched the outside of the box for it and then tossed the boxes next to the others that had been discarded. Some scoffed but turned away and stuffed the package into backpacks or pockets. We left to give them a chance to talk and think and come to their own decision.

For me it was a long night. What if we had completely misread the situation? What if no one showed up? Would that mean our approach had been wrong or that we hadn't given it enough time? Would it mean that the other pastors had been right? I'm not sure which one of those possibilities bothered me more.

CHAPTER SEVEN

The next day Cyrus and I went to the gathering point, where eight people were sitting on the ground waiting for us. Behram was one of them.

Behram stood to greet us. "There were more who wanted to come, but they weren't sure if they could trust you."

I wasn't surprised by that sentiment. But it didn't matter. The fact that there were eight people meant the idea was a success. And there was the possibility that others would join us too. We had to try again.

That night we took a van back to the building and filled it with five hundred more meals and just as many portions of hope. Behram and the others who had arrived at the lot helped to distribute them. Everyone was welcome to eat. Once the van was empty, we invited those who wanted to accept the opportunity we were offering to get in the van and come with us. People piled in and others jockeyed for position to get in next. There were far too many. I had the others get out of the van.

"Alright, if you're serious about change, give us your name," Cyrus said. In just a few minutes, we had over a hundred names.

Our lot in the city was far too small. Even if there had been enough space, the police would have noticed a gathering of that many homeless and addicted people in a new location and would have been certain to ask questions. We couldn't go back on our word though. We had offered a glimmer of hope.

We had to find a way.

That night Cyrus and I made a plan. He would find another location with more privacy outside the city, preferably flat, but that was something that my workers could fix if it was needed. We knew that the people on the list would need medical treatment through detox, so I would go to an addiction treatment center to arrange that.

The next morning, we both went to work.

I knew Dr. Ahmady through my uncle Husein on my mother's side. I trusted him to know what to do.

He was surprised to see me, but he made time for us to sit down in his office.

"It's good to see you, but what brings you here today?" he asked.

"I have a group of addicted people whose treatment I want to pay for."

"How many?"

"A hundred and ten."

He laughed. "No, seriously, how many?"

"A hundred and ten," I repeated and held up the paper. "Here's the list."

He took it from me and looked at the names. I could see him turning over the possibilities. He handed the list back to me. "I have sixty beds, and only a third of those are available. For the others, I can help you find beds at other facilities."

I shook my head. "No. The group already has connections to each other. I don't want to separate them. What would it take to make a temporary location work?"

He studied me for a moment, then said, "You're serious about this."

"Of course! Give me a list of what you would need, and I'll make sure that it happens."

He tapped one finger on his desk. "Alright. Wherever this location is, you need enough space for that many people to sleep, and for them to have space to move around and pace when they need to." He began to count off on his fingers. "You need showers and a kitchen, and we find that having music playing helps calm those who are detoxing. There should also be people there to watch over the group. You don't want those who are addicted to feel like they're in prison, but there will be times when their craving overwhelms better judgment. Having someone there who can convince them to stay through the difficult times is important too."

I jotted down what he said and then looked up. "What about medications?"

"I can give you a list," he said. Then there came a knock on the door. Before he could speak, a woman came in.

"Everyone's waiting. Did you forget about the meeting?"

CHAPTER SEVEN

I held up my hand. "Do you mind? He's meeting with me right now." I didn't have much time to get this set up. The rest could wait a few minutes.

She drew back.

"I'll be there soon," Dr. Ahmady assured her.

She looked at him and Dr. Ahmady gave her a little nod. She turned but kept anger-narrowed eyes on me as she left the room. I didn't care what she thought. I had to find a way to fulfill the promise Cyrus and I had made to a hundred and ten people.

"She's right, I do have a meeting." He scrawled a quick list. "These are the basics. Let me know where you're located, and I'll stop by to see how you're doing."

His requirements were straightforward enough. Now we just needed a place to bring it all together.

I still don't know how Cyrus did it, but by noon he had found a spacious garden outside the city. "It's the right size," he said. "But it isn't flat."

"I'll take care of it." I took my workers off the current project to prepare the site. By evening, it was flattened and had poles in place to support a canopy. An outdoor carpet was put down so that people didn't have to sleep directly on the ground. Next to that was an open area where people could walk and gather. It wasn't finished, but the weather was still pleasant. It would suffice for the night.

Then we began to ferry those who were on the list to our temporary recovery center. By the next day we had set up a temporary kitchen, canopy, and bathrooms with showers for men and women.

Dr. Ahmady came by to look at our facilities. "You did all this in such a short time?"

"You still thought I was kidding?" I asked as we walked to his car.

"Not anymore," he replied.

"So, it's good?"

"Very nearly. You need more electrical outlets. Detoxing can put a great deal of stress on the body even when a person is in good condition. Sometimes people who aren't healthy to begin with will need additional medical support. If that happens, I'll need power for the emergency equipment that's easy to access."

"Consider it done," I said.

"I'll be back with nurses and medications in a few days," he said, then hesitated before he continued. "Until then, they're going to go into withdrawal unless they have access to their drug of choice."

I had the connections to make that happen. When Ali had been with me in Tehran we had gone to a party. For me, it was just a way to have fun. Ali observed the wealthy young men buying drugs and how much they were willing to spend, as if money meant nothing. An idea formed. The plain his family had owned for generations was perfectly placed to be a route for drugs coming into the country. His new venture went from observation to success in a remarkably short time.

I called him and told him what I needed.

"Are you having a party? I didn't think you did that anymore."

"I don't." I explained what Cyrus and I were doing. "Can you supply me?"

"Of course," he said.

After that I made the arrangements for the outlets. I walked back into the gathering, and I knew that these people had trusted Cyrus and me to help. I felt the weight of that responsibility. We wanted to care for their spiritual needs, and we wanted to give them the opportunity to regain their sobriety, but we also had to take care of their bodies. They needed clean clothes to wear and towels for showers. That was my next task, but before that, I had to at least put in an appearance at work for a few hours.

I was heading out of my office to see what I could do when my friend Samad arrived.

He owned a smaller company that specialized in tile. I had often hired them, and we were working on a project together at the time.

"I'm sorry," I said. "I was just leaving."

CHAPTER SEVEN

"To the job site?" He walked with me to the parking lot. "I'll go with you."

I wasn't sure what to say. The complete truth would raise questions I didn't want to answer. I shrugged. "No. It's just a charity thing."

"Oh really? I'd like to help." In a way that didn't surprise me. Samad was my age, but he'd spent his life taking care of other people. He worked hard and dedicated just as much time to helping others.

"I said I would provide some clothing and towels for a large group. I'm just not sure where to get the best price."

"Oh, that's easy. There's a great secondhand store I know of. A lot of their stuff is like new."

In less than an hour and for a lot less money than I had expected, we were supplied.

To be able to bathe and change into clean clothes was a luxury that many of them had not been able to indulge in for a very long time. It didn't change their addictions, but I like to think it began to change their outlook.

Chapter Eight

A FEW DAYS later Dr. Ahmady called and invited me to the treatment center's annual benefit. I could have just sent him a donation, but if I went, I might learn something we could use.

When I arrived, the low hum of conversation already filled the lecture hall. The rows closest to the front were filled, so I sat in the back. A few minutes later, Dr. Ahmady walked up to the podium and began his lecture. He began with the prevalence of addiction, what kind of support was needed to keep people drug free. His statements were punctuated by PowerPoint slides while he emphasized how the good to society far exceeded the cost of providing treatment.

At the end of the lecture, I went over to one of the long tables set up along the walls to write a check. People passed by, some to leave, others to chat with friends, but I wasn't paying attention until I heard a familiar voice.

"This is a new friend of the center," a woman said. She was the one who'd interrupted us in Dr. Ahmady's office. She came over to the table with a younger woman. She was smiling, but it was a tight smile that didn't reach her eyes. "We didn't meet properly the other day. I'm Zohre, one of the psychiatrists at the center, and this is my sister, Sahar. She's just finished her bachelor's in engineering."

"It's nice to meet you," Sahar said, holding my eyes as she spoke.

I sat back in my chair and looked at her for the first time. She was tall and slim with long hair and dark eyes, and she was still watching me, a sure sign of more than just a casual interest. "It's good to meet

CHAPTER EIGHT

you too. Please, sit," I said to both. Sahar sat next to me. Her sister sat on the other side of her. "So, you have your degree. Are you working as an engineer?"

"Not just now. I think I want to get my master's in mechanical engineering. Right now, I'm working in my sister's office at the clinic."

"Why? You have your degree; you should be independent." I could see anger flicker through her sister's eyes. A smile tugged at Sahar's lips, but she tilted her head to conceal it from her sister. She leaned closer as we chatted.

Even in those short few minutes of small talk in a crowded room, the mantle of calm that she pulled around herself was evident as were the careful silences that others might have missed. The room began to empty out, and I was getting ready to leave and put the conversation down to a pleasant encounter after a mostly dull lecture.

"We should stay in touch," Sahar said. She took out her phone. "Can I get your number?"

I hesitated. I hadn't been involved with anyone since I became Christian and I wasn't looking for anyone. But I gave her my number anyway.

I had only been home for a few minutes when my phone buzzed. I didn't recognize the number, but I could tell who it was from the message. *It was great meeting you and seeing your smile.* I smiled again as I read it.

It was good to meet you too, I texted back and sat on the sofa, the phone next to me. Her reply came a few minutes later and I responded. Soon I was sitting with my phone in my hand, anticipating the tone.

You know, her message said, *we should get together sometime. Maybe have tea, or coffee if that's what you like.*

I didn't hesitate. *We could do that. Did you have somewhere in mind?*

When she sent the address, I knew the place immediately. I'd been there before. We went back and forth about a convenient time and day and settled on Thursday at four in the afternoon.

It felt like the time would never pass.

The air inside the Median Coffee Shop was perfumed by the sugary scent of fresh pastries sparkling in the richer smell of brewing coffee. Several tables were filled with people deep in conversation while others who sat alone at the edges created their own space with books or newspapers. Sunlight shone through the wide windows and gilded the edges of light wood tables and curving backs of chairs with golden highlights.

Sahar and I found a table by the window. We'd only had a chance to greet each other when a woman paused next to the table. She was familiar, but I couldn't recall her name. First she turned a hard gaze on me and then she fixed appraising eyes on Sahar. "I wonder what your expiration date will be." She turned on her heel and walked out.

After a moment of silent surprise, Sahar looked at me. Curiosity danced in her eyes.

For a moment I couldn't think of what to say, but the beginnings of impatience had begun to creep into Sahar's eyes.

"I used to be that person, but I've changed over the past few years."

"Oh? How?" she asked, and a little smile tickled the corners of her lips. Maybe she believed me, maybe she didn't. At least she was willing to listen.

"My life changed when I became a Christian," I said. At that point I wasn't so concerned about her reaction. I wanted to make sure she knew the truth before the relationship went any further. She shrugged off the revelation and I went on.

"That's how I met your sister. I was talking with Dr. Ahmady about arranging treatment for a group of people."

"That's what Zohre said, but she didn't tell me how all that came about."

I told her about the months spent living in the abandoned building for part of the week and the offer that we'd made to the people we'd met.

She told me a bit about her family, and I got the sense that there

CHAPTER EIGHT

was some friction or unhappiness there, but she didn't go into detail and I didn't ask. We wandered through my work, what drew her to mechanical engineering, and her aspirations all tied together with laughter and the sense that I didn't want the conversation to end.

We spent four hours in the café before we moved to a restaurant for an unhurried dinner and after that a late-night walk in the park. By the time we said good night, it felt as though there was so much more to say.

In the next few weeks, I split my time between work, the recovering homeless, and Sahar. We used the example of the Good Samaritan to help those struggling with their addictions to see their own worth, to see that they were important to God, and that they had the power to positively affect the lives of others. It was a journey we defined in ten steps. Some didn't make it. Others felt the power of God moving in their lives and knew that their addiction had been replaced by something far stronger than any drug.

It wasn't easy, even for those who wanted it. More than once Cyrus or I sat with someone when they sobbed and begged for their accustomed relief. We did our best to give them something to hold on to and to help them find a reason to resist the clawing need for a fix. Even though Behram was struggling with his own long addiction, he was instrumental in the day-to-day successes of so many.

Sahar found a role for herself as well. Her expertise wasn't in addiction recovery, but she did understand the computer system the recovery center used to track patient records. She created a similar system for the group in the garden, making sure medications and other critical data were tracked and monitored.

Outside of the garden, Sahar and I saw each other three times a week. The hours always slipped away far too quickly when we were together. I looked forward to her texts and imagined the words spoken in her voice. I'd never felt like this with anyone else. I was falling in love with her, but I wasn't sure if she felt the same way about me. I thought she did, but that brought its own set of concerns. I decided I needed to put some space between us for a few days.

The first forty-five days of recovery for our new friends were rapidly coming to an end. Those who had completed their treatment had earned their success, and I thought that success needed to be marked in a special way. We planned a small celebration after I got back from a three-day business trip. That trip was also the time and space Sahar and I needed.

The first night I was away, she called me. After some small talk, I began to tell her what had been on my mind.

"You know we're getting serious," I told her, "and I wasn't looking for that. Now that it's happened though, you have to understand some things."

"I understand," she insisted.

"No, you don't," I said.

"But—"

"Would you just let me finish?"

She fell silent.

"You know I'm Christian. You don't know that I'm an outcast in my family. My parents won't be able to meet yours."

"I don't care," she said. The answer was too quick. She couldn't have thought about it. Not the way she needed to.

"I'm not so sure this is a good idea. Maybe we should stop seeing each other."

"No!" I could hear panic in her voice. "If you did that, I'd…I'd kill myself."

That made me pause. Before I became Christian, I wouldn't have cared, but now my view had changed. I took a deep breath. "If I commit to this relationship, that's it. We're married in the eyes of God. I won't go back on that promise. You need time to think about that."

"No, I don't."

"Yes, you do. Give me your answer at the party when I get back."

"I don't need to wait that long. I promise I'll never leave you."

"If you're so sure, it won't matter if you wait for a few days. I'll see you when I get back."

When I ended the call, I hoped that she was still so certain. Even

CHAPTER EIGHT

if she wasn't, I would rather know that sooner than later.

I lost track of how many times she called or texted me after that. I do know it was impossible to read all the texts. I didn't respond to any of them. I was determined to give us both time to think.

When I got back, I went to work as usual and then to the garden in the evening. Sahar was there, working on patient records. I greeted her, but I had too much to do to get into a serious discussion at that point. I sat with Behram and some of the others. Each time I caught a glimpse of Sahar, she was trying not to look at me. When I finished, we found our way to each other in a quieter corner of the open space.

"The texts I sent while you were away—"

"I deleted them all," I said.

I could see the relief on her face. "Good. The last few were... well...I was upset. I wanted to tell you—"

"Have dinner with me tomorrow night. We'll talk about it then."

Tension rippled through her shoulders, but she agreed.

I knew what she was going to say, and I knew what my answer was going to be, but there was still a tiny part of me that wasn't sure I could trust her. I don't know why. She'd never done anything that I could point to as dishonest, but I couldn't help how I felt. I had to be certain that she really meant what she said.

The next night, dinner wasn't long enough to contain the conversation. We drove around the city for hours. I was afraid to lose her, but, at the same time, my doubts made me afraid to commit. I had to hear her tell me that she was sincere. Perhaps it sounds cruel, but I tested her as we rode slowly through the brightly lit streets of Tehran.

Was this something she really wanted? Did she really understand what it meant? What would she think in five years of not being able to live together? Ten years without children?

The same questions in different forms tumbled into the space between us, and for each one she gave me reassurances of her commitment to me and to our relationship. I had to hear her say it. I had to know that, even if the relationship ended, those words had come from her lips.

In the small hours of the morning, my doubts still lingered, but she had given me every reassurance that she could. I thought that if it wasn't right, God wouldn't have put her in my path. But would she still want to be with me if the police threw her in a cell? I couldn't bring myself to ask her.

"Alright," I said. "I believe you're serious, but I still think you need time to be sure."

"I have thought about it and I am sure. What do you think the last few hours have been about?"

"I'll take you home tonight, and we'll make it final tomorrow."

"And how many more steps after that?"

"Sahar, this isn't something to rush into. A day won't matter."

She stared out the window in silence, her arms crossed, all the way back to her family's house.

The next day, I was in my office just finishing up a meeting before lunch when Sahar walked into the outer office. The sharp, staccato sound of her high heels clearly conveyed her mood as she walked across the tiles. She surveyed the space and then met my eyes through the glass wall of my office. The people in the meeting looked at each other and then at me.

"Let's pick this up again after lunch," I said, ushering them out and Sahar into the office. I picked up my lunch. "Come up to the conference room. It's more private." I wasn't happy that she'd shown up at all. It was sure to create all kinds of speculation and gossip.

She sat across from me. "I think you're playing with me." Her legs crossed; her eyes demanded that I justify myself.

"Sahar—"

"No! You leave town and threaten to break up with me. You come

CHAPTER EIGHT

back and for hours I explain every way I know how that I understand what I'm getting into and that I want to be with you. When will it be enough?"

"We're planning a party for the recovered group in about ten days, right?"

Her eyes narrowed just a fraction. "Yes."

"Since those people are why we met, I thought we would promise there."

She looked at me and smiled a little. "You couldn't have told me that last night?" She leaned forward and picked up my fork, taking a bite of my chicken and rice.

I shrugged and felt myself smile for her and her alone. "You might have changed your mind."

I still wasn't completely sure that I was doing the right thing, but that one percent uncertainty was silenced by my plans for the evening. For hours I thought about what I could do to mark the occasion. I could have filled the garden with flowers, but the party was in honor of those who had worked so hard to recover. I didn't want to make the evening about Sahar and me, so I dismissed the idea. I could have gotten Sahar a ring. I even chose a gold band that looked like three narrow bands stacked together, but she wouldn't be able to wear it all the time without raising difficult questions. In the end, I dismissed that idea as well. Symbols and decorations were for other people. Sahar and I had each other, and that was all that mattered.

The night of the party was filled with joy. I'd hired jugglers to provide entertainment, but there was also music, and those who were recovered provided their own entertainment with dancing. Laughter surrounded all of us, and I couldn't help but think about how far they had all come. They stood straighter and looked at the world with clear eyes filled with purpose and intention.

As the evening went on, the laughter gave way to testimony. Those who finished the program shared their stories of what had pulled them down into addiction, recalled their worst moments, and then shared what had allowed them to climb out again.

Behram had been a leader when he was still in the midst of his own addiction. Now that he was sober, the frail man I'd met now radiated confidence and newfound strength. After his testimony, he looked at me.

"You've given us the chance to begin our lives again. Now, we want to begin to take some responsibility for our lives."

"What would you like to do?" I asked.

"You have people here to watch the entrance and others to cook for us. In the beginning, we needed those things and we are grateful, but those are things we can do for ourselves now," he explained.

The more I thought about it, the more sense it made. These people needed purpose and control in their lives. I sat back and watched as they decided among themselves that the women would take over the kitchen. Several of the men took over the door. The only person whose task wasn't reassigned was Sahar.

After all the laughter, testimony, and discussion, it was getting late and people began to wander off to relax or talk together in smaller groups. Before long, Sahar and I were sitting alone next to the kitchen.

She was so beautiful that night. The black and white dress she wore was the exception to her usual uncomplicated style. Around her wrist, a black band held a narrow gold plate with the word *Heaven* engraved on it in delicate Farsi. The engraving sparkled in the soft light like so many diamonds. People who were still awake could see that this was more than a conversation. They gave us a wide berth.

"We accomplished something amazing here," I said. "We gave them a chance to change their lives, and they changed this into a holy place, the Garden of Heaven. Are you ready to promise?"

She smiled and it was like seeing the sun rise early. "Yes."

I held out my hands and she put her hands in mine. "God said, if you promise, I'm the witness. Do you want to be my wife?"

She nodded. "Yes. Do you want to be my husband?"

CHAPTER EIGHT

"Yes. I will be with you through the hard times and promise I will never betray you."

"I won't betray you, and I'll be with you, no matter what happens, good times and bad."

That was it—in my mind and my heart, Sahar was my wife. We stood and hugged. Those around us felt something shift. Esther, the oldest woman in the group, came over to us.

"I know something just happened here, but I don't know what it was," she said.

"We just gave each other our promise," I said. "We're married."

Esther cupped her hand over her mouth and began the Kel. The joyful sound echoed around the camp, drawing everyone's attention. Before long we were surrounded by the others, everyone speaking at once to offer congratulations. As Sahar and I walked to my car that night, she paused and looked up at the stars sparkling overhead. "Thank you, God, for tonight," she whispered, entrusting her prayer to the soft breeze. In a garden where men and women whom society had rejected struggled to begin a fresh chapter, my own had begun.

Chapter Nine

DESPITE WHAT WE felt and what I believed in my heart, Sahar and I were still an unmarried couple. In Iran it's a serious crime for a man and woman to live together outside of marriage. Both partners could be lashed and then forced to marry, whether they would have chosen to or not, a humiliation for both families. The best we could manage was to be together for a week or two at a time. Her mother and sisters knew about me, and they knew where she was. Her father and brother couldn't know without putting both of us in danger. When she stayed with me, she lived a hidden existence.

To carve out those precious weeks together, we had to treat our relationship like a shameful secret. Her arrival and departure had to be hidden. Her things had to be concealed. Not even a toothbrush could be left out for a casual observer to find. It wasn't the way we wanted to live, but it was the best we could do.

Those former addicts who were recovering were doing well, but Dr. Ahmady let me know that, unless they could work, they would be vulnerable to relapse. Sobriety wasn't enough. Those men and women needed a way to support themselves and prove to their families that they'd made a permanent change. So, I hired all of them.

One of the first things I had my new workers do was add another floor over the workshop to be a lunchroom and kitchen. It took about a month and a half to finish, but when it was complete, my staff was able to eat together as a group, with some of the women from the camp doing the cooking.

CHAPTER NINE

It was important to me that everyone see each other as part of the same team no matter how long they had been with the company or what their position was in it. I assigned everyone to a table and changed the rotation daily. We were all sharing the same meal at the same time. For that hour job titles or seniority shouldn't matter.

While they were still getting used to this change, I changed something else. Traditionally, Muslims eat before praying. But Christians pray first and then eat. When my staff came into the lunchroom for their midday meal, I stood and said a short prayer. "Thank you, God, for this food. Please let it give us energy to do good things and show love to people."

Those who were becoming Christians weren't surprised. The others were shocked, not only by the timing of the prayer, but also by the words, because the mealtime prayer they were accustomed to stopped with a simple thanks. For a moment there was silence, and then the buzz of a whisper swept through the group. I didn't try to explain. I just let them speculate amongst themselves.

Soon enough, surprise was eclipsed by laughter and lunchtime gossip. Some prayed after the meal as well, but that was their choice, and they were free to make it. I continued to pray each day before lunch. The shock faded and my employees came to appreciate the logic of thanking God for the food before the meal was eaten. A week later, when I called for volunteers to lead the prayer, I was pleased to see how many there were.

Behram did his best to work along with the others, but he wasn't suited to be a laborer. He was a leader and organizer. I opened a small company for him in a storefront on the south side of Tehran and provided him with workers who knew the job when he needed them. He was so excited when he got his first contract. It was smaller than anything my company had ever taken on, but for him it was a thrilling start.

As I got to know them all, I learned that there were several of the women with solid computer skills. They went to classes in design. Others had an interest in health care, and so they trained as nurses.

BECOMING JOSHUA

The further they moved along their paths, the more confidence they gained, and the more they were able to rebuild their lives.

In those months, I spent a great deal of time reading the Bible and trying to answer the questions the formerly homeless had, but what Cyrus and I did was based on realism and practicality, not religion. They were growing in their faith, but there were no miracles. Those who succeeded had earned their rebirth through their own hard work and the acceptance of a loving God.

Without Cyrus's willingness to help me, none of this would have been possible. He was the one who taught me how to see past the dirt, pain, and desperation to the humanity that was too often ignored. He taught me to speak so that I would be heard and to listen with my heart. My time in that abandoned building taught me more than any university ever could, and I will always be grateful for my mentor.

A few months after everyone had finished their treatment, I was sitting down to breakfast at just after seven in the morning when my doorbell rang. No one had said they would be stopping by, and I doubt I would have agreed to it at that hour anyway. I hadn't even gotten up from the table when another knock, sharp and insistent, sounded. The bell rang again. That was not a good sign.

I opened the door to the courtyard, and there were three police officers waiting for me. They grabbed me as soon as I stepped outside. There were two more armed men on my roof. I didn't know what they wanted, but I was grateful that Sahar wasn't there.

A fourth man held a document before me. "We have a report that you are keeping alcohol in your house. This letter from the court gives us the right to search."

Possession of alcohol was a serious crime, but the response seemed too big for that. It was a ridiculous accusation anyway. "Really? Go and look, but I want to see the letter," I said.

CHAPTER NINE

"You can read it inside."

They walked into the house ahead of me. I read through a document that spelled out exactly what I had been told; they were looking for alcohol. As I watched them search through all my books, I wondered exactly what kind of alcohol they were looking for.

"Who made this complaint?" I asked. "What kind of investigation did you do?"

The one who seemed to be in charge looked at me with indifference. "If you have any questions, you'll have to go to the courthouse and speak with Tofigh."

They didn't find anything, but they took my phone and computer anyway.

I followed them out and forced myself to hold back the insults that formed on my tongue. Who had contacted the police in the first place? I'd had many girlfriends. Maybe one of them had a husband who wanted to get back at me. When I got into the street, I noticed two unmarked police cars and bearded men in high-buttoned collars. Neighbors looked out of their windows and stood in curious little knots on the sidewalk wrapped up in eager whispers about what might have happened to disrupt the quiet of the neighborhood.

I went back in the house and finished getting ready and went to the courthouse instead of to my office. The fact that nothing had been found meant that I had the basis to file a complaint against the court official who signed the authorization to search. After I got answers, I had every intention of doing just that.

I asked the soldier at the reception desk for Tofigh. He directed me to his office and told me I could wait in the hall. For two hours, I sat on a metal bench and tried to unpick the knot of my suspicions with a hand made unsteady by upset. The only thing that made sense was a grudge, but why wait so long and who would have enough influence with court officials?

Finally, I was told that I could go into Tofigh's office. It was small, drab, and cheaply furnished with a view to nothing more than governmental utility. Behind his desk hung the same photos of Khomeini and Khamenei that cast a pall over offices in every government building in Iran.

Tofigh was past his prime, with circles under his eyes and a bit of a belly. Even though he didn't stand, the way he slouched in the chair gave me the impression that he was tall. The dark jacket he wore was too big for him, and it bunched around his folded arms. *Tasbih*, a string of prayer beads, in green and orange were wrapped around the fingers of his right hand.

"Please, sit," he said.

I sat and dropped the letter on his desk. "Your agents came and searched my house looking for alcohol. I want to know who made the report and what kind of investigation you did, because they didn't find anything."

He scanned the letter, then leaned back in his chair, and a little smile that I could only interpret as relief moved over his features. He gave a little nod. "I'm glad you didn't have anything."

The look on his face, the tone in his voice, this had all been misdirection. Without the name of the accuser, without even a cursory investigation, no official would sign an authorization to search. It would look like a personal attack, and a complaint could be made against the official that could jeopardize his position. Someone had enough influence to force Tofigh to sign the authorization with no evidence, despite the consequences to himself.

There were no answers here.

I drove back home with the incidents of the morning running through my mind. The cars in the street, the men on the roof, the way my books had been searched, and the confiscation of my computer and phone. Alcohol had nothing to do with it. This had been a warning.

The next day, when I told Sahar about the search, she was as confused as I had been. "Alcohol? Who would say such a thing?"

"I still don't know," I said and told her about my meeting with Tofigh.

For a few days neither of us mentioned it, but Sahar was turning

CHAPTER NINE

over the implications. Her anxiety was what made me decide that I had to move.

Because of my work, I had connections with real estate brokers and was able to quickly find a large apartment. I had my laborers pack for me, but I hired another company to accomplish the move. There were only four people who knew where I was living outside of Sahar and me, and those were the people I trusted most: Farhan, Behram, Cyrus, and Ali.

Even after Sahar and I settled into the newly redecorated apartment, the memory of being surrounded haunted the shadows and quiet spaces in my thoughts. No matter what I did, the specters lingered.

The newly recovered had begun to share God's message with others on a scale I couldn't have imagined. They created underground churches and traveled far to study. Some became pastors. When Cyrus and I began to calculate how many new believers had come from those sixty-five who finished the recovery program, it amounted to over two hundred. It was overwhelming, but it meant that there was always a pressing need for Bibles.

I told Farhan that our group was growing, and we needed Bibles for our new members.

He understood, then paused in thought before he said, "But you're not a part of our organization anymore. You know how precious Bibles are. We only have enough for our own people."

We were all Christians. We all believed in Jesus. Isn't that the only organization that matters? I sat back in my chair and reminded myself that getting upset wouldn't solve the problem. I spent the rest of the day formulating a plan.

When Cyrus stopped by that night, I told him my thoughts over tea.

The glass had been halfway to his lips. He put it down again with a sharp sound before I had gotten very far. "You mean they refused?"

"Yes, they refused. I'm not part of their organization anymore. Apparently, it doesn't matter that these people are Christians too. We're not *their* Christians." My own tea slowly cooled before me.

"We've made promises. Maybe we can make a few copies."

I shook my head. "I have a friend out of the country. We'll see if they'll sell to someone other than me. If they do, I'll use my Kurdish contacts to get them here."

"How many?" He brought the glass back to his lips.

"Ten thousand."

Cyrus began to choke on the sip of tea. I waited until he recovered. "Ten thousand? Do you know how much that'll cost?"

"A lot, but I have an upcoming job that should cover it."

"Ten thousand?" he repeated.

I nodded.

"You don't do things by halves, do you?"

While I was busy with those arrangements, Cyrus and Behram were making arrangements of their own. They had grown closer in those few months, bonding over their shared past and absolute faith that divine intervention had brought them through it.

While my friend and I put our bit of subterfuge into practice, Cyrus and Behram were collecting money from the newly recovered. A few days later, both stopped by my office after hours.

"Well? Did you get your ten thousand?" Cyrus asked when we were settled in my conference room.

"Of course," I said. "As long as my name is kept out of it, they're more than willing to sell."

Behram shook his head. "I still can't believe they would be so petty."

"If they want to be petty, we'll be creative. I'll get in touch with my Kurdish contacts tomorrow to make those arrangements."

Cyrus and Behram exchanged a look. "We know this is going to

CHAPTER NINE

cost a lot," Behram said. "We want to help with that." He took a small notebook and a pen out of his pocket and wrote a figure on it.

I stared at the number and then at a smiling Behram. The figure he'd written was nearly half the cost. "Where did all this come from?" I asked.

"All of us," he said. "We are over two hundred now. We're working, getting our lives back, and we wanted to contribute."

"But this much?"

"Some gave half their wages for the month," he said. "This is important to us."

"Thank you," I said. Even after all this time, these people were still amazing to me.

I went to Sulaymaniyah in the still-peaceful Kurdish region of Iraq to arrange for the Bibles to be brought into Iran. To bring in such a large quantity of Bibles, I would need to contact several people. My uncle Ako had put me in touch with many smugglers. I had worked with Khalid several times; he was reliable and had a network. I called him again.

"Ten thousand?" He went silent for a moment. "Yeah, I know a few people, but it's going to take a couple of days to set it all up."

And so, a few days later, Khalid and several others got together for dinner. Before we began, I said a prayer before we ate. They were surprised that I wanted to bring in Bibles because they knew my father. Even more of a surprise was that most of the money came from people who had been homeless and addicted only a few months before.

"And this is what they give money for? Bibles?"

"It's important to them," I said.

They didn't ask anything else that night.

All the smugglers we hired survived the treacherous crossing over the mountains from Iraq into Iran, but that left the problem of transporting the Bibles to Tehran. To move so many would be a challenge. In the past I had hired others to drive the route from the border to the city. The volume meant that ten or fifteen cars would be needed, and they would travel at different times of the day and night. I hired some drivers, but people in the group also offered to drive. I even made one of the trips myself.

Whether or not a person is stopped at the checkpoints is largely a matter of luck. Not every car is searched, but after midnight, the soldiers who did the inspections were more selective. I passed through the checkpoint at Bijar without any problem. When I arrived at Zanjan, it was a different story.

I slowed down for the speed bump as I approached the checkpoint, then wove through the two barriers when the soldier directed me to pull over. There were seven hundred Bibles in my trunk. There was no way they could be missed. When they were found I would be going to jail. I opened the window as he approached.

"Good evening. May I see your driver's license, please?" the soldier asked. While I got it out, he looked in the windows of the empty car with a flashlight. I handed him the license. He looked at the photo and then back at me, then walked around the front of the car and looked at the number plate.

"What do you have in the car?" he asked. There was a tone of certainty in the question.

"Nothing." I did my best to keep my voice even.

"Can I look in the trunk?" It wasn't a question, and refusal wasn't an option.

I pulled the trunk release and watched in the wing mirror as he walked behind the car. I tried to stay calm, but I was sure that this was it. How long would I go away for this time? Years? Longer? What would happen to Sahar?

The trunk thumped closed. The soldier walked up to the window again. He handed my license back to me. "You can go."

I just stared at him for a minute. "I can go?"

"Yes," he said. "Go on."

"Thank you. Have a good night."

I have no idea if he saw the Bibles and didn't say anything, if he saw them and thought they were just books, or if he didn't see them at all. No matter the reason, God protected me that night. That didn't

CHAPTER NINE

mean it was over. I still had a four-hour drive ahead of me. Every kilometer that passed I worried that I would be stopped. To me, each one of those Bibles represented the person who would read them and the person who carried them across the mountains. I was responsible for them.

The safest place we could think of to store the Bibles was in the garden. Those who had recovered had continued to assist others to free themselves from their addictions, so there were ten or fifteen people living there. When I arrived, the oranges and pinks of sunrise were streaking the sky. Cyrus and Behram were waiting for me.

"You'll never guess what happened to me," I said as we started to unload the trunk.

"What?" Cyrus asked, taking one of the cartons.

"They searched the car," I said.

They both froze. "What do you mean they searched the car? How did they miss them?" Behram asked.

"I have no idea. He looked in the trunk; he must have seen them. It had to be a miracle."

"Miracle or not, you can't do that again," Cyrus said. "What if you're not so lucky next time? What would we do without you?"

"You'd do what you're doing now. You don't need me to create underground churches. You've done that already. You don't need me to spread the message. Your group more than doubled before I even knew what was happening. You don't need me to help other people recover. You can do that on your own too. This isn't an organization with leadership and hierarchy. You're all leaders. I'm not any more important than any one of you."

A few weeks later I got a call from Khalid. "The others want to talk to you," he said.

"What about?" I asked.

"I think your story about the homeless addicts interested them.

They want to know more about Christianity."

I sat back in my chair. "I can't get away right now, but I'll send someone else."

I knew exactly who should go. The smugglers had been so surprised to learn that formerly homeless and addicted people had contributed so much money for Bibles, they were the perfect people to answer their questions. I asked Cyrus and Behram for suggestions. The two of them agreed on Saeed and Abdullah. Saeed knew the region and was familiar with the language. He listened more than he talked and was good at keeping things hidden. Abdullah was Kurdish, though he was Kurmanji, not Sorani. He was still an obvious choice.

"We need to send a woman as well," I said. "Wives are respected in Kurdish communities. If you want a man to convert, convince his wife that she should. You need a woman to spend time with the families."

They looked at each other. "Who would be willing to go?" Cyrus asked.

Behram thought. "I can think of a couple, but I think it should be Saba. She makes connections with people more quickly than the others. I think that would be an asset."

When I first asked them to go, none of them quite knew how to respond. They knew what I was asking them to do was important, but it was also dangerous. The Kurdish people want their own country, so when Kurdish people are caught by the government, they are often labeled as terrorists. If Saba, Abdullah, or Saeed were arrested, they could be executed. They decided to go anyway. At least one of the three would be in contact every night to let me know how things were going.

A few weeks later, during one of those check-ins, Saeed said, "They want to be baptized. Can we do that?"

I'd had to wait for baptism for three years until the leadership decided it was time and then it required someone high up in the organization to do it. This wasn't an organization. "Do it."

"Really? But I've only been a Christian for a few months."

CHAPTER NINE

"How do you know that? Your soul might have been Christian for twenty years. You're there and they want to be baptized. Do it."

It struck me that they had baptized others when they hadn't been baptized themselves. I suggested that they baptize each other, but they refused. They wanted me to do it. I resisted at first, but finally agreed. One by one, I baptized all sixty-five who had been part of the first group.

Chapter Ten

IN THE MONTHS that followed, my life was full of wonderful things.

The business was flourishing and helping the newly sober to learn a trade and get their lives back. As they grew in their faith, they shared it with others. Often, they went back to the south side of Tehran to find others who were ready to change their lives. When their numbers grew, they began their own underground churches. Cyrus and I had to look twice at the numbers to believe what we were seeing. Those sixty-five who had completed treatment had grown to hundreds.

Sahar's presence wove through all of it. Her father might not be ready to agree to the match, but the complicity of her mother and sisters gave me time to find a way to make it work.

That autumn was a time of beginnings and firsts. I began a sculpture of Sahar. It was the second time I had spent my birthday with her, but it was the first time I trusted her completely. She might not have realized that lack, but I did. At dinner that night, I told her about my doubts, and that they had been erased.

It was the first time we traveled together. We spent three days at my vacation home on the shores of the Caspian Sea. While we were there, I called Farhan and invited him to visit for the day. Until that point, I hadn't told anyone that Sahar was living with me part of the time, but as soon as he arrived, it was obvious.

We stood in the living room and watched Sahar walk along the sandy beach. "This isn't right," Farhan said. "You two aren't married."

"And how are we supposed to get married?" I asked. "Should I lie

CHAPTER TEN

and marry as a Muslim?"

"No, but you can't just live with someone. I'm not the only one who thinks so either."

I didn't need him to explain who the rest were. "So, Sahar and I are supposed to be alone until we can marry as Christians, even if that takes the rest of our lives? No. When we made our promises to each other, God was our witness. According to Malachi 2:14, that's all we need. To me, she is my wife."

He wasn't happy, but he knew he wouldn't win the argument, not when I had the Bible on my side.

Before we left, Sahar and I took photographs together for the first time. Those photos were as closely guarded as the fact that we lived together.

When we got back to Tehran, I began to feel the itch of anxiety. The group Cyrus and I had unwittingly created had gotten far larger than we could imagine or control. We had taken precautions to keep our identities a secret, but word of mouth carried the story of a group of Christians who were willing and able to help homeless addicts. I knew the government couldn't ignore that for long. Eventually those rumors would lead back to me, and the police would have enough to act.

I just didn't know when.

It was just after four on a sunny afternoon when the possibility of arrest became a certainty.

I had gotten home from work and decided to walk through the park near my apartment to the market. On the way back, I came around a bend in the path and saw a white van and an unmarked police car behind it. The van had at least five men inside.

A man in plain clothes got out of the car while others ran toward me. I felt another man step behind me.

The one from the car opened his jacket and showed me his gun.

Only the police carried guns. It was as good as a badge. "You have to come with us."

As many people as they brought, I think they were expecting a fight, but I didn't resist. One took the bag of groceries from me before they put me in the back of the car between two policemen. I thought I knew what was coming.

One of the men in the front handed a length of cloth back.

"Put your head down," one in the back ordered.

A blindfold went tight around my head. I felt the car pull away and merge into city traffic. From that moment on, the ride was completely silent. I couldn't imagine what they were doing. I had been arrested. We must be going to the police station and then I'd go to court. What did they think they were accomplishing by hiding that?

The car went around and around one of the numerous traffic circles, then negotiated several sharp turns in a row, and then went around another traffic circle. I was familiar enough with the city that I might have been able to work out where we were by timings, turns, and stops on an ordinary ride. This intentionally mysterious tour through Tehran left me disoriented after only a few minutes. Occasionally, I could hear the short sound of a car horn being tapped to urge on someone slow to respond to a traffic light, but with my head down, the usual sounds of the city were muted and changed.

I can't say how long the ride lasted, but eventually we turned onto a sloping driveway and then I heard a garage door close behind us. While the mechanical sound was still filling the space, no one moved. Then the rattling mechanism stopped. They left the blindfold in place and took me out of the car. Metal handcuffs dug deep into my right wrist when they secured my hands in front of me. Chilly air moved against my skin. From somewhere overhead a cat meowed. This couldn't be a police station. They took my arms, one on either side, and led me away from the car. Wherever this was, it was something far worse.

"Stairs," said the one on the right.

On the next step I reached forward with my foot to search for

CHAPTER TEN

a rising stair tread or an absence that would indicate a step down. I found the latter and began to carefully descend the flight of stone stairs, one person next to me, the other still holding my arm, but walking slightly behind us. When we got to the bottom, they pulled me to the left and spun me around several times before leading me down a hall. I heard a heavy metal door scrape open and then another, lighter door opening. I was pushed into the back of what had to be a room. The scent of plastic soundproofing hung thick in the air. The blindfold came off and I was met with utter darkness. Before I could truly process what had happened, the door closed, and I was left alone in a kingdom of silence.

No light leaked into the space. I reached forward with my cuffed hands and found the chilly wall. My fingers traced it to the left and found a corner of the room, fingertips sweeping carefully over the concrete wall until they caught the squared-off edge of a low opening. This wasn't a police station, and it couldn't have been a prison. There would have to be a court order for that. I wasn't even sure who had arrested me. Maybe they were going to kill me.

I braced my fingers against the wall and shifted my weight from one foot to the other. The universe beyond those points of contact might be endless and unknown, but the wall against my hand and the floor under my feet were solid and certain. Cresting panic gave way to a kind of cool, defiant logic. There might be a camera in the room. If they wanted to see a display of desperation and fear, they would have to look elsewhere for their entertainment. I took a few steps away from the niche and sat on the rough concrete floor with my back against the wall.

How long was I left there? Long enough to begin to discern the language of the silence that surrounded me. Long enough to feel the pressure of the darkness wrapped around me. Long enough for the chill of the wall and the floor to seep into my body. Where did I end and where did it begin? I couldn't tell.

In all that time, nothing had violated the silence of the space. No one moved outside the door. Plumbing didn't tap or rattle; electricity didn't hum through concealed wires. There was nothing but the sound of my own breathing. I was beginning to think that's all there was when a laugh, hard and mean, broke the illusion of complete isolation. The door opened and light from the hallway flooded in, blinding me. A moment later a light in the room came on.

I shielded my eyes and listened to people come into the room. When my eyes adjusted, I saw three men in the opposite corner from where I was, the light shining from the wall above their heads. Two were seated in folding chairs, and one stood by the closed door, his arms crossed. I looked between the three of them. The one seated to my left was a little older. The other was turned slightly toward him, his posture deferential. It was an arrangement I recognized. The man on the left was in charge.

He spoke first, calling me Mister and saying my name with a politeness that concealed sarcasm. "And how was your journey to us?"

"How do you think it was?"

"Your name is 'Dog' because you're dirty and we pray we don't have to touch you," the one seated to the right said, his words dripping with venomous contempt. He leaned forward a little as he spoke, as if ready to pounce. "We know all about you, Dog. We know that you were in jail for claiming to be Christian, but then you confessed that you weren't." The one on the left just watched me, his eyes appraising.

"That's right," I said. "Now I am a Christian."

He looked as though he was going to speak again when the one on the left spoke, his voice calm, the barest hint of a smile on his lips. "Give me one reason why you became a Christian. What's the difference between Christianity and Islam?"

"Just one reason?" I asked.

The one standing by the door stepped forward, his fists clenched. "Let me teach him how to answer with respect."

"I don't think that will be necessary," the leftward man said. His eyes were on me, though he was clearly speaking to the standing man. Not a ripple marred his practiced calm. "I'm certain it was just a mistake." Then he spoke to me. "Yes, just one reason."

CHAPTER TEN

"The difference is," I replied, my eyes on his, "according to the Qur'an, you will go to heaven for imprisoning and killing me. According to Christianity, I will go to heaven by forgiving you. If you have something to write on, I could give you the verses. You could look them up later."

They knew exactly who I was, and they knew my Islamic background. They knew they wouldn't be able to trip me up with verses.

He shook his head. "We don't want to kill you. We want you to repent and come back to Islam because Islam is a peaceful religion."

My gaze didn't waver. "If you are a good Muslim and you believe what the Qur'an says, you have to kill me. Of course, Islam isn't a peaceful religion, and you know it. You can lie to the rest of the world about what's in the Qur'an, but you can't lie to me."

He put his head down and sighed. "I wanted to help you, but apparently you don't want my help. The rest is out of my control." He took a breath, slapped his hands against his thighs, and stood, smoothing the front of his cream-colored shirt. A look passed between him and the other seated man before he moved behind him and out the door.

The other seated man stood and clapped his hands and rubbed them together in anticipation as he came toward me. "Take off your clothes." It was an efficient order.

I didn't move. I just watched him.

"Don't look at us. Look down."

The other walked over to me.

"Where are the basement churches? How many people go there? Who are the leaders?" he asked.

They hadn't brought anything with them to write on. This wasn't about confession or information.

I stayed silent.

He squatted in front of me, his eyes as flat and black as a shark's. "How long do you think you'll keep that arrogance? How long before I have you begging to tell me every name, every location, every detail I want to know? How long before I have you whimpering like the dog that you are?" He stood. "Take off your clothes."

I took off my pants.

"More," he demanded.

I took off my underwear as well, but the handcuffs made it impossible to take off my T-shirt. The two of them lifted it over my head and used it to pin my arms.

"Get in there." The one on my right pointed at the small niche. My shoulders were wider than the opening.

"The space is too small," I said.

"We'll make you fit."

They pushed me back into the tiny space, kicking the front of my shoulders and pushing my head down and back. The floor inside was three inches lower than the rest of the room, creating a lip. They kicked my feet and shins until my legs were folded up to my chest and my feet were inside the lip of the cavity. To keep me in that position, they put a metal bar behind my knees, securing it inside the tiny space and ensuring that I wouldn't be able to move.

I became wrapped in pain. My shoulders and back burned from scraping over the rough concrete. The extreme angles overstretched tendons in one direction and shortened them in others. My neck and spine painfully compressed. The bar not only kept me in place, but it cut off my circulation. I couldn't take a full breath. Each shallow gasp I managed pushed my legs into the bar, cutting off my little remaining blood flow. My hearing faded, then disappeared completely. The pressure in my eyes became agony. Numbing cold enveloped my feet and toes.

That became my world. The cold, the pain, and the storm my shallow breaths created inside my head, buffeting the single thought I still had—*How can I get through this?*

I don't remember losing consciousness, but when I awoke again, I was lying on the floor outside the hole. I was alone, but next to me was a bowl of rice and tomatoes. It was the first food I'd been given since I arrived, so I ate. My hearing wasn't right, the pressure was still in my eyes, and the pain throbbed through my body with every heartbeat.

When my captors came back, they looked down at me, their heads tilted. "Where is the basement church?"

The sounds of the words were altered, as if I was hearing them through water. I had to decode what he was saying.

I stayed silent.

"I'll be back and then I want the names."

When he came back, he didn't ask anything. They just forced me back into the hole.

This time I remember being pulled out. I remember the blinding pain of shortened tendons and sinews snapping back to their normal length as my body unfolded.

"I want the names," he said.

I stayed silent.

This was my new reality and I would learn how to survive. I focused on one thing—breathing. I lost track of how many times I was forced into that tiny space; maybe it was fifty, maybe a hundred. I began to envy the dead. They were only put into their graves once.

Eventually my captors decided I was surviving too well. The next time they came in, they filled the shallow void with sewage water to the level of the cell floor. This time, I struggled to get out, as the stench and the filth surrounding me made it almost impossible to draw breath. I began to bang my head on the top of the space. I could feel blood soaking my hair and trickling down over my face. I wanted to die.

It would be easy to say that in the darkness, in the cold, in the pain, I prayed. It would be easy to say that I gave them nothing because Jesus was with me, that Jesus gave me strength and supported me through all of it. It would be easy, but it would be a lie.

There were times I had flashbacks of distributing Bibles and sharing the Gospel and I thought it was all wrong. I thought, *I'm here because of you. Where are you? Are you hiding?* I didn't ask God for release because God wasn't there.

I didn't stay silent because God gave me strength. I stayed silent because the men and women I had helped had trusted me. Maybe they'd trusted in God too, but God wasn't there. I was. I couldn't betray them. I couldn't take away that hope.

When the door opened for the last time, I expected more pain, more questions, more insults. Instead I was given back my clothes. After I dressed, I was blindfolded. The handcuffs on my wrists were exchanged with a different set, one with a rigid bar linking them. They took me out of the room and spun me around several times before taking me back upstairs again. They put me in the back of a small van, pushed my head down, and began another circuitous and seemingly aimless journey around Tehran. Whatever was happening, it could have been better. It could have been worse. I had no way of knowing.

I don't know how long we'd been traveling when the van stopped, and the doors opened. The vehicle shifted as people got out. I didn't know what to expect. They'd taken me somewhere, but where and why?

The blindfold was yanked off. The van was parked outside of a police station. A young soldier was looking in at me. I was relieved. Now everything was legal and recorded.

They put me into a holding cell. For the first time since my arrest, I was able to see a clock. It was around eleven in the morning. I was alone again in a concrete cell, but at least I knew where I was. I could still see the clock. The measured movement reassured me that I had emerged from my disappearance. I watched an hour tick away before one of the soldiers gave me a sandwich. As before, the blanket I was given was filthy, but it didn't matter. I wrapped it around myself and waited for whatever was going to come next.

There was no bathroom in the holding cell, so that evening

CHAPTER TEN

another soldier showed up to take me down the hall. At first, he just stared at me, the shock evident on his face. He had to help me walk the short distance.

"Where were you?" he asked, his nose wrinkled against the odor of all that I'd experienced since my arrest.

What could I say? For all I knew I had been next door to the police station the entire time.

"I'm only supposed to give you ten minutes, but if you take longer that's alright," he said when we walked into the bathroom.

I stood at the sink and let the water run over my hands. I watched it strip away the strata of dirt and desperate uncertainty that had built up over the time I had been in that place. The soldier's humanity and the deep purple-black bruises that encircled my wrists where the handcuffs had been stood out in vivid contrast to each other. I leaned against the sink and washed my face and upper body as best I could. I barely recognized the reflection looking back at me from the polished steel. My hair, already long, was wild and matted. The beard that had grown was another strange change. I no longer looked like myself. I looked like one of the homeless people I'd spent so much time with.

The soldier waited there far longer than the ten minutes I'd been given before he helped me back to the holding cell.

"You'll be in court tomorrow morning at ten," he said and left me alone for the night.

Chapter Eleven

THIS TIME I wasn't allowed the dignity of walking unshackled and escorted by a family friend. At 8:30 the next morning, handcuffed and fettered by a short chain between my ankles, I was led across the street by two soldiers to a much larger courthouse than the one in Arima. One Security Policeman followed with the documents pertaining to my case. I knew people were staring. I kept my eyes on the ground in front of me, the sounds of the chains between my ankles a soft, bright clink amid the bustle of the street.

Once inside, the clink of the chains and our footsteps were the only sounds as I was led into a small, empty waiting room. There was an inner door opposite to the one we came in. My eyes were fixed on the bland tile between my feet.

The clerk of the court came out. The Security Police officer didn't look at me when he introduced me as "the accused" and held out the documents to the clerk. We were told to wait, and silence deepened. Each minute that passed felt like a weight resting on my neck and shoulders. Each tick brought me closer to being sentenced.

The inner door opened again, and I was brought into the courtroom. It was a larger room, which held a polished air of formality that had been lacking in the courtroom I'd been in before. I stood at the podium with a soldier slightly behind me. The judge on his elevated bench was flanked on either side by the court reporter and the clerk of the court. All of them were framed by a yellow wall. None of them looked at me at first.

The judge said my name before he lifted his eyes. "Do you know

CHAPTER ELEVEN

why you're here?" he said. The man sat very straight in his chair as if he wanted to look down on me from as great a height as possible. The traces of unconscionable acts carried out under the auspices of the law were written across his heavy, square features.

"Do you know why you're here?" he asked again, his impatience putting a sharp edge on his voice.

"No," I answered.

The judge glanced at the man to his left as if explanations were beneath his exalted station.

"You've been charged with acting against national security and leading underground churches," the clerk said, a disinterested tone in his voice.

"Now, do you know why you're here?" the judge asked.

"Yes, because I'm Christian," I replied. Something in my tone shattered the brutal efficiency of this court and replaced it with shocked silence. All eyes in the courtroom were suddenly on me. I seized the opportunity. "What should I be proud of except Jesus' name? I'm not a slave anymore. I'm a son of God."

"Twelve months," the judge said.

I had been expecting a much longer sentence. "God, Jesus, please forgive him because he doesn't know what he's doing." I spoke softly, but in the quiet courtroom, the judge heard me.

"Fifteen months!" His sharp voice was heavy with the threat of a longer sentence.

I stayed silent. The additional three months weren't so bad. I had been expecting another year.

"You'll have time to think in prison. May Allah bring you back."

The soldier led me back to the waiting room. For thirty interminable minutes we waited for the wheels of bureaucracy to turn, for the orders formalizing my sentence to be signed and sealed and presented to the Security Policeman. He flipped through the documents, assuring himself that it was all in order before they led me back downstairs to a car and two different soldiers. The Security Policeman came with me. The papers never left his hands.

They didn't tell me where I was going, but there were only two options. The silence of the ride left me alone with my racing thoughts. I was alive. I knew what my sentence was, but there was still so much I didn't know. Of all the lines that made up my life, Sahar stood out bold among the others. I had been gone for months already. Anything could have happened to her. Had she been arrested too? I couldn't ask. Not without revealing that she existed in the first place. Then there was the business. Who was looking after everything? Was it even still mine? It might have been seized by the government. I had no way of knowing. This fathomless anxiety coiled around me and made it hard to draw breath as we approached the imposing fortress of Evin Prison.

There are two gates into the prison. The part of the facility reserved for detention was for those who were being held pending sentencing. I was taken to the other part of the facility; the part for those who had been sentenced to a prison term.

It took several hours to be processed in. As part of that, I was allowed to shower for the first time since I was arrested. I stood under the hot spray, and for a moment relief flooded in. Then fiery pain sliced through my scalp. I had forgotten about the wound on my head, and the water had dislodged the scab.

I washed the blood out of my long hair carefully with one hand while I protected the wound with the other. Afterward, I dressed in the gray uniform they'd given me. When I emerged, I was issued a number that would serve as my identity for the next fifteen months.

The Security Policeman was still there when I emerged. He followed the soldiers who escorted me through the seemingly endless hallways to the cell I had been assigned and stayed until I stepped inside. He'd been with me all day, but I don't think he looked at me once. Perhaps that meant he didn't have to think of me as human.

CHAPTER ELEVEN

The cell was certainly larger than where I'd been held most recently, but I wasn't sure what to expect of the twenty-five men who faced me. Strangely, there was none of the naked aggression that I'd felt walking into the jail in Arima for the first time. A tall, thin man with a long beard stepped forward.

"I'm Saber."

I introduced myself, my eyes still darting from face to face. Some were young men, some old, but the only thing written on their features was curiosity. He followed the direction of my gaze, then gestured to the others. "We've all spoken out against the government in some way. So, we were banished here."

"I'm a Christian," I said.

He shook his head. "Oh, the last thing we need in here is a mullah."

I didn't know how to respond.

Saber smiled and humor crinkled the corners of his eyes, and I remembered what it was like for a smile to be something other than mocking. He apparently knew my look all too well. "I'm joking. Come, meet the others."

My cellmates were all highly educated men who enjoyed a good conversation. It was almost like being on a university campus. With so many of us in the same cell with so many opinions and ideas, there had to be a system so that each person had the opportunity to choose the topic. The rule was that each person had twenty minutes to speak about whatever he wanted. They listened politely, even though they often didn't agree with each other. Mostly, they chose to talk about politics. I could remember most parts of the Bible, so I did the same thing I had when Cyrus and I had stayed with the homeless. I used verses without mentioning Jesus.

These men were not homeless or addicted though. Their curiosity and focused minds broke through my simple ruse in only a couple of days. The Bible was still new to them, so they were eager to listen and ask questions. The questions they asked most often were about the idea of the shepherd. They especially liked the book of Psalms.

Each night, the lights were turned off at 10 p.m., and a thick darkness would descend. For a few minutes silence reigned.

Each night I lay there waiting.

"Repeat it," a voice from the darkness would say. Sometimes I could tell who it was, sometimes I couldn't. What they were asking for was always the same.

"The Lord is my shepherd; I shall not want. He maketh me to lie down in green pastures: he leadeth me beside the still waters. He restoreth my soul: He leadeth me in the paths of righteousness for His name's sake. Yea, though I walk through the valley of the shadow of death, I will fear no evil: for thou are with me; thy rod and thy staff they comfort me. Thou preparest a table before me in the presence of mine enemies: thou anointest my head with oil; my cup runneth over. Surely goodness and mercy shall follow me all the days of my life: and I will dwell in the house of the Lord forever." I kept my voice just beyond the far side of a whisper, but it still carried far enough in the dark silence that men in other cells heard me too.

"Again," someone else would say.

I repeated the verse.

The guard was listening, he always was, but he was also silent. Most nights I repeated the verse two or three times, no matter who asked or what cell the voice came from.

I have always had the gift of memory, but I had never really appreciated it until those first days in prison. Speaking to those men, hearing their questions and feeling the way the conversations shifted from politics to what it meant to have a relationship with God, I began to see what a powerful gift my memory truly was.

In those early days I fell easily into the routine of prison life. Breakfast and dinner were brought to the cell. Saber, the boss of the cell, portioned out the food to everyone. Lunch was the only meal served in a common dining hall. Each day, we could walk in the yard. Some of the inmates could work and earn money, but that was at the discretion of the guard. Those who had money could use the prison store to buy canned chicken or beef to supplement the food

CHAPTER ELEVEN

the prison supplied. When there wasn't enough to go around, those who had bought extra would share with the others.

After about ten days I was offered the chance to contact someone on the outside. I was still worried about Sahar, but who could I contact and how could I ask what I wanted to know without revealing too much to the authorities? I decided that it would be safer not to contact anyone.

It was about twenty days into my sentence when, just before dinner, two soldiers came into the cell with a man who wasn't in uniform and didn't need to be. One soldier called my name. "Let's go," he said.

"Where are you taking him?" Saber asked.

"You don't need to worry about that," the soldier said, pushing past him. There was nothing to do but go.

I didn't know where they were taking me, but if they had been moving me to another cell, I would have been ordered to collect what few possessions I was allowed. They led me down a flight of stairs, then another and another, going down deeper under the prison until we got to a door. The soldier on the other side knew we were coming. He opened the door as soon as we got there. Lights glowed every twenty feet or so. They bathed the long, blue and gray hallway in dirty yellow light. Our footsteps were the only sound that filled the space.

We walked in silence down to a "T" intersection and turned to the left. The guard gave a sharp knock on the first metal door on the right. It was opened by a soldier. We turned in to a smaller hallway. About ten feet down, small metal doors lined either side of the hallway with tiny ports that could only be opened from the outside. We stopped in front of the third on the right, and my escort opened the door with a loud squeak.

The top of the door barely reached my chin. I had to bend down to enter. The ceiling was a couple of inches higher than the top of the door, but I still couldn't stand up straight. It was five feet to the back of the cell. Next to the door, there was a hole in the ground to use as a toilet with a tap for water over it.

As soon as the door closed, this became my world.

It was a world of absence. An absence of light and sound that became an absence of time. When they opened the port in the door to give me food, the light was painful.

"Where is your God?" a voice mocked from the other side. "Do you still want to talk about Jesus?"

Days might have passed, or weeks come and gone, when the horror that had filled each of my cells spun and twisted and grew to unbearable proportions. Being silent wasn't helping. I focused all of my energy and began to scream.

"Release me!" I shouted at the oppressive walls and the invasive darkness. "Release me! Release me!" I sank down onto the cold cement, my energy spent. The horror that had filled me had been shaken off my skin like so much filthy water. No one could hear my voice, not even God. He had abandoned me to the darkness and silence.

As my existence in this place outside of time stretched longer, the absence drew me deeper into itself. I could feel the cold concrete of the floor. I could move from one side of the space to the other. I could sit or lie. I could trace the walls with my fingers, defining seams and corners and the change in texture as my hands skated from the wall to the door. But everything else was gone. Sometimes there were footsteps in the corridor; sometimes another prisoner would scream as I had or beat the wall or doors. It must have been their first day. Once I tried to speak to one of them. The guard threatened to stop bringing me food.

I stayed silent.

This strange alchemy of loss continued. It ate away at the outside of myself and insinuated itself into my pores. Was I still there? How could I know? I couldn't see myself. Maybe the darkness and the silence had consumed me. Maybe it was more insidious than that. Maybe it was remaking me in its own image as I slept. The pain of being forced into that tiny hole had been horrible, but it had given me something to fight against. How do you fight absence?

I don't know how long I had been in that cell when I saw light

CHAPTER ELEVEN

beginning to gather. Not the harsh light of the hallway, not the yellow light of the sun. It was a soft purple that reminded me of the inside of a flower. The light from the ports was painful, but as that purple glow grew, I could open my eyes and look around. I could see every corner of the room. I could look down and see myself. More than that, I could feel the light surrounding me with a pressure akin to water.

Seeing that light, being with that light, it was a miracle. I felt Jesus there with me. I don't know how long the light lasted, but it faded into a calm withdrawal. After that I began to sing and to repeat the psalms, especially the twenty-third psalm. I began to introduce myself to myself. I gave my biography to the darkness and used memories to fight the way the vicious absence threatened to consume me.

When they took me out of the cell where I had been entombed, I had lost forty pounds. The pain throbbed through my back and knees and made it impossible for me to stand up straight. I hobbled down the long hallways and up the stairs still struggling under the weight of the darkness and silence. Before they took me back to the cell, the soldiers and guard allowed me to shower and gave me a change of clothes.

"How long?" I asked one of the soldiers. My voice in such an abundance of space sounded strange to my own ears.

"I don't know," he said. He'd probably had numerous assignments since I went into the cell, and fetching me out of the darkness was just another one of them. So, I asked the guard.

"No idea," he said in the same exact tone of the soldier. That was a lie. The guards knew everything that went on with the prisoners they were responsible for.

When they brought me back to the cell, my cellmates stared in what was for them an unfamiliar silence.

Saber was the first to speak. "Where were you?"

"In the dark," I said. "How long was I there?"

Saber glanced at the calendar he kept. "One hundred and twenty days," he replied. Concern had replaced the familiar humor in his eyes.

It had been so long since I'd spoken to another person that I just nodded and went to bed. I lay on my back and tried to get used to the sounds of more ordinary life again. I listened to my cellmates talking to each other, to them moving around inside the cell, to the soldiers walking in the hallway. Sounds that I hadn't even noticed before seemed intrusive. They were too big and too loud and too many all at once. The pain that throbbed through my bones provided a bass line for all of it.

I woke up the next morning with a burning pain in my back and a numbness sifting through my leg. I had to use the frame of the bed to stand up straight. My cellmates tried not to stare, but I could see the concern on their faces. Saber was the only one who spoke.

"Let me help you," he said.

"No," I said quickly. "I'm fine."

I used the walls to help me move around. I couldn't sit up to eat, so I lay on the floor, and then I went back to bed. I hadn't been able to stand up straight or stretch out when I lay down in months. I thought moving would help, so every hour or so I got up and walked around in the cell.

It didn't help.

A few days later I told one of the soldiers I needed to see a doctor.

"Why?"

"Pain in my back and legs."

"I'll let them know," he said.

Days passed while I waited, and I was getting worse. I couldn't walk to lunch with the others, so my meal was brought to me. I couldn't go out in the yard, so I remained inside. Two weeks later, and with the intervention of Saber, I was taken to see the doctor.

The medical facilities were clean, but outdated and bare. A bored-looking doctor asked what was wrong. I explained and showed him where the pain was.

"How long have you had it?" he asked.

"Since I came here."

"I'll give you something," he said, the bored tone of routine never leaving his voice.

CHAPTER ELEVEN

He didn't tell me what he was going to give me, but he drew up an injection. They let me stay there for about an hour and then took me back to the cell. My gait was still halting and careful, but the pain had eased.

"Are you feeling better?" Saber asked.

"Some. I don't know what they gave me though."

He waved dismissively. "They never tell you. They worry that if you like it, you'll pay one of the soldiers to bring it in for you."

I went back to bed again.

After a few days, Saber came back to me and offered me a cup of tea. He and the others tried to draw me into conversation. I had been immersed in the dark and the silence for four months, and I wasn't the same man. Even when the guards made fun of how being locked away for those months had changed me, I said nothing. They wanted to put me back into the darkness. I let them hurl their insults and pretended I didn't hear them.

The others would ask me to repeat the twenty-third psalm, but I wouldn't do it. I knew what would happen as surely as I knew that going into the water would make me wet. I went into the silence and I became silent.

A few months later, Saber and I were walking in the yard. "I understand why you don't want to say it every night. I really do and I don't blame you. The government is not above putting agents into prisons. For all you know, I could be informing on everyone."

I gave him a sidelong look, but I didn't say anything.

"Do what the others do. Talk about business or other safe ideas. But I do find that verse to be so beautiful. Will you say it one more time, just for me, so that I can write it down?"

I nodded. That afternoon, I sat next to him. My voice was just above a whisper. He wrote the words with a careful hand in a small notebook.

After that, the days were all the same. I could be drawn into the conversation on occasion, but only to talk about ordinary things and never about the Bible. Ten months into my sentence, the guard told me that I had a visitor. That was impossible. I hadn't contacted anyone, and the only people who would have been allowed to visit were blood relatives.

"Who is it?" I asked.

"Come and see," he said. His eyes glittered with relish.

Maybe it was some sort of trap, maybe it wasn't. There was no need to take the chance. I shook my head. "Whoever they are, I don't want to see them."

I never found out who it was.

Saber was not only the boss of the cell; he had designated himself timekeeper. He had a much longer sentence than anyone else and so he kept track of how long each of us had been there as well as when we were due to be released. On my last night in prison, Saber put together a little celebration for me. People came from other cells, and Saber even created a special meal for me by augmenting the prison rations with the most luxurious item that could be purchased in the prison store: canned tuna.

I wish I could say that I enjoyed it. The truth was, I didn't feel anything, didn't taste the food. I didn't even feel any excitement about getting out. The darkness and silence had killed something inside me.

The next morning, Saber woke me at four thirty with a cup of tea. The others were still sleeping while he and I sat next to each other for the last time.

"I have a cousin," he said softly. "He's a talented computer programmer, but no one will hire him."

"I don't even know if I own the business anymore, but if I can help him, I will."

He nodded. "Thank you."

It wasn't long after that the soldiers came for me.

Chapter Twelve

BEING PROCESSED OUT of prison took as long as being processed in. After all the paperwork had been signed and officially recorded, I was given a small amount of money and went to stand by the door with a soldier. I was to be officially released at seven in the morning, and they weren't going to let me out a second before.

The soldier kept looking at his watch. At last he glanced up at me. "Fifteen seconds," he said. I think he was hoping to make me smile, but there wasn't a smile in me. I looked at him and waited for those final fifteen seconds to tick by. Once they had, he opened the door and I stepped outside into a cold, windy morning.

Behind me, the door closed with a solid thump. The first, singular moment of freedom stretched into another and then another. What was I going to do next? I wasn't the same man who had gone for a few groceries a year and a half before. If I wasn't the same man I had been a few months before, what was left of the rest of my life?

There were always taxis waiting just down the street from the main gates of the prison. No doubt the drivers knew those being released would have a bit of money and a need to get home. I got into one and asked to be taken to northern Tehran.

The driver looked at me in the rearview mirror. "Are you sure that's where you want to go?"

"I'm sure," I said and gave him an address near my office.

He didn't ask any more questions. He just drove to the address and dropped me off.

They wouldn't be open yet. It was too early. I walked the last few blocks through the wakening streets, feeling the air on my skin and looking at the ordinary world playing out its daily dramas before me. As I got closer, I crossed to the opposite side of the street, went into a store, and bought some milk, walking out in the opposite direction before turning back again. By the time I came back, they should have been open. What if they were? What was I going to do? Walk in ready to start the day as if nothing had happened? My heart began to pound in my chest, and buzzing filled my ears. I hid behind a large pine tree. My fingers found their way into the crevices in the rough bark as I watched through the gaps in the passing traffic. People were moving around inside the building. I recognized all of them, but would they still recognize me? What would they say? For a moment I leaned into the tree and closed my eyes, the sharp, sweet scent filling my lungs with every inhalation. I had to find out if it was still mine and watching from a distance wouldn't tell me that.

I stood up straight and pulled a confidence I didn't feel around my shoulders. I crossed the street and went inside as if this were just an ordinary day.

The janitor, Arash, was making sure that the floor was clean for the start of the day. He stared at me for a long moment, then greeted me with a warm smile.

"Where were you?" he asked after greetings were exchanged.

I didn't want to tell him. "On a trip," I said.

He nodded. "I heard about that."

He'd heard about that? I walked into my office and Arash followed me. My desk was no longer as I had kept it, but I could tell it was still mine.

"Ali comes in regularly," he said. "He doesn't know what to do but he's learning. Behram comes in too. He thinks he's the boss, but he's not."

It was all so ordinary, as if I really had just been away on business or to study. There was no certainty in any of it, though. In any moment, it could all be taken.

CHAPTER TWELVE

"Are they coming in today?" I asked.

"Yes, they should be," Arash said.

"Good. I'm going up to the conference room," I said.

I climbed the stairs and sat down in one of the comfortable chairs. I leaned back and closed my eyes. All the familiar scents of the room were there. I could put my hands on the smooth table in front of me, feel the give of the chair, hear the imperfect quiet. It was all there, but I wasn't. Not really. One thought chased through my mind: protection. Protection for the company, but also protection for Sahar, for myself, and for all the others who were close to me.

This could not, would not, happen again.

At five to nine the door burst open. "—said he was here," Behram said, looking over his shoulder as he opened the door.

"No. He'd want to go home. Wouldn't he?" Ali said. The two of them tried to come through the door at the same time and managed it as well as physics would allow. I stood up to greet them.

They both just stared at me, as if I would disappear again if anyone spoke. Ali didn't speak. He swept forward to hug me. I knew he was glad to see me after so long, but I couldn't hug him back. I stood there with my arms at my sides and retreated back further into the numbness. In the space of a few heartbeats, Ali recognized that I wasn't responding to him. He stepped back.

"Where's Sahar?" I asked when we sat down again.

"She's fine," Behram said quickly. "She's been coming in a couple of times a week to deal with the books."

"Cyrus takes care of writing checks and making sure everyone is paid," Ali said.

"I negotiate contracts and set up the work," Behram added.

"I make sure everything goes like it's supposed to," Ali said. I saw the look Behram shot him, but I didn't say anything.

I just nodded. "How did you know?"

"Cyrus figured it out. We knew you wouldn't just leave without saying anything to anyone," Behram said. "We told everybody you were studying out of the country. Let me call Sahar—"

"No. Don't call anyone yet," I said. "I need some time."

"Then I won't tell her you're here," Behram said. "I'll just ask when she's going to be in with the bank statements."

I nodded. It was so ordinary, but I could still feel the world shift beneath my feet with every breath I took.

I was relieved when she said she wouldn't be in for a couple of days.

They both started to tell me everything that had happened since my arrest. I sat back and listened, while they laid out who had done what.

Twenty minutes later, Sahar came in. She paused in the doorway, her eyes on mine. Relief eased the tension in her shoulders. Behram and Ali hadn't called anyone, but Arash was calling everyone.

A look passed between them, and they left Sahar and me alone. Once the door closed, she hugged me, her head resting on my shoulder as she sobbed. I hesitated as I had with Ali. But the tears that fell won through, and I put my arms around her. It was what she needed, but I knew she felt the difference. She didn't pull away until her cheeks were dry.

We sat down. I didn't know what to say. She didn't know where to start. The silence was familiar, and unbearable.

"What happened?" she asked.

"I was arrested," I said. I couldn't say any more and I think she could see that.

She nodded. "Cyrus guessed that's what happened. We kept everything running as you wanted." She pulled her laptop out of her bag and started logging in. "People still eat together every day. A different person leads the prayer. The others are still getting new contracts." She turned the screen toward me so I could see the bank statement.

My eyes were on the screen while she talked about how they had all come together to take care of the business. They'd done a good job, and it was clear that I had people around me who I could trust. When she asked a question, all I could give her were one- or two-word answers. She finished taking me through the accounts, and

CHAPTER TWELVE

silence settled around us again.

"Come on," she said. "Let's go home. I'll make you something to eat—"

"No."

"But—"

"I need time."

She didn't say anything; she just reached into her bag and put my car keys on the table. "It's still in the lot out back."

I nodded and wrapped my hand around them. "I'll walk you out."

We'd reached the door when one of my employees, Marzie, stopped and stared at me. "You look so much older. There are wrinkles around your eyes now."

The rest of them must have noticed the changes in me, but no one had said anything. Sahar and I both stared at her, the look on Sahar's face conveying more anger than words could have. Marzie tried to laugh it off. "I suppose that's what working hard does to us all." She put her head down as she walked away.

I spent the rest of the morning looking at the accounts while Ali and Behram talked about ordinary things and tried to draw me into conversation. Most of it didn't even register. I kept my eyes on the numbers in front of me. Ali and Behram might have stepped in without really knowing what they were doing, but they had known enough to grow the business. Why was I jeopardizing everything? I had a thriving business; I had my freedom; and I had Sahar. All those things could have been lost in the stroke of an official's pen. Maybe now was the time to focus on living an ordinary life.

After I left the office, I spent hours driving around the city. What would it be like, I wondered, if I were to simply stop talking about Christianity? The others could make their own choices, but hadn't I given enough? I could have lost everything and for what? For an idea? Maybe I had been wrong all along. The turn onto my street was approaching, but my heart began to pound again. I couldn't go there. What would I find if I did?

I drove past.

I drove past three times before I could make myself turn onto the street but not the entrance to the parking structure. On the fifth try I made it inside.

For a few minutes I sat in the car taking deep breaths and reminding myself that if the apartment was no longer mine, Sahar would have said something. Wouldn't she? What if she had and I hadn't heard her? I wrapped myself in the same kind of false confidence I wore when I walked into the office.

It was after midnight when I walked into the apartment. I ran my fingers over the counters and along the backs of furniture, refamiliarizing myself with the space and the things that occupied it. There was no dust. Some of the furniture had changed, but for the most part everything was the same. I walked into the dark bedroom and put my back against the wall next to the bed and shifted over to the corner. Then I slid down to the floor, my knees drawn up, my head resting against them.

I had become a ghost. Haunting the familiar spaces of my former life, I moved from room to room more dead than alive, just eating and sleeping. Most days I went into the office but only for an hour or so. The others still ran the business. They wanted to help me come back to myself, but I didn't want to see any of them.

They left notes for me on my desk where I was sure to see them. They varied their schedules to run into me about once a week. They talked about work and about what jobs were current and upcoming. I listened until I could leave.

Behram often invited me to see what he'd done with his company, but I couldn't make myself go. I was still ensnared by the numbness. For the first few days the phone rang. I didn't answer it. The person they wanted to reach wasn't there anymore. After a while, the only ones who still called were Cyrus and Sahar. She and I went to dinner a couple of times, but the bustle and humming sound of a restaurant

CHAPTER TWELVE

abraded my already raw nerves. Our conversation came out stilted and strange. Each time she reached out to me, I retreated.

I told her I needed a few weeks, but I wasn't sure if that was going to be enough. What if a lifetime wasn't enough?

Eventually, I ran out of excuses not to visit Behram's company. He'd persisted, no matter how many times I said no. A visit seemed the easiest way to keep him from asking again. And so, I stood outside the large window and looked in. He had a lot more space now. Two designers worked near the entrance, and his desk sat toward the back. We'd barely greeted each other when a customer of his walked in.

"I'll tell him I'll call him later," Behram said. "He's a good customer, he'll understand."

"No, no. I'll look around while I wait," I replied.

Behram had set aside a large area to display examples of sculpture and other design elements that customers could choose from. I wandered from one attractive display to another while he negotiated with his client. When that conversation was winding down, I went into the kitchenette area, where the office manager was making tea.

"So, what's he like as a boss?" I asked.

The man stood up a little straighter as he looked at me. "He's not my boss," the office manager said. "We work together."

Something sparked inside me. It was a little flash of remembered warmth, but it was more than I'd felt in months.

Behram walked his client to the door, and I sat down in the chair the client had vacated. The office manager brought the tea over when it was finished.

"He said you're a good boss," I said to Behram.

Behram looked at the man with a touch of surprise. "Did you say I was your boss?"

"No. I said we work together," the office manager corrected.

These were the ideas that I had planted so many months ago, and they had borne fruit I couldn't have imagined. It reminded me of who I had been. I felt myself smile for the first time in months. Behram began to laugh. The warmth and heat of the camaraderie began to burn

131

off the chill fog that had consumed my life. It was the beginning of my journey back to myself.

That night I called Sahar and suggested we go out. Before then it had been her who had always initiated our evenings. When she asked, I told her about what had happened at Behram's. In turn she told me about other times when people had used my words to live a better life. Her pride in that was unmistakable. That night, we talked almost like we used to, and the hours slid past as they hadn't since my release.

Chapter Thirteen

IT TOOK ABOUT a month before I was ready to talk about the group. Behram, Cyrus, and Ali came by the office most days, but they knew I wasn't ready. They avoided the topic. When I wanted to know more, they began with generalities.

"So, how are you all staying safe?" I asked.

Cyrus and Behram looked at each other, as if deciding how much to tell me, how much I was ready to hear.

"When you say 'all,' how many do you think we are now?" Behram asked.

"I don't know," I replied. "There were two hundred when I was arrested. Maybe four hundred?"

"Higher," Cyrus said.

"Six hundred?"

Behram shook his head. "More than that." Pride beamed from their smiles.

"How much more?" I asked.

"We have over fourteen hundred now," Cyrus said.

I couldn't believe it. All at once, too many questions flickered brightly and I couldn't just choose one. "This isn't a conversation. We need to have a meeting."

We eventually found a time that worked for everyone. Meanwhile, Behram and Sahar kept hinting that there had been changes to the garden. No one would tell me what they were. All they would say was that it was Samad's surprise. Samad had come with me to drop off the towels and clothes all those months ago. When he saw what we were doing, he wanted to help in a bigger way. His company finished the space, and he began spending time there. Hearing Cyrus talking about the Bible led to his own conversion. I couldn't imagine what the surprise was, but from the excitement on their faces, I could tell it must be something big.

"Would you like to go out there?" Behram asked.

Of course I agreed.

On a sunny afternoon, Sahar drove the familiar route to the garden. As soon as we came around the sinuous curve in the road, I expected to see the canopy and temporary structures. Instead there was a large building connected to an open-air but walled space. I leaned forward in my seat, trying to get a better view. "They did all that? In seventeen months?"

"It was Samad that started it really," Sahar said. "They wanted to buy the garden, so they collected money. Except when they totaled it all up, it was way too much. So, he talked to the owners of the adjacent plots, and they built this."

She parked and I got out of the car, only able to stare at the spacious wedding venue. Cyrus, Behram, Ali, and Samad were waiting inside.

"Who designed it?" I asked.

"Your company," Samad said. "Do you want a tour?"

"Of course," I said.

He opened the door and turned on the lights to reveal a large space with empty, round tables arranged on either side. Much of the floor was carpeted, and there was a dais for music beside a tiled space for dancing. The echo of our voices and footsteps followed us as we moved through the main room. There were comfortable playrooms for the children of the wedding guests and a gleaming kitchen.

After they'd taken me on a tour of the building, Samad pointed out how to get to the garden itself.

Sahar took my arm. "This is my surprise," she said.

CHAPTER THIRTEEN

The others waited while we walked out into the walled space. In place of open ground and temporary amenities, there was a pond that sparkled in the sunshine. Everywhere I looked there were lush flowers, grapevines, and tall trees. On the spot where Sahar and I had made our promise, the chairs we'd sat in had been connected to each other to form a bench and framed by white stone columns.

"I didn't want to change it," she said. "No one did."

We sat on the bench together with all that flourishing transformation, and it settled onto my heart. I was ready to throw myself into ministry again.

When we got back, I focused on the meeting and thought about how to manage and protect a group of well over a thousand. So much had happened in the time I had been away, I had to understand how we were functioning with so many people. We were able to bring together fifteen people, the leaders among the leaders. I wanted to talk about our supply of Bibles and teaching eventually, but safety lay at the top of my list.

The conference room wasn't large enough. The ones who arrived first sat around the table. Cyrus and Behram both ended up across from me. Ali and Sahar sat on the other side with me. The later arrivals stood where they could.

"There aren't enough chairs," one of them commented.

I had too much on my mind to worry about where people were going to sit. "Take some from the lunchroom, or from downstairs somewhere." The ones who were standing left and came back with chairs and filled in the empty space in the conference room.

The more people who came into the room, the louder it got. Everyone was glad to see me, but most didn't know where I'd been for nearly a year and a half. They believed I had been away, studying. They were eager to tell me about how many they'd shared the message with, how many new churches those new believers had formed.

I wasn't hearing anything about responsibility for those new believers they'd brought in.

I was still overwhelmed by the numbers. When I had first talked about my idea of sharing Jesus with the homeless, the expectation had been between eight and twelve new believers. To be over a thousand in such a short time seemed impossible.

As I listened to the happy chatter and the pride that filled their voices, I could tell that they hadn't considered anything beyond increasing their numbers.

Initially I just listened. But eventually my anxiety could no longer be held in silence. "Explain to me how you manage a group this big," I asked. "How many warehouses do you have now?"

"Two," Behram said.

"There were two before I left," I noted. "You've got a bigger group and more materials, and you're concentrating them in the same two locations?"

"It's worked well so far," Cyrus said.

"Do you hear yourself? You're telling me that you are willing to risk thousands of Bibles at a time because it's worked well enough so far? All the people who risked their lives to get them here, and you stack them up like they're not worth any more than old telephone books?"

Ali looked away, but I caught the little smile before he did. I wondered if he'd said the same thing and been ignored. Ali preferred action to discussion, but of the people in that room, he was the only one who had any experience keeping an illegal enterprise from being discovered. The rest shifted uncomfortably in their chairs.

Cyrus watched the light reflect off the bracelet as he moved it around his wrist. "I'll admit, I didn't think about it quite that way."

They were all thinking about it now. Later, once they'd had a chance to think, we'd talk more about it. I was a little worried about how they were going to answer my next question, so I let the silence stretch just a bit longer than I usually would have before proceeding. "What about house churches?"

CHAPTER THIRTEEN

"We did it the way we always have," Cyrus said. "No more than twelve or fifteen per group. When there are more than that, one or two members form their own house church."

"And each has its own leader," I said.

"No," Behram said. "We still lead them."

"So, all of those people know you," I said. "What's the difference between having a dozen house churches led by a single person and having a single church of over a hundred led by that person?"

Their silence was the answer.

"Nothing," I said. "Each of those churches should act independently. They need to choose their own leaders. All of this needs more planning than you think." I could see that they were all embarrassed. I decided to move on to other things for the moment.

"How are you getting Bibles?"

"Samad's been keeping us supplied," Behram said.

"Khalid asked where you were, but Samad always told him you were busy. I don't know if he believed it, but it seemed to keep him happy," Cyrus added.

"That's all good, but this is so big," I said and thought for a moment. "You have the space to do it. I want to bring everyone together, but I don't want them to know who I am. I was already away when most of them converted anyway."

Ali leaned forward. "If you want to do this, you're going to need security."

Ali wasn't the type to speak at meetings. He came, he listened, but to hear his voice was a rarity. It made people listen more closely, and I was no different than anyone else.

"What are you thinking?" I asked.

"You need people inside to keep an eye out for anything that looks suspicious, on the outside to make sure only the people who were invited get in, and people stationed on the road in pairs at five-kilometer intervals beginning at about twenty kilometers out, to make sure there's enough warning to give people a few minutes to get out if the police are on the way." He might not speak often, but when he did, he spoke with confidence.

The others looked at each other. No one protested.

"Agreed," I said. "But who's going to do it?"

"My men," Ali said. He must have seen worry on my face because he continued. "I'll make sure they look presentable."

I had to suppress a laugh. I'd seen his men. It would take more than a change of wardrobe to help them blend in, but they were trustworthy.

I left that aspect alone for the moment. "We need to think about some dates."

We selected Thursdays because it was the most popular day for a wedding and settled on a date between five and seven weeks away. That would give us time to properly prepare. "Talk to your leaders and have them talk with their membership. We'll see what works best for everyone."

"You should really do it on Wednesday," Ali said.

"No one gets married on a Wednesday. It'll look suspicious," I said.

"Only if they know," he said. Everyone looked at him curiously and so Ali continued. "Look, the police expect weddings on Thursdays. They'll be more likely to drive by, looking for anything suspicious like dancing or drinking. Why would they go by on a Wednesday? The place should be empty. If someone tips them off that something is happening, you'll probably have two or three hours' advance warning. Besides, there's no law that says a wedding can't happen on a Wednesday; it's just not common."

It made sense. "Anyone object to a Wednesday instead?" I asked.

No one raised any further objections. We agreed to meet again to fix the date.

That meeting changed perspectives and got everyone thinking about ways to be safer. A few days later, Ali, Cyrus, Behram, Sahar,

CHAPTER THIRTEEN

and I were talking. We got together most days, but that day I could see that Behram had something very important to say.

"After we met yesterday, Cyrus and I were talking, and he reminded me of a book I read recently about the Armenian Christian persecution. They changed the names of the leaders. No one outside of a very small circle knew who the leaders were. If anyone is arrested, they can give the names they know, but those names don't lead anywhere. The leader is free to walk around, acting like any other member of the group. None of them know him for who he really is." His eyes were sparkling.

This was my anonymity. The biggest part of the group had never met me. They might have heard that I was away, or they might not have heard of me at all.

"I like it," I said. "But if we do it, we all need new names, all sixty-five of us."

"What about Ammin, for you," Sahar said to me.

It meant "the one you can trust." I nodded. "I like it."

We came up with a few more, but people left with instructions to choose and let the rest of us know.

———∞———

At our next leadership meeting, we set a firm date. The planners at the venue went to work arranging for a meal as well as preparing and sending out invitations. Most people knew that someone at the company was the one who had taught the Bible and brought everyone together, but because I had been in prison, they didn't know who. The others spread the word that it had been Ammin, and we made sure that the name Ammin appeared on the invitations as well.

I spent the six weeks leading up to the "wedding" putting my life back in order. The company had been acquiring contracts and completing jobs based on my name and reputation. My clients had to see me and know that I was still present and involved.

Sahar and I were living together as much as we could. She was worried about losing me again. I was worried about that too, but we had a good plan in place.

As a part of that plan, we came up with a list of questions that attendees shouldn't ask each other. People could give false names, but anything else that could lead to identification, such as what kind of work a person did or where they lived, was strictly off-limits.

Cyrus and Behram began to tell me more about some of the things that happened when I was in prison. I knew about the expansion of our group, but when they told me that halfway through my sentence, Farhan had been so jealous of our numbers that he'd approached Cyrus about rejoining Yale, I had no idea what to say.

I couldn't believe it. A few months before that we weren't even worthy of Bibles. But as soon as he thought there was an opening, he had moved in like a starving jackal. His offer had been rejected, but it showed me how low he would sink.

The day of the meeting was my personal tour through all the different shades of anxiety. I was excited to see everyone, to meet them, to have them meet me, and yet they were all strangers. How could I—or any of us—know who we were really speaking to?

On the day of the meeting, Ali positioned his men on the road leading up to the venue. They worked in teams of two. If they saw the police approaching, they'd call the others who were stationed inside. The art of concealment was second nature to them. The men and their vehicles became a part of the landscape. Ali had done his best with the ones who were inside, but clothing alone couldn't conceal the hard faces, vigilant eyes, and razor-sharp gazes that scanned the room.

If anyone noticed the incongruity of a street gang protecting a group of Christians, they didn't say anything.

People were invited for seven with speeches to start at eight. Tables were laden with fruit and flowers. Several of the women were

CHAPTER THIRTEEN

providing childcare in two of the rooms that had been designed for that purpose. Sahar and I arrived at seven thirty and stepped into a room filled with conversation, laughter, and worship music.

We mingled and circulated from group to group. That first half hour was over far too quickly. At five minutes to eight, the music ended and Behram asked for order. We sat and participated in the three minutes of silence he asked for. He didn't ask for prayer, but the feeling of focused worship filled the space with a palpable presence that surrounded and sat with us as we listened to the speakers.

They shared the changes their faith had brought about in their lives. Someone who had been invisible a few years before could command the attention of over a thousand. A person not trusted by his family gained a new community. Even though I knew them, knew their stories, knew that a few short years ago, they had been sleeping in an abandoned building and wondering where their next fix was coming from, I was moved by the power of it. Bringing everyone together might have been my idea, but it was their night.

With Sahar by my side, my anxiety began to lift for the first time since my release.

At nine thirty, there was another moment of silence before a buffet dinner was served and the speeches continued. Several of the speakers used the same verses I'd spoken to them during those long, dark nights when we sat together on an unfinished floor in the time before I had been able to tell them that the verses that gave them comfort and made them think were about Jesus.

Behram, Samad, Cyrus, and the others all spoke from the heart as if they were born to it. I didn't like the message about tithing at the end of one of the speeches, but I'd never given them an accurate picture of how money should be handled. I decided I would do that at the next leadership meeting.

After the speeches ended, I listened to people talk about what they had heard. We also took the opportunity to visit with those who arrived later. Many were curious about Sahar and me. They stuck to the list of approved questions, but I could see how difficult it was for some of them when I said I'd been converted for several years. More than one person said to me they'd wished Ammin had been able to come. I agreed, as if they weren't speaking to him. The few who knew said nothing. The rest were more than willing to accept and embrace the idea of an absent leader. In so many ways, it was perfect.

In that beautiful place, surrounded by so many people, I felt a profound sense of healing.

A few days later, the fifteen leaders gathered in my conference room again. Everyone counted the wedding gathering as a success, mainly because it showed people that they weren't alone. There were over a thousand others who thought and believed as they did. I agreed that was an important thing, but I didn't want to just leave it there.

"I think we need to talk about tithing," I said. "I don't want any money filtering back from the house churches to the mother church."

"But a church doesn't run for free," Samad said.

"No?" I asked. "We don't have buildings to maintain because we meet in people's homes. Those who preach aren't paid; they work and support themselves. When we need Bibles, we find a way to get them. What else is there?"

"You're saying they shouldn't give anything?" he asked.

"No. Each person can contribute if they want to, but those donations stay within each house church. The people who gave the money in the first place should decide how it's spent. Control of the account should be held by two people, and those two people change every six months."

"Not everyone has a talent for that. If members elect someone—"

"This isn't a permanent position, and a house church shouldn't be a permanent group," I said. "People should be gaining experience of handling the finances, of preaching and teaching so that in a year or so they can start their own house church. If someone doesn't know how to do one of those things, you teach them. If someone is struggling, you help them."

Chapter Fourteen

IT TOOK BARELY three weeks for that fragile sense of normalcy to be shattered.

Two men walked into my office. The short one in front moved with the strutting air of authority. He didn't need to speak. There was a circular scar on his forehead, meant to be an obvious sign of how much time he spent with his forehead pressed to his prayer mat.

I put my pen down.

"Would you come with us, please?" It was a politely given order. He had a soft, jowly face, but hard eyes studied me from behind glasses.

"Why?" I asked.

He handed me a letter. "You're under investigation. As we speak, we have officers searching your home, and this gives us authorization to search here as well."

I had a moment of panic until I remembered Sahar was out for the day. I scanned the document. "How are you in my house when I'm here?"

"There was no time to lose," he said.

It took me ten minutes to read through the paperwork he'd given me. As I read, others began to open drawers and take computers.

When I looked up from the document, he gestured to the door with a whisper of a smile on his lips. "Please."

They walked me out, past an office full of employees. There were three others waiting outside along with two cars. I was put into the back of the second one and handcuffed. This time there were no blindfolds or circuitous routes. I was taken directly to a police station and past the desk sergeant. The one who arrested me took off my handcuffs and had me sit at a small table where I was told to fill out a form that verified my name. The sergeant came to collect it.

"Why am I here?" I asked him.

He looked at the forms. "Acting against national security. Acting against the government. Establishing underground churches and distributing the Bible." His tone was flat, as if my crime had been no more than shoplifting.

"And did you find anything?" I asked.

"That's for the judge to decide. Do you want to call anyone?"

"Yes. Jamshidi, my lawyer," I said.

"Write down the name and number. We'll call him."

I wrote it down and was escorted to a bare holding cell.

Then, the waiting began.

There were already several others in the cell when I arrived. Old and young alike were sitting on the cement floor with their backs against the wall in a loose cluster. When I arrived in the cell, two of them were involved in a conversation that seemed easier than I would have expected for strangers. I wondered if they had been arrested together or if they knew each other some other way. I sat against one of the other empty walls. All three of them looked at me with suspicion. I had been arrested in my office and was formally dressed. I don't think they quite knew what to make of me. After a moment of assessment, we greeted each other.

"Why are you here?" the oldest one asked.

"I'm Christian," I said.

He glanced at the others. "But why are you here?"

"That's it."

I could see the surprise on their faces. It wasn't the kind of crime

CHAPTER FOURTEEN

petty thieves understood. They were all waiting for their turns in court.

I was waiting too. Waiting to go to court or to at least see my lawyer. The days passed. Court dates were changed and pushed back, and I was stuck waiting in a bare concrete cell with a parade of people arriving and leaving, sometimes after a day or so, sometimes after a few hours.

I had been in the cell about a week when two others were brought in. They didn't look any different than any of the other men who'd spent time in the holding cell.

They introduced themselves as Javad and Mohammad.

The two of them sat together and asked me what I was there for. I believed I was going to court soon and that they would be bailed out like all the others, so I told them.

Javad was curious. "A Christian? How is that possible?"

Mohammad rolled his eyes. "You don't want to get him preaching. It's bad enough to be stuck in here. We don't need to listen to a sermon too." The statement reminded me of Saber's, but all the warmth and humor that had been present in my former cellmate's words had been replaced with biting disdain.

They had been arrested for shoplifting. I waited for them to be bailed out or go to court, but these two stayed. They told me all about the difficult situation that led them there. Poverty, no family, no one to care that they'd been arrested or to help them with bail. I didn't trust them, because I didn't trust anyone, but we started to speak more about the ideas of Christianity. Javad would ask questions and Mohammad would make fun of the answers I gave. Javad started out curious and he remained that way, while Mohammad maintained his sarcastic approach to anything he heard.

I had been in the cell for two weeks when I was told that Jamshidi was there to see me. They opened the door and I found him standing in the hall outside of the cell. The soldier stood there the whole time we spoke.

"What's going on?" I asked. "They keep telling me I have a court date. Then the day gets here, and I'm told it's been rescheduled."

"I've been trying to find out. They called me the day after you were arrested. I've been at court every day, but no one will see me."

"I'll put up the deed to my apartment for bail—just get me out."

He nodded. "The judge will decide if that's enough, if I ever get to see one."

"What do you mean if?" I asked.

"I mean it's entirely at the discretion of the court. They can keep you in holding for years without setting a court date." He must have seen the look on my face because he hurried on. "I'm sure it won't come to that. I'll keep going. Someone is bound to see me eventually. To get me to go away if nothing else." He tried to smile, but it didn't reach his eyes.

I walked back into the cell and sat down on the concrete floor, my back against the wall. How long was I going to be there?

Javad and Mohammed had been there for several weeks. Mohammad seemed to have something snide to say about just about everything. It wasn't my goal to get him to accept what I said, but the derision had gotten to be too much.

"There were two thieves crucified with Jesus," I said. "One accepted Jesus and trusted him. Even then, Jesus promised the thief that he would be with him in heaven. The other rejected Jesus. Why do you want to be the one to miss the opportunity?"

He didn't say much for the rest of the day. The next morning Mohammad came over and sat down next to me. That was unusual. He and Javad tended to occupy the opposite wall of the small space. When I looked closer, I could see that he had tears in his eyes. He hugged me and told me that he'd had a dream and that I had been right all along.

I couldn't tell him that he was lying, but there was something about the whole thing that didn't feel right to me. I can't define what it was, but I know I felt it. After that, we spent more time talking. The

CHAPTER FOURTEEN

sarcasm that had been there throughout the weeks they'd been there was gone now, replaced by curiosity and questions. It was during that time that he began to tell me about his life.

"Why shouldn't I steal?" he asked me one day. "I grew up in the streets. No one cared where I was, or what I was doing. I was out of school more than I was there. I had to feed myself somehow."

"You have choices now," I said.

"Do I? I don't have any skills. I know if I had work, I could be a good person, but who will hire me?"

"I know someone who will." I gave him a name and address. "When you get out, go there and tell them I sent you."

The subcontractor I sent him to was Christian too. He'd be hired as casual labor so that we could see how he lived, how he worked. If Mohammad was serious about Christianity, the people who spent time with him every day would know. Words could lie, but actions couldn't.

They weren't in the cell very long after that. When they were released, they'd been in the cell with me for a month and a half. After that, no one stayed long.

The police station wasn't meant to house people for more than a day or so. Bathroom facilities were down the hall, and prisoners had to be escorted by a soldier. Those in holding sat and slept on a single blanket on the bare cement floor. Food was unpredictable. There were times when I was brought a meal, but the others in the cell weren't given anything. I couldn't just eat in front of them, so I shared what I was given.

There were no shower facilities for people in holding. Every few weeks I was allowed to shower in the soldiers' locker room. Each night I spent on the cold concrete, the pain in my bones sharpened until there was nowhere I could go to escape it.

New people came and went. Some said nothing and would glance about with suspicion. Some spoke to hear themselves, the sound of their own voices staving off panic. Most knew they were going to court soon, so they drew the quiet around themselves and waited.

My court dates were scheduled and canceled. Scheduled again and then postponed. Jamshidi came to see me a total of five times. Each time we met outside the cell, in sight and hearing of anyone who happened to be passing. The first four meetings he hadn't been allowed to see a judge and had no news.

The fifth time there was an eagerness in his voice. "They want some kind of assurance that you won't leave town."

"How much do they want?" I asked. Bail or bribe didn't matter at that moment.

He leaned a little closer and quoted me a number.

"Yes. Go see Sahar. She'll give you the deed to the apartment. It's worth more than they're asking for," I said and signed the document he handed me.

He took it back and pretended to study it while giving the nearest soldiers a sidelong glance. "Just because you're getting out doesn't mean the investigation is over. You'll be under closer scrutiny than before, and if you're arrested again, they'll want a lot more than this."

He held my eyes and I nodded. He had said enough. They were coming after me and they weren't going to stop. I had bought myself a little time, but that was all. The next thing they'd want to take was the company. I couldn't let that happen. Too many people depended on it for their livelihoods.

I'd signed the document Jamshidi presented me with at around nine thirty in the morning, but I wasn't released until after two in the afternoon.

First, I was taken to sign paperwork, and the sergeant gave me a list of what I was allowed to do. "Under the conditions of your bail, you can't leave town. You can't sell your apartment. You can't rent the apartment to someone else." I listened to his bored voice telling me all the things I wasn't allowed to do with my own property; then I was escorted across the small courtyard to a property room to collect the few possessions I'd come in with, including a dead cell phone.

"Will you call a number for me?" I asked the soldier behind the desk.

CHAPTER FOURTEEN

He shook his head and turned back to his paperwork. "I can't do that."

"Please, I just need to let someone know that I've been released."

"It's against the rules." He did his best not to meet my eyes. Out of shame or indifference I couldn't tell.

I studied him for a moment, noting the breadth of his shoulders and the way his uniform fit him. "You're an athlete?" I asked.

He looked up at me and shrugged. "Not so much now."

I nodded. "When I was younger, I was an internationally ranked wrestler."

He looked at me, his pen tapping against the desk. I don't know whether he believed me or not, but it didn't matter. He held out his hand. "Give me the number and wait outside."

I stepped out of the police station seven months after I'd been brought in, released on bail secured by the home Sahar and I shared, and I knew I had to walk away from all of it.

—∞—

Sahar picked me up and took me to lunch. She told me about how things had been going at the company, and about how the others were doing. Most of what she said focused on how well everything was going. She talked through the entire meal, which was good because I was hungry and didn't have much to say. There were only crumbs on our plates when she started to fill in the shadows around the highlights. Ali had been doing his best to run everything, but he hadn't had as much support this time. Cyrus wasn't helping him the way he had been.

"Why not?" I asked.

She hesitated. "He and Behram were both arrested when you were."

"Are they still in jail?" I asked.

"No. Behram was released first. Then Cyrus a few months later."

There was more to it, but Sahar had already moved on to other topics and I didn't want to pursue it then.

When I got to the office the next day, I didn't linger outside. For the moment anyway, I knew it was still mine. For months I'd lived in a concrete box and waited for a court date that never materialized, and in the interim Ali and Behram had been doing their best to keep things going.

Behram arrived shortly after I did. This time I was able to accept the hug he offered.

We exchanged a few pleasantries and sat down.

"Who was that guy you sent to work with the tile contractor?"

"What guy?" I asked.

"He showed up about five months ago asking for a job. He said you sent him."

Those five months were a blur. I had been so focused on getting out and protecting what I still had, I had forgotten about Mohammad and Javad. "Just someone I met in jail who said he needed work. Why?"

"I think he already had a job," Behram said. "With the government. He spent more time asking questions than working. When he realized he wasn't going to get any answers, he stopped showing up."

I shook my head. "I thought his 'conversion' was suspicious at the time." The incident proved that our system of watchful waiting before inviting someone into a house church worked, and that the government was working hard to find something against me. "Where's Cyrus?" I asked.

"I don't know. He left the city," Behram said.

"Just like that? Without telling anyone where he was going?"

Behram looked down at his hands for a moment, then back at me. His voice was taut. "You weren't the only one arrested this time. I was arrested, but so was Cyrus and his wife. I told them I didn't know anything and acted like I needed a fix. They must have been convinced

CHAPTER FOURTEEN

because they released me after a couple of days. Cyrus and Deborah weren't so lucky." He chewed on the inside of his cheek. "From what I understand, Deborah was raped in custody. After they were released, they left the city, and he hasn't contacted anyone. When we try to contact him, he doesn't respond."

He kept talking but I looked away. My stomach turned and I thought I might vomit. Rape was a common tactic used against women who belonged to groups who were enemies of the government, regardless of religion when they were arrested. I was afraid for Sahar and everyone else I was close to. What Cyrus and Deborah had been through was worse than anything I had suffered. Jamshidi had been right. I needed to get out of the city, for my own safety and the safety of the people I cared most about.

Sahar was afraid too, but she didn't want me to leave. I tried to explain the danger I was in, but she didn't understand the urgency of the situation. Leaving wasn't easy for me either. I could find a new place to live, but she wouldn't be able to come with me.

Before I made any permanent moves, I called a last meeting in my conference room. I could build another company somewhere else. Behram and several of the others had established their own businesses. Only one question remained.

"I'm selling the company," I said.

Immediately there was protest from everyone.

"They're not going to stop coming after me and anyone they think is associated with me. You all know that. But I can't sell the garden." Technically, the company owned it, but it belonged to all those people who had been brought back to life there. It belonged to all the people who had worked so hard to improve it.

"What are you going to do with it?" Behram asked.

"Someone has to own it. I think it should be Samad's cousin, Isaac."

BECOMING JOSHUA

"Why? He didn't build it."

"No, but you have to admit, he's fearless about his faith."

"He's too young. You can't just hand him something like that."

"I'm not looking at his age, just whether or not he's ready. I think he is," I said.

I could see the pride on Samad's face. Yes, his cousin would be fine. The rest of them would just have to live with the decision.

The next few weeks were consumed by my preparations to leave. I had to be discreet, but I couldn't afford to drag my feet. My uncle Ako lived in the city of Urmia in northwestern Iran in a largely Kurdish area. I'd planned to go there.

If I'd had the luxury of time, I could have sold the company for what it was worth. Half the value was good enough. I couldn't sell the apartment, so I planned to take only what I needed and walk away from the rest. The day before I left, I sold the car. It would be too easy for the government to track it.

I didn't care about leaving things behind. Things could be replaced. What I hated most was leaving Sahar. Even before I left, I told her we would have to work out a way to be married. I know she wanted to, but that meant she would have to leave her family. For the moment, she would be safer away from me.

When the day came, she drove me to the bus station. There were no tears, not then, but I could see the tension in the set of her shoulders. She stood near me in the empty bus station, facing me but not meeting my eyes.

"We'll work this out," I said. "We'll call, we'll text, and when I find a place to rent, you'll come and visit. Samad or Saba or one of the others drives the route every few weeks. You can ride with one of them to Urmia."

She nodded, more in acknowledgment than agreement. No matter what I said, how convenient or appealing I made it sound, the move meant that we would be separated. I couldn't hold her in public, so we stood there, separate and silent in the empty bus terminal, until it was time to board. When I stepped onto the bus, I

CHAPTER FOURTEEN

knew this wasn't going to be the last time I moved, and it wouldn't be the furthest I would go. I sat by the window, my eyes on Sahar's. When the bus pulled away, I wondered if I would ever see her again.

Chapter Fifteen

MY UNCLE AKO owned the same kind of company I did, only on a much smaller scale. I didn't really know how much smaller until the next day when he showed me around the tiny, rundown storefront in a seedy part of the city that wore a permanent coat of grime.

"You work here?" I asked, looking around the awkward, cluttered little space. I had storerooms that were better organized.

He shrugged. "It has everything I need."

I shook my head. "Where's the best part of the city?"

"Why?"

"Because you need to move, as soon as possible," I said.

"Do you know how much that'll cost?"

"Clients who have money to spend aren't going to come here. Your offices are your first advertisement for what you can do. You're wasting that opportunity."

He looked around. "Well, maybe we could do something to the place."

"No," I said firmly. "It's too small and it's in the wrong location."

He looked like he wanted to argue, but he knew how successful my company was. "Well, maybe it wouldn't hurt to look."

He took me on a tour of the better part of town. Finding a space that would work was difficult. Everything was either too small, too poorly laid out, or unavailable. I managed to find a much smaller space than what I had left in Tehran, but it had potential and that would be a start.

CHAPTER FIFTEEN

"Find the owner and see how much he wants to rent it," I said.

When Uncle Ako looked around, he saw cost and not potential. "He might not want to rent it out."

"Just talk with him," I said.

I rented a house under an assumed name and Uncle Ako found the owner of the space we found and negotiated a price. As soon as I was sure we had the space, I spent the next few days designing. It was difficult to fit everything I needed into the more compact area, but, with a little creativity, there was space for everything, including fireplaces and computer workstations for client meetings. I took out several half-walls and changed them for floor-to-ceiling glass to bring in natural light and a sense of openness. Uncle Ako's battered furniture would have ruined the look and had to be replaced. Once the plan was made, I called Behram and had him send the materials I would need.

Sahar was studying for her master's, so for the first month and a half that I was in Urmia, she couldn't visit. I got the office set up and renovated Uncle Ako's approach to work. I changed the way he dressed, the way he spoke to clients, and even how he got to work. If he hadn't been so sure that I knew what I was doing, I don't think he would have agreed to any of it.

As soon as Sahar had a break in her classes, we planned for her to come to Urmia. Not counting my time in prison, that month and a half was the longest time we'd been apart since we married, and I was looking forward to seeing her.

Her visit didn't get off to the best start.

She took the bus as I had a few weeks before. It was supposed to be an eleven-hour journey, but the bus was two hours late. She arrived tired and frustrated late that evening. She wasn't impressed with the car I'd bought and registered in my uncle's name; it wasn't as nice as the one I had sold. I wanted to show her the newly finished office. She took a brief tour around the quiet space and pronounced it not as big or as nice as the one in Tehran. That was true, but I put the brusqueness down to her being tired.

Sahar liked the city itself. It was small yet surrounded by ruggedly beautiful mountains. That time, she stayed for three weeks.

My gamble with location paid off for my uncle's company. I got one wealthy client and he recommended me to others. Within a few months we were busy most of the time. Khalid, my smuggling contact, knew a few people who had converted, and he introduced them to me. My home became a house church almost immediately.

Every few weeks Sahar came to visit me. The second time our visit went more smoothly and not just because the bus was on time. The long journey was difficult, and we talked more about getting married and how to bring her family around to the idea.

Since we had the wedding venue, we decided to put it to good use. We planned a "birthday party." It wasn't as large as the first gathering, but aside from size, it all went much like the first. Sahar and I sat in the crowd and listened to the others speak, enjoyed the fellowship of other Christians, and heard people say that they wished they had been able to meet Ammin.

Whether we were on the phone or together, Sahar and I talked at length about what came after our marriage. She didn't want to lose her family and she didn't want to lose me either, but she began to see that inaction was only keeping us apart. I had to meet her family. We began with her mother and older sister, Zohre. I had met Zohre several times, but she'd never moved past her first impression of me. We decided to meet at another clinic where she worked, near my vacation home.

Sahar and I talked often, but in the days leading up to that meeting, Sahar began to tell me how I should behave around her family. "Remember to cover your tattoos." "Don't bring up religion, but if she says anything positive about Islam, just agree." I didn't know where this was coming from, but the more she talked about it, the angrier I got about the whole thing.

"I'm not a child who has to be told how to behave. You think I could run the business and not know how to talk to people?"

"This isn't just 'people,'" she said. "This is my mother."

CHAPTER FIFTEEN

This was important to her. I bit back a retort that, while true, might have ruined things. I agreed to what she wanted.

Sahar and I had always been able to talk through our disagreements. This new facet to our relationship troubled me.

Just about every time we talked about the planned meeting with her mother, we got into an argument, and in the end, I always did my best to just agree with whatever she wanted. I didn't care what her family thought, but I knew it meant a lot to Sahar.

From the moment I walked into that meeting, it was obvious that I was meant to be on the defensive. Sahar and I sat on a sofa in the comfortable office, and Zohre and her mother, Yalda, sat facing us. It was hard to believe that this dark-skinned woman with a self-absorbed cast to her roughly hewn features had given birth to pale, graceful Sahar. I reminded myself of the goal.

"You want to marry my sister, but what can you offer her? You had your own company, a home, and now what do you have?" Zohre said.

"The skills I had made that company a success in the first place," I said. "Now that I've had the experience of building a business, I can build another."

"Even if you can provide for her, you want to take my daughter so far away. How is that fair to me or the rest of her family?" Yalda said. Before I could respond, she turned to Zohre. "How would you feel if your sister was hours and hours away? You'd hate it, wouldn't you?"

Zohre nodded. "Of course I would. A family shouldn't be separated like that."

I gestured to Sahar. "We're going to be a family," I said.

"I wish you weren't Christian," Yalda said. I opened my mouth to speak, but again she turned to Zohre. "I think that's nothing more than selfishness really. Even if they were still living in the same city, she'd still be lost to us if she married a Christian."

Zohre nodded. "Selfishness or a desire to draw attention to yourself."

I began to wonder if I was meant to be involved in this conversation.

157

It went on like that. Yalda would ask me a question and then turn to Zohre for an answer. Once the two of them had their few moments of agreement, I was allowed to justify whatever aspect of my life was being picked apart. I kept my answers polite and short.

After a contentious discussion, Yalda sighed. "Well, even if I were to agree, your father has to give his permission."

"Then let's set a time to meet," I said.

Yalda looked at Zohre. "I don't know—"

"I'll marry him anyway." Sahar's voice was firm.

Zohre didn't bother to conceal the anger that flashed through her eyes.

Yalda studied both of us, calculation visible in the set of her mouth. "I'll talk with your father, but it'll take some time. We'll meet again in a month or so."

A few days later, the date for the meeting was set.

The meeting was the topic of conversation between Sahar and me for the next few weeks. Maybe they could overcome my lack of family connections, but not the fact that I was Christian.

"What would be the harm in saying that you're Muslim? We're not going to live near them. How would they know?" I could hear the conspiratorial, cajoling tone in her voice, even over the phone. I couldn't believe she would even make such a suggestion.

"I would know. Any time we were around them, I would have to pretend. It would be one lie on top of another, and not just any lie—a lie about who I am. I won't do it."

"You won't do it? You'll be lying? What about me? I've wanted this for so long, and now, when we're finally so close, you're going to ruin it. But I suppose as long as you've got your principles, that's all you need."

"You knew," I said because it was the truth she was shying away from. "You knew who I was from the beginning. Why didn't you ask me to lie then? Because it was easier? Because it was exciting?"

She didn't answer.

"I wasn't a liar then and I'm not going to start lying now."

CHAPTER FIFTEEN

Throughout those days, I still arranged for Bibles to be brought into the country. In Tehran I never would have considered keeping thousands of Bibles in my house, even for a short time. Urmia was different. It was in a mostly Kurdish area, and the attitude toward illegal goods in general was far laxer. Nothing was in my own name. I felt more comfortable about storing Bibles and other Christian materials in my house for a day or so until they could be moved on. The system worked well, for a while.

I was staying with a friend, Yousef, in another city a couple of hours away to arrange for another shipment. It was less than a week before my much-anticipated meeting with Sahar's father.

The sun was barely up when my landlord called me.

"Where are you?" he asked.

"Staying with a friend, why?"

"Someone broke into your house last night. We locked your door, but the police need you to come down to the station to make a report."

It was strange, but I thanked him and hung up.

"Are you going to go?" Yousef asked.

"I don't know. I've been storing the Bibles there. If the police were there already, they've seen them."

While I was still making up my mind, my phone rang again. This time, it was one of my neighbors.

"How did you get my number?" I asked. This was someone I'd said hello to if we were both outside at the same time, but I didn't know him at all beyond that.

"From your landlord. Didn't he call you? The police need to see you about the break-in," he said. I could hear nothing but concern in his voice.

"I'm on my way," I said and forced myself to remain calm

All the calm, helpful tones just added to the disquiet that gathered in my stomach. My friend Ahmad lived a few houses down from me, so I called him.

"Was my house broken into?" I asked after a few pleasantries.

"What? When?" he asked.

"Last night." I explained about the two phone calls. "I don't know what it is, but something just feels wrong. Could you go over and check the house?"

He agreed and hung up. I held my phone in my hand, staring at the screen and waiting for it to ring. If they were watching the house, would they let him in? Would he be arrested? That few minutes felt like hours. The phone vibrated in my hand.

"There's nothing wrong at your house," Ahmad said. "The door is locked, just like you always leave it. The windows don't look forced or broken. I don't know what they're talking about."

I thanked him and hung up.

I looked at Yousef. "No one broke in."

He sat up straighter and took a deep breath. "I don't know, this sounds like a way to get you to come to them. You must leave. Now. You can be in Turkey in a few hours."

"I can't just leave. I'm meeting Sahar's father in a few days. It's taken months to get this far with her family—"

"And how are you going to marry when you're dead or disappeared? You're Kurdish. If they catch you, they're not going to bother with a trial. They're not even going to mention that you're Christian. They'll kill you and say you were a terrorist."

He was right. If I went back, a long prison sentence was the best I could hope for. But how could I leave Sahar?

I was still standing there, struggling to figure this out when Ahmad called me back. I could hear the pressure of worry in his voice. "I was wrong before. All I did was look around the house, and it was all locked up. But before that apparently there was a van parked outside and the police had been carrying boxes out."

My legs gave out. All my doubts evaporated. If they had been in the house, then they'd found the Bibles I had stored there. That was

CHAPTER FIFTEEN

it. The only thing that had saved me from a longer prison sentence before was the complete lack of evidence. Now they had more than enough to lock me up for a decade at least, and it had been my own fault for becoming complacent and giving it to them.

I called Sahar and told her everything.

"Yousef is right, you have to go," she said, her voice firm.

"If I go it's permanent. I can't come back. I can't meet your father. We can't marry."

"That's not true. I'll join you in Turkey in a few months. We can get married there and start our lives with all of this behind us. None of that will happen if you don't keep yourself safe to start with," she said with a confidence I didn't feel.

She was right. I knew she was right. But it was still another loss, and there had already been so many. I had lost my family, my freedom, my home, my company, and now I had to give up my country as well. Just how much did God want to take from me? I didn't want to do it. Not right then. I called Ali and the others. All of them offered me money, but I didn't feel right about taking it. There were so many things, larger and more important things, swirling through my head.

If I left, I would have nothing. No home, no job, no money, not even any friends to call on. Is that what God wanted from me? To be destitute in a country where I knew no one and didn't even speak the language? Why? What had I ever done to him?

As evening deepened into night, my thoughts began to wander down other, thornier paths. I could call my father. I could tell him that I was wrong, that I regretted everything. I could beg for his forgiveness. If I were contrite enough, if I were sincere enough, if I groveled enough, he would welcome me back into the family. He was a powerful man. He'd use his influence to convince the court that I had come to realize that Christianity was nothing more than deception. Sahar and I would be able to marry and start a family like we'd planned for so long.

It would be so easy to say I renounced Christ.

The trouble would be living with it.

If I said all those things, convinced my father that I was wrong, he would own me like he owned a rug. I would have a comfortable life again. A life free of worry and running and looking over my shoulder, but it wouldn't be my life. It would be his. And he would never let me forget that I'd come crawling back.

I couldn't do it.

I wouldn't do it.

Why was God always testing me? At every turn there were more roadblocks, more obstacles, more problems knotted with anxiety and danger.

Dawn began to touch the horizon, bathing the world with shades of pink.

You want to test me? I thought. *Alright, I'm going to test you. I'll go, and I'll trust you, but this is your journey.*

My trip was only planned to last a day or two. All I had with me was a small backpack, a change of clothes, and my Bible. It was all I had to start a new life. Thinking back, I probably should have left it behind. Holding so tight to a few material possessions made it seem like I trusted God less.

The next day, we left Yousef's house at ten, heading for the Turkish border. I wasn't sure what I was going to do once I got there. I didn't have enough money to travel anywhere else. Yousef told me to get to the UN. He'd heard that they'd helped other people. I hoped he was right. I crossed into Turkey and made my way through the long border station to a parking area where buses were waiting. I thought there was a UN office in Van, so that's the bus I selected.

Before I got on the bus, I looked back over the mountains of Iran. They loomed in the distance. The air was chilly, but the early afternoon sun added sparkle to the veins of snow atop the rugged gray peaks and softened the green of the lower hills surrounding them. On the other side of those mountains was everything I knew. They were between me and the family I had been born to, and the one I had created for myself. They were between my wife and me, and maybe they always would be. They were all I could see of the world I knew. As I stood there, my backpack slung over my shoulder, I knew I wouldn't be this close to Iran for many years. It might never again be safe for me to be so close.

I turned away and stepped onto the bus.

Part II
Turkey

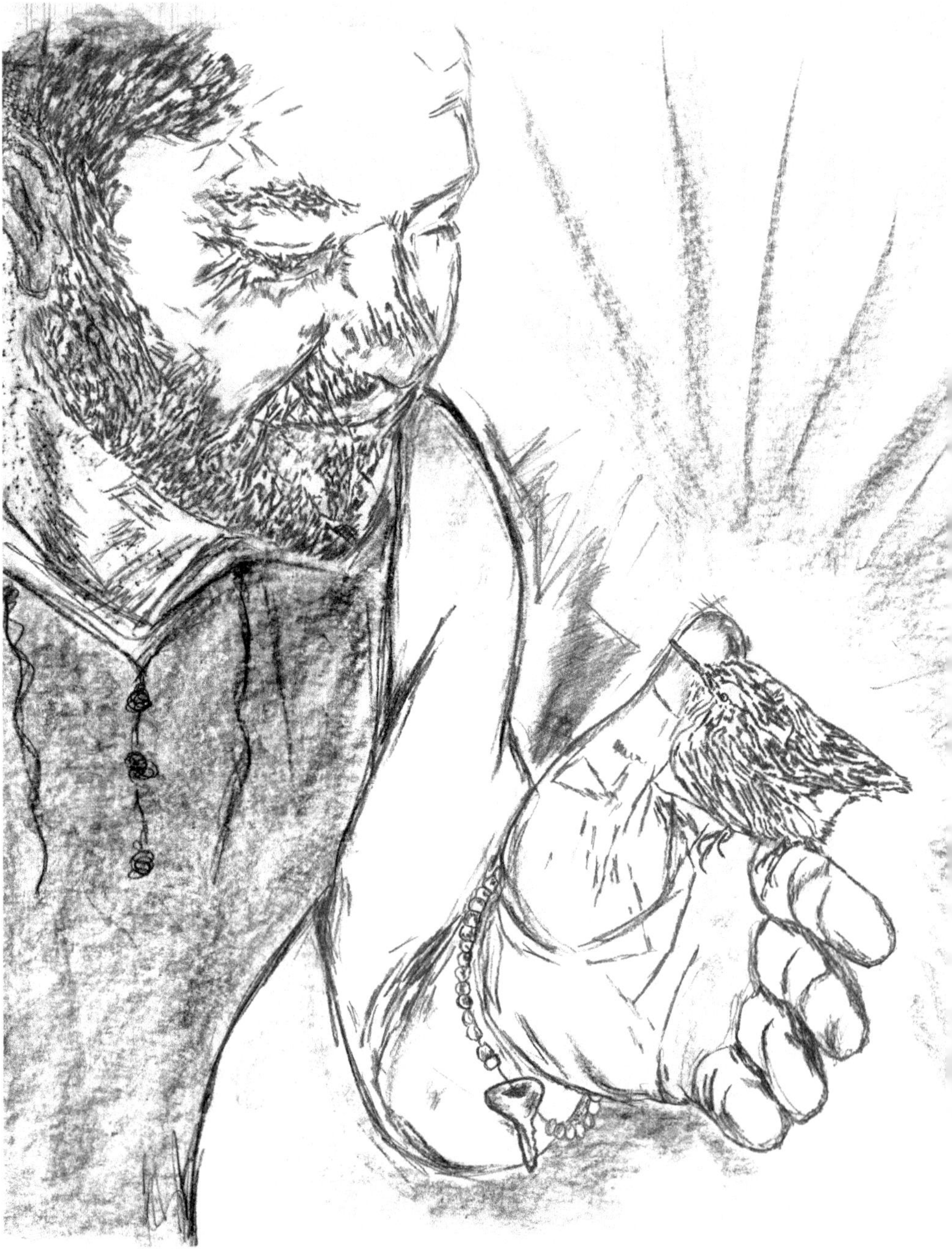

Chapter Sixteen

WHILE I WAITED to leave, I texted Sahar. I told her that I was alright, that I was safe, but I'm not sure that was completely true. I remember that I wanted to cry, but there were no tears. Shock had taken them. The bus sat at the border until it was full. When we began to pull away, I let Sahar know that I'd be losing my signal soon, but not to worry. I'd find another phone. We had only been traveling for ten minutes when I lost that fragile link with my home.

I was alone.

There wasn't much to do but think as the bus traveled deeper into Turkey. Half-formed thoughts slid over the broken shards of incomplete plans. All the way to Van, the latter abraded the former until only raw uncertainty remained. When I got to Van, I learned that the UN offices there had closed a few months before. I had to go to Ankara.

Buses to Ankara filled quickly and usually required booking in advance. I was lucky that there was space available on the next one. It cost most of the money I had with me to buy one of the least desirable seats in the back row.

The person sitting next to me began to talk almost as soon as we left the station. He was Kurdish as well, but he was Kurmanji, and I am Sorani. Some of the words were similar enough that I was able to understand some of what he said. Most of the time I just kept my answers short and polite while my mind turned over the implications of where I was going and what I was doing. Twice he let me use his phone to message Sahar. I couldn't say much, but the last she knew

BECOMING JOSHUA

I was on my way to Van. I wanted her to know about the change in destination and to let her know that I was safe. As my seatmate and I talked, I told him why I was going to Ankara. He taught me my first Turkish word, *yabanji*, meaning foreign.

I spent the rest of the day and night on the bus wedged between two strangers. The rumble and vibration of the engine underscoring all of my questions and musings. What was next? I was alone, my pockets were nearly empty, and I didn't even have a clear plan. At times the exhaustion of the last few days overtook my active mind for a few minutes, and I was able to drift toward sleep, but that respite never lasted very long.

When I arrived in Ankara the next morning, I was tired and hungry, but at least I had a destination in mind.

The first thing I did was to find a taxi. I couldn't understand the driver, but I said *yabanji* and he understood. It cost me a quarter of the money I had left, but he got me to the UN. As soon as I arrived, I could see people of all ages lined up along the sidewalk next to a wrought-iron fence and a pair of white kiosks. Some were sitting, some standing. They turned to each other in small groups, watching the new arrivals with curiosity or suspicion. Many were clustered around piles of luggage. I began to wonder if I was the only person who ran without prior planning. I could hear some of them speaking Farsi.

"What are you waiting for?" I asked one of them.

"To get our assignments," someone said.

"That'll be awhile," someone else answered.

"You'd better enroll," another advised me and gestured to one of the kiosks. "Over there."

I looked at the small window.

"They just ask for your name. If you have documents, you show them. If not, that's okay," a woman said. She spoke with confidence, but there was also reassurance in her voice.

I went to the first kiosk. The man inside greeted me in Turkish and asked what country I was from.

CHAPTER SIXTEEN

His suit and beard triggered memories of so many government officials who'd been involved in my arrest and imprisonment. I stood in anxious silence. He stared at me, waiting for an answer.

"Iran." I injected confidence into my voice.

He held up his hand, indicating that I should wait. A few minutes later someone else came back.

"How can I help you?" he asked in Farsi.

"I want to apply for refugee status," I said.

He studied me for a moment. "Do you have documents and identification?"

I handed over my ID.

He glanced at it, then handed it back. "We'll call you."

I went back into the crowd and sat down next to an elderly Armenian man and his wife. I didn't know how long I would have to wait. I began to chat with them a little to pass the time. A little while later, the woman who'd explained how to enroll came over and introduced herself as Mozhde.

"May I ask if you're Christian?"

"Yes I am."

"So are we!" Excitement laced the exclamation. She gestured to her husband and children with a proud smile. She leaned a little closer. "Be careful here. People will try to take advantage."

I thanked her and introduced myself.

"If they ask where you want to go, say Kayseri. We have people there."

I had spent some time studying in Turkey, but the way the classes were scheduled didn't leave any time to explore the area. I hadn't thought beyond getting to the UN, so I accepted her suggestion. We spent the next few hours getting to know each other.

At 2 p.m., no new refugees were allowed to enroll that day. They began to call people's names to receive their city assignments.

When my name was called, the man in the window asked, "Do you know what city you want to live in?"

Mozhde's suggestion came with a tenuous connection to others, something I knew I needed. "Kayseri," I said.

He stamped a paper written in Turkish and handed it over to me. "You have three days to present yourself to the police in Kayseri. If you fail to present yourself at the police station, you can be arrested. While you're in Turkey, you can be asked for this paperwork at any time. If you fail to present it, you can be deported in less than twenty-four hours."

By the time that I had finished, Mozhde and her family, as well as the Armenian couple, had their assignments. We had all been assigned to Kayseri.

My new friends and I made our way to the bus terminal to buy our tickets. When Mozhde found out how little money I had, she bought my ticket, and we shared a meal while we waited for the bus. It wasn't anything special, just flatbread sandwiches with chicken and vegetables, but it was the first meal I'd had since I left Iran two days before. To me, it was a feast.

We got into Kayseri at eleven in the evening. It was too late to try to find the police station, so we found a hotel for the night. The next day we went to the police station. It was my first experience of introducing myself as a refugee. The sergeant at the desk looked at us with suspicion. He gestured for us to follow him and be fingerprinted. We were told we'd have to come back for a police interview in a couple of months and that we'd have to come to the police station Mondays and Tuesdays to sign in. This was for the safety of the refugees as well as an issue of compliance.

"Do you know where you're staying?" Mozhde asked when we left the police station.

"No," I admitted.

"I'll contact Hesam. He's single, and he knows some churches as well. He's not Christian, but he's a good person," she said, and sent a text. We didn't have to wait long for a reply. "He's at work until four. I want to look for a house to rent. Come to the real estate office with me, and he can pick you up from there."

Hesam welcomed me warmly into his home. He was a political

CHAPTER SIXTEEN

refugee. Even though he was a Muslim, he knew several pastors and churches. That Sunday, he took me to a service at one of the house churches in the area. Afterward, he introduced me to the pastor.

The house church was affiliated with Yale, but the pastor, Qassem, didn't know me. As soon as the pastor found out I had converted in Iran, he asked my name. In the short time I had been in Turkey, I had learned that names were closely guarded. I gave him a false name. They asked who I knew in Iran, where I had lived, and about the underground churches I had attended. I said I had lived in the northwest but was deliberately vague about the rest. He didn't push the point and invited me to a Bible study the next night. I wasn't sure I could trust them, but I wanted to see what path they were on.

The study group only consisted of six or seven people. Once the discussion began, I started to quote verses from memory. They each began to leaf through their Bibles to check my quotations. When I had to check something, they could see that my Bible was filled with notes.

I know that got them thinking, but so did the way that I lived.

After a life under the restrictive Islamic law in Iran, Turkey offered freedoms that many had never considered. Alcohol could be purchased in grocery stores. Young men and women could spend time together and date. Some couples even began to live together before they were married. The easy availability of everything that had once been forbidden overwhelmed some and led to addictive indulgence.

None of that mattered to me. I was married to Sahar and waiting for a time when she could join me in Turkey. That attracted as much attention as my understanding of the Bible.

Yale offered the opportunity for a few Farsi-speaking people to study the Bible in Istanbul. There were only twelve spaces available, and I was offered one of them.

I accepted and thanked him for the opportunity because I was always curious to learn more.

"Usually we want to baptize the people we send on these courses," he said.

I couldn't tell him that I had already been baptized without revealing too much of my history with Yale, so I agreed.

I had been in Kayseri for less than two months when I was baptized for the second time. Before I went to Istanbul, I had my first police interview. The first interview is conducted by the police in the city a refugee is assigned to. A Farsi-speaking police officer sat across from me and asked why I had to leave Iran and why I had come to Turkey. Each question was delivered with sarcastic boredom and each answer treated with suspicion. I was lucky and they believed me. Some refugees had to go through this humiliating process multiple times.

The three months I spent in Istanbul were busy but wonderful. Classes were held in the basement of an Armenian church. The eight men and four women were accommodated a short walk away, the men in one apartment, the women in another. Our food, lodging, and such were provided, meaning that we could focus solely on our studies. We worked and studied from four in the morning until ten at night on most days. Thursdays and Fridays, we took Bibles to the European side of Istanbul. We walked around, talking about Jesus and handing out Bibles to those who wanted them. We saw a great deal of the beautiful city we were living in that way.

I can't say I agreed with everything that was taught. The importance of attendance numbers was emphasized. Getting people into the church and keeping them there was paramount. They treated human beings who wanted to know God like commodities. To Yale's leadership, that's all we were.

When I got back to Kayseri, Qassem offered me a position as a pastor in the organization. That Sunday he asked me to preach to introduce me to the congregation. I had a choice, make a deal with an organization I disagreed with and be comfortable, or stick with my principles. Both would give me a chance to help, but I wasn't sure which one would give me the chance to do the most good.

I hadn't been back long when I ran into Mozhde. She was glad to see me, and she invited me to her house. I was happy to accept. I

CHAPTER SIXTEEN

thought I was going to be spending an evening with her and her family. When I arrived, there were ten strangers in her living room. Some were old, some were young. I found out all of them were waiting for me. I didn't know how they'd even heard about me. After a few minutes I found out that they had all been injured in some way by Qassem. The first one to speak was Aziz, a man of about seventy who looked as though he'd rather be anywhere else.

He couldn't quite meet my eyes, his discomfort evident in the way his hands moved over and around each other in his lap. "When my family and I came here," he began, "my son, he..." His fingers gripped each other. "He doesn't want to have a natural relationship with people. I was in shock. I didn't know what to do. I still don't." He fell silent for a moment. I knew what he meant. Even though the Iranian government liked to say that homosexuality was unknown in Iran, that isn't the case. People who leave find the freedom to express their religious preferences, and sexual orientations as well. I waited until he was ready to speak again. "I went to Qassem. I don't know what I was expecting. I know he couldn't fix it. I know it's my son's choice. I guess I was looking for some comfort or advice." Tears began to slip down his cheeks. He shook his head. "He looked at me like I was disgusting. He told me that if I couldn't even manage my own family, there was no help for me. Like it was my fault. I don't know. Maybe it is. Maybe I don't belong with everyone else."

I couldn't believe what I was hearing. This man had been looking for help and instead had been insulted and rejected. "No," I said. "Jesus told us to love one another, and that means everyone. We're meant to accept each other as Jesus accepted us. There isn't a list of exclusions."

The others began to speak as well, telling me similar stories of how they'd been badly treated or rejected by the one group that should have listened with compassion. Even Mozhde had a story. By the time people had finished speaking, most of those present were in tears.

I had thought that maybe I could find a way to work with Yale while I was in Turkey. After seeing these people and hearing their stories, I couldn't do it. The church was using the refugees' need for community against them. If I agreed, I would be condoning that behavior.

"So, stop going," I said. "There are enough of you here to start your own house church."

They looked at each other. "We can't do that. Can we?"

Most of them only had experience with Yale. They believed they needed the pastor and all the other trappings that Yale provided. "Instead of going to church on Sunday, come here. Next week we can talk more about how it works." I turned to Aziz. "And everyone who wants to attend is welcome."

A few days after I got back, I had to go to the police station in Kayseri for my second police interview. This one was conducted at the police station by a representative of the UN. When I arrived, a small group of people were already waiting there. Most were chatting to each other in Farsi. I was surprised to see Qassem arrive. I had no idea he was a refugee as well, and from the look on his face, he didn't want anyone to know.

We were given a form to fill out where we had to describe our reasons for coming to Turkey. Those of us who were there spread out at the tables along the edges of the room to fill in our forms. I wrote a paragraph or so about the danger I was in from the government and the reason. After I had finished and set my pen aside, Qassem came over to me.

"No one needs to know you saw me here today," he said and gave a little smile. "I mean, it's not really anyone else's business. Is it?" A cajoling thread wove through his words.

My name was called. I went in to meet with the representative without answering Qassem's question. The interviewer didn't treat me with derision this time. He looked from the paper to me and back again.

CHAPTER SIXTEEN

He scanned the document and flipped it over, looking at the blank back page. "This is it?" he asked.

"You said you wanted the reasons. That's what I wrote," I said.

"It's so short. Most people write a page or two at least. Are you sure this is all you want to say?" He handed the page back to me.

I added a couple more sentences, not because I felt like I had left anything out, but more to appease the interviewer. In the end, he accepted the page as it was.

Yale held their services in an apartment with a spacious living room. Chairs were arranged in rows around a central aisle. There were two doors off a central entry hall. The door closest to the lectern was closed off. Those who came for services entered through the far door. That Sunday morning, I was sitting in the front row, waiting to be introduced as a pastor. The plan was for me to give the sermon that Sunday. I had every intention of following through with that plan, in my own way.

I hadn't outlined what I was going to say, but that was nothing unusual. I knew I would say the right thing in the moment. During the first half hour of the service, I listened to the announcements and the music and prayed that God would give me the right words when the time came.

Then, Qassem introduced me. Everyone's eyes were on me as I walked the few steps to the front in jeans and a T-shirt, my Bible in my hand, and stood next to the lectern. I could feel the expectation in the way the congregation was watching me.

For the span of a few breaths, I was silent. "Why are you here?" I asked them. I could see them give each other sidelong glances. "Why do you come here every week? Why do you listen to someone preach? Why do you do it?" They were starting to shift uneasily in their seats now. "Do you think that coming here for an hour once a week makes you a Christian? You show up and repeat all the right words and you've

BECOMING JOSHUA

done everything that Jesus wants?" I shook my head. "Jesus doesn't want churches filled with people who have no desire to know him better. He doesn't need people coming to take up space. He doesn't need money or grand gestures of devotion." I walked down the aisle as I spoke and made eye contact with the people I passed. "If you try to live by the teachings of Jesus in your homes, in your work, in the way you interact with friends and family and strangers, then keep coming. If you keep your relationship with Jesus at the center of your life, keep coming. If you're here for any other reason, don't bother." When I finished, I walked out the rear door into the hall.

For a moment, everyone was silent. I knew they were probably expecting that I was just giving them time to think. Qassem would know better. I didn't want to have the discussion that would follow. I could hear the rest of the congregation beginning to whisper to each other. I picked up my bag and was almost at the door when David, a member of the congregation, came out into the hall with me.

"I don't know what that was about, but evil sometimes speaks through the children of God. You should think about where that speech really came from," David said. He and his fiancée, Bahar, were two of the few church members who had converted in Iran, but they had been with Yale since the beginning.

I shook my head. "I think you need to open your eyes."

I didn't give him a chance to respond. I opened the door and walked to a park a few blocks from the church. I hadn't planned what I was going to say, and I hadn't planned what to do after either. I had been sleeping at the church since I got back from Istanbul. That didn't matter. I couldn't have lived with myself if I had sacrificed my principles for comfort. I had been there for most of the rest of the day when David found me. He paused for a moment a little way down the path. There'd been more than enough time for him to talk with the pastor about what his approach should be.

"What are you doing here?" David asked.

"Did you really think I would still be staying there after this morning?" I asked.

CHAPTER SIXTEEN

"Fair point, so where are you going to go?" he asked as he sat down beside me.

"I don't know," I admitted.

"Come on, you can stay with us."

I shook my head. "I don't think so."

"You can't stay here. Come back with me, at least for now."

I nodded and picked up my bag.

"Do you have work?" he asked as we walked out of the park.

"No," I said.

"I'm working at a furniture factory. I'm sure they'll hire you too. Come with me in the morning."

David lived with his fiancée, Bahar, and her mother, Molok, in a small, run-down apartment building not too far from Mozhde. The place wasn't big enough for four people, but they welcomed me anyway and let me sleep on the floor of David's room.

I'd met Bahar and Molok at church, but I didn't really know them. I could feel the uncomfortable tension in the atmosphere as soon as I walked in. At first, I thought they resented me for being there, but as soon as David and I were alone, the real problem was revealed.

"Molok thinks I'm not good enough for Bahar. She does everything she can to make my life miserable," he said.

I didn't want to get involved in their personal problems, so I stayed silent and hoped to be able to find somewhere else to live before tension erupted into an argument.

The next morning, I went to the factory with David. They did hire me. The same day I went to work making furniture that was sold in stores all over Turkey. The wages weren't much, and the hours were long, but it was honest work. That evening, Qassem arrived at David's house.

We exchanged a few pleasantries and sat down in the small living room. I knew why he was there, but I was going to wait and see how he brought it up.

"Well, I'm sure you can guess that your sermon stirred up quite a bit of discussion."

"Good," I said. "They should be thinking about what they hear."

He smiled, a little. "They should, and I like that you challenged them, but I think that many of them didn't realize that you were only doing it to be provocative."

"What makes you think that it was just a challenge?"

He gave a little laugh. "Well, you couldn't have seriously been advising people to stay away from church," he said. "I'm sure you didn't mean it that way, but that's how many of them heard it."

"I told them the truth, and that's exactly what they heard."

He looked down at his hands. "You're passionate and that's exactly why we want to work with you. I think that you're just not used to how we do things. We still have a position—"

"No! I've seen how you do things. I'd rather sleep in the street than work with you."

I could see the surprise flicker over Qassem's face. Then his mouth set into a hard line. "Well, that's your choice," he said.

The next evening, Qassem came by again with the same false warmth as the night before. Despite the good-natured pleasantries I knew he wouldn't be there at all if my speech hadn't been effective.

"I gave you my answer last night," I said.

"I know, but I think you're being a bit hasty. Take a few weeks to think about it and then come back and explain what you really meant." He smiled at me as if he weren't asking me to stand in front of that congregation and take back everything I'd said.

"I said what I meant, I'm not sorry, and I haven't changed my mind."

One finger tapped against his leg. "I want you to work with us, but I can't keep repeating this offer indefinitely. If you don't accept, I won't be back again."

"I didn't ask you to come here at all. My answer is no, and it's not going to change," I said.

From the beginning, David, Bahar, and Molok all welcomed me, but the tension I sensed that first night only grew. David complained to me about Molok. Molok complained to me about David. I watched

CHAPTER SIXTEEN

the two of them do passive-aggressive battle over everything from window boxes to Bible verses. Sometimes the tension around them shattered into arguments, and when that happened, I didn't have many options for escape. The longer I stayed, the more the upset of the household began to infect me.

That Sunday I went to Mozhde's house while David and the others went to church as usual.

This was more of a meeting than a worship service. They worried about everything from where to get chairs to music to who would be pastor. I explained how a house church should work. They heard me, but I left with the feeling that they would need a little more direction. They agreed to meet the next Sunday to talk more.

Refugees always had a difficult time earning money, but Christian refugees in mostly Muslim Turkey had an especially difficult time. Employers might refuse to hire us, or we might be hired but then the employer would refuse to pay the wages that were earned. If that happened, the refugee had no recourse. For that reason, most kept silent about their religion. For women, the situation was worse. Many were harassed by employers who knew they had few options. David didn't want Bahar and Molok subjected to that, so they didn't work. As hard as he and I worked, there wasn't enough money coming into the house. By the end of the week, there wasn't enough food for all of us.

We gathered at the table in the drab kitchen. What little we had to eat was placed in the middle. Anyone could see that it wasn't enough for four people. We talked about the Bible to distract ourselves and tried to chew slowly to allow others to have more. I couldn't look anyone in the eye. They had fed me and given me a place to stay. Because of it, they had less for themselves. It was clear that this arrangement was not going to work.

By the questions my boss at the furniture factory was asking me, it was clear that he suspected I was Christian. I was paid, but I worried that if I stayed, I wouldn't be paid again. I decided I wouldn't go back. The day after I got paid, I thanked David, Molok, and Bahar for their kindness, but said that I had to go. Molok came outside after me.

"David didn't give me any money for the rent this month. Do you think I should go to the church and ask for help?"

I couldn't send anyone to Yale for anything. "How much do you need?" I asked.

"Two hundred lira," she said.

That was the amount I'd been paid, so I handed it to her.

"No!" She pushed my hand back. "This is all you have."

"I've lived with you; I've eaten with you. It's only fair," I said. "I'll be fine."

"I'll be fine." It was a confident statement, and I had no way of knowing if it was true. I had just a few coins in my pockets, no job, and nowhere to live. Who was I? I was homeless, faceless, nameless in a country where I couldn't string together a sentence in the native tongue.

I spent the next twenty-one days in a corner of a park far from the area where refugees usually stayed. Living among the homeless in Tehran hadn't prepared me for the reality of being homeless myself. During those long nights I always knew I could go home. Home to get a good meal, a hot shower, and clean clothes. I could go to work, and people looked at me and saw the owner of a large, successful company. Sleeping in an abandoned building as part of a grand plan didn't change any of that.

Now I was truly homeless. I was that person no one wants to look at. I was the person who begged for food from strangers. I was the one who had loud arguments with God in the corner of a park as people tried not to stare.

I was sure that everyone had forgotten me. I had no contact with Sahar or anyone at home. Mozhde hadn't forgotten me though. She had become good friends with Noran, a Turkish real estate agent. Many Iranians rented properties from her because she spoke fluent Farsi. It was Mozhde's practice to stop in and chat with her for a bit

CHAPTER SIXTEEN

each day. During one of these chats, Mozhde was telling Noran that she was searching for me. Another man who happened to be there to list some of his rental properties heard the conversation and agreed to help her look.

I don't know how he knew where to look, or even what inspired him to want to, but he did find me, stretched out on my back, looking up at the sky, deep in another one of my arguments with God.

He didn't speak Farsi, and I didn't speak Turkish, but he said my name and Mozhde's name. It was enough to get my attention. Beyond that we both had to gesture and pantomime. Eventually, he made me understand that Mozhde was looking for me, and he asked that I go with him. If he hadn't used my name and hers, I wouldn't have even stood up. He introduced himself as Baris, and I followed him.

Chapter Seventeen

THE CAR BELONGED to a rich man. When he opened the door for me, I could smell the leather. It was all so strange. Why would he be so kind to me? What if my father was somehow behind it? He gestured for me to get in. I decided to see what he would do. He pulled out onto the divided highway. Commuter trains ran in the median, passing the car every few minutes with a hiss and a rush of air. Baris kept looking over at me and smiling to reassure me. I kept smiling too, but I wondered where we were going.

I thought he must be taking me to a shelter, or maybe to Mozhde, but the streets we were travelling on were lined with trees and flowers. Well-dressed people in designer clothes walked on the wide sidewalks and relaxed at outdoor cafés. Luxury cars were parked along the streets. We were heading into one of the most exclusive parts of the city. A shelter there would be a three-star hotel. A few minutes later he parked on the street in front of an older apartment building. The kind where reputation turns wear into charm.

The doorman didn't even look at me as we walked into the quiet lobby, but I began to feel uncomfortable. If Baris was taking me to his home, what would his family think of me? I'd been living in a park. I hadn't showered for weeks. I couldn't even speak to him and his family to apologize for my appearance or for interrupting their routine. I hesitated in the doorway. Still smiling, Baris gestured for me to follow him into the kitchen.

CHAPTER SEVENTEEN

His wife, Laila, was a diminutive woman with an equally welcoming smile. She made me a plate of sujuk, a spicy beef sausage, sliced and fried, bread, and large black olives. It was a meal that was well beyond the budget of a refugee, let alone a homeless person. I couldn't understand what they were saying, but they were relaxed, and that helped me to relax. They wanted to help. I could tell that much even without knowing the language. While I ate, Baris made a phone call. I found out later that he was calling Noran to let her know that I had been found and was safe. Then he made me a cup of strong, flavorful Turkish coffee.

After I finished eating the best meal I'd had in weeks, I was shown to a guest bathroom where I could shower. Baris's eleven-year-old son gave up his room for the night, and Baris loaned me a set of his own house clothes so that I could have something clean to put on. It was early in the evening, but after weeks of uncertainty I was exhausted. I went to bed and slept until well after nine the next morning, well past the time when most people were already at work. I must have disrupted their morning and I didn't even have a way to apologize. I hoped I hadn't made them regret their kindness.

I opened the door into the quiet hall and thought about what gestures I could make to ask forgiveness. A television played from elsewhere in the apartment, so I followed the sound to a living room decorated with antiques. A palette of golden tones and turquoise accents tied the comfortable room together under a coved ceiling. It was a beautiful space, but very different from the clean, modern lines and bold colors of the apartment I had left in Tehran. Baris was sitting in front of the floor-to-ceiling windows, the view of the city and snowcapped Erciyes Dagi beyond. His morning cup of tea steamed in his hands. My feet sunk deeper into the thick carpeting as I stepped closer. I was about to say something when he noticed me.

He smiled and gestured for me to follow him into the kitchen, where he made me breakfast. I did my best to convey my thanks, but he brushed that off.

After I'd finished, he gestured for me to follow him to the car. I thought he would take me to Mozhde, or to someone she suggested. Instead, he took me a little way out of the city to a spacious walled compound. Inside lay a large, two-story villa with a wide balcony set among fruit and almond trees. A stream flowed among the trees, the sound melding with birdsong. It was so peaceful. Baris let me know that this was where I was going to live. The produce from the trees was mine to use as I wished, and there was already food in the fridge. I couldn't believe he would be so generous with a perfect stranger.

Through Google Translate, he asked if there was anything else I needed.

"Internet," I said, thinking of Sahar and explaining in the best way I could why I needed it. I'd managed to email her a couple of times when I was at David's, but I hadn't liked to ask to use their computer. The whole time I'd been living on the street, I hadn't been able to contact her.

Baris nodded and made a phone call. We sat in the living room, and he explained as much as Google Translate could manage about the house. When he left, he loaned me his laptop. By that evening I was able to message Sahar on Skype and tell her to call me. I turned up the volume on the laptop and walked from room to room in the quiet house while I waited for her to respond to the message.

At first, we were both talking at the same time. She wanted to make sure that I was safe and well and to know where I was. I wanted to reassure her that I was fine. Once our mutual anxiety had been assuaged, I held the laptop in front of me and took her on a tour of the house.

"The bottom floor is mine," I said. I stood in the middle of the living room and turned. "The kitchen down here has no appliances, but there's another one upstairs that I can use." I went up there next, showing her the open living area with a wood-burning stove and then out through the French doors to the balcony that overlooked the fruit trees in the expansive garden and the view of Erciyes Dagi etched in purples and blues in the distance.

"He just gave it to you to live in?" Sahar asked.

CHAPTER SEVENTEEN

"His family only uses it once a week. I think they want someone to be here the rest of the time." I sat on the balcony. "I have a place that I can use as my own. Baris doesn't mind if I have guests. When are you coming to see me?"

"I'd love to, but I'm in the middle of the semester." She looked away from the camera. "When it's over, I can come."

The Friday after I arrived in Baris's garden, I invited Mozhde and the others to the house. Baris offered to bring over extra food, but I said no because everyone was bringing something, and there was always the fruit and almonds from the trees. He came over with bags full anyway. Baris and his family were Muslim, but he welcomed the church group in the same way that he'd welcomed me: with unwavering generosity.

We spent the day relaxing together next to the stream that ran through the shady orchard. It was a beautiful day that lasted well into the evening.

That first Sunday, I went to Mozhde's house for another meeting. It still wasn't a service, but it gave us the opportunity to begin to make assignments. Mozhde would be the first to give the lesson. One of the members with a laptop was assigned to provide the music. Some took on the role of getting the space ready, and another would care for the children. Even though tithing wasn't required, we still needed someone to be the treasurer to account for any money people contributed. I assigned Aziz to that role. I'm not sure they were confident when we parted that evening, but at least they knew what was needed and what their roles were.

When I got back to Baris's villa, I found that Baris and his family were still there. Sundays were the only days that Baris used the house. I was going to give them their privacy, but they insisted I join them. Even though we still couldn't speak to each other, they made it clear that they thought of me as a member of their family.

I appreciated all their generosity and compassion. I didn't want to just take advantage of such kindness, and so the next day I began to clean up and improve the yard and the outdoor space of the balcony, planting flowers and creating flower beds along the edges of the house.

Most evenings I talked with Sahar. After so many weeks of not being able to see or speak to her, those video chats were a luxury that I looked forward to. Each one of those chats made me miss her more. I was counting the days until her semester ended and she would be able to come and see me.

At the next week's service, the decision was made to find a cheap place to rent for the church. Since Mozhde was closest to Noran, she oversaw finding somewhere within our modest budget.

While we waited, we used Facebook to create events for other refugees in Kayseri. We hosted backgammon tournaments, ice cream socials and other things we thought people would enjoy. These events were open to anyone who wanted to connect with and spend time with a community. We talked about our church if anyone asked, but religion was never the focus. Everyone was welcome.

It took some time for Mozhde to find a place we could afford. Once she did, she called me, asking if I would come and look at it. We set a time and I met Mozhde and Noran there. As soon as I got there, I could see that this wasn't going to work. The layout of the apartment was fine on its own, but it was upstairs.

"I think you're going to have to keep looking," I said.

"It's taken me this long to find this place. There aren't a lot of choices at this price," she said.

"I know, but there are some who will have a hard time with the stairs," I said. "I don't want them to feel like they can't come because of it. I think we can find something better."

"There is one other place that might suit you," Noran said. "It's a little bigger and on the ground floor. It's a bit out of the range you gave me though."

"By how much?" Mozhde asked.

CHAPTER SEVENTEEN

When Noran told us the figure, Mozhde shook her head. "We can't raise that every month, not from the number of people we have now."

"It's been available for a while. The owner might be open to making a deal so it isn't sitting empty."

"We should see it anyway," I said.

Noran drove us to the other property. It was a newer, more modern-looking building and far larger than the other property. We came into a small entry with open shelves separating the door from the main part of the space. The spacious living room could be closed off by pocket doors when services were going on. The kitchen opened off it with a long breakfast bar. The arched cutout could be closed with a shutter, making it perfect for tea and coffee after services. There was a restroom and another room that could be a playroom for the children. Upstairs there was space for community gatherings.

It was perfect, but perfection was beyond our means. Mozhde could see that too. Excitement about the possibilities and financial reality chased each other over her features.

"You know what we can pay," Mozhde said to Noran. "Will the owner accept that for, maybe, three months?"

"Possibly. Let me check," she said.

Mozhde and I wandered around the apartment, seeing potential in the stark walls and empty rooms while Noran phoned the owner. She spoke in Turkish, but the tone sounded generally positive. She ended the call and told us that the offer had been accepted.

We had a building and our faith. It was a good start.

Word spread about our church and our approach to faith. Our congregation began to grow. People left other churches in Kayseri, including the Yale church, to attend ours. Refugees from other cities began to follow us on Facebook, and some even traveled to attend our services. It was a great compliment. For those who were from out of town, we invited them to arrive on Saturday and spend the night. The men stayed with me, and the women stayed with Mozhde. By the end of those three months, our congregation had more than tripled, and we'd had to add services. Paying the full rent was no longer a problem.

A few months later Baris hosted a party in the garden. The children ran and played among the fruit trees while the adults ate and visited and enjoyed each other's company. Noran was there as well. She and I took a walk along the edge of the small stream that flowed through the trees.

"How's the church doing?" she asked me in Farsi.

"We've grown bigger than I thought we would in such a short time. I really appreciate the break on the rent for the first few months," I said.

She shrugged. "The owner didn't mind getting the rent from two different sources."

"What do you mean?" I asked.

"Baris made up the difference for those first few months." She must have seen the surprise on my face. "You didn't know?"

"No, I didn't." I looked over to where Baris played with some of the younger children. He was having as much fun as they were. I could wait until we were alone to ask him.

That evening, when things had begun to quiet down, Baris and I drank tea on the balcony. I put the Turkish I was learning to good use.

"Baris, I know about the rent on the building—"

He shook his head and flicked his fingers in my direction in a dismissive gesture. I'd seen him do it before. It always meant that it was nothing and he didn't want to discuss it. Maybe it was nothing to him, but it meant so much to us. I would find a way to repay his generosity.

———∞———

Over the next few months, I got to know Baris and his family better. His mother, brothers, sisters, and cousins all treated me with the same warmth and kindness that Baris had, including me in all the family events held at the garden. He introduced me to his wealthy friends and included me when they visited him at the villa. He treated

CHAPTER SEVENTEEN

me like an honored guest instead of a refugee who'd been found living in a park.

My Turkish gradually improved, and Baris and I were able to have easier discussions, even if the exact words eluded us sometimes. We often spent evenings at the villa, talking about anything and everything. I knew he was wealthy, but he didn't like to talk about that, or about how influential he was in the city—a certain sign of both. The refugee community often benefited from that far-reaching influence. Not only did he help us get the building for the church, but he helped others find work. When employers refused to pay refugee workers, Baris made a few phone calls, and people received their wages. Without him, those people would have had nowhere to turn.

I also learned that Baris loved animals. In addition to the two dogs that lived there already, I added chickens, ducks, and quail outdoors, as well as two watchdogs (Tik and Tok) and seven cats that moved between inside and outside. The cats and dogs curled up together on chilly nights and protected each other as they slept. The first time I saw that, I was surprised. I had always believed that cats and dogs could never live so peacefully together.

My dog Tik taught me the most. When he was three months old, he made a mess in the house. It made me angry that I had to clean up after him. I yelled and banished him to the yard. Before my anger had cooled, I went outside and Tik came trotting over, pressed his head against my leg, and wanted to be pet. I shoved him away, but he just came back, tail wagging as if his accident had never happened. This time, I pushed him away but not as far. He came back again, his head tilted, brown eyes fixed on me. I realized that if I loved him, I had to accept that he was flawed and forgive his mistakes. He had already forgiven me.

It's the same for people. They're flawed, they make mistakes and they live in ways I don't always understand. None of that matters. Love one another meant just that. The animals taught me more about unconditional love and acceptance than any person I'd ever met.

BECOMING JOSHUA

I had been living in the villa for three months when I was scheduled to go to Ankara for my main UN interview. Interviews and the bureaucratic process of being a refugee were a frequent topic of conversation among members of the church. People asked for prayers when they were scheduled for an interview. Those who had been through a particular step in the process shared information with others about what to expect. I was no different. I listened to those who had been through this interview talk about the aspects of it in the weeks leading up to the appointed time.

The interview was scheduled for nine in the morning. I didn't want to spend the night in Ankara, so Baris gave me a ride to the bus station at two in the morning. It was too early for conversation, but he wished me luck and told me to call when I got back. This time I knew where I was going and what to expect when I arrived. I didn't sleep on the bus, but the stress that had accompanied my first arrival in Ankara was only a memory.

When I arrived at the UN, people and luggage were already lining the sidewalk, and a tapestry of languages filled the chilly morning. This time I moved past the line and went inside the quiet building. I showed the receptionist the letter I had with the interview time on it. I was led to a small waiting area and told that someone would be down to get me soon. I'm sure there were dozens of refugees through those offices every day, and they made me feel like I was one of those faceless dozens.

I sat with a couple of other refugees and thought about what the people at church had said. Some of them had been interviewed by the same person I was scheduled with. They told me that she was suspicious and often rude in the way she questioned interviewees. I wasn't looking forward to that, but I trusted that the right words would come to me.

It didn't take long before the interviewer came to get me. She led me upstairs to a gray hallway with small interview rooms arranged on each side. Each had a window set high enough in the wall that a person passing couldn't see who was inside. The look of them reminded

CHAPTER SEVENTEEN

me of interrogation rooms in a prison. I was brought into one of them and asked to take a seat facing the door. I could see a camera in the corner of the room. One of the church members had told me that there were others watching the interviews as well. I tried not to stare at it and to keep my anxiety under control. I told them enough to prove that I was indeed a refugee, but no more.

After I got back from Ankara, I learned that my case was accepted. Less than a month later, I went to Ankara to let the UN know if there was any country I would refuse to go to. I told them there wasn't. Soon after that, I was told that the United States had accepted my case.

I was glad for that, but I worried that Sahar would have a difficult time joining me. I had been in Turkey for a little less than a year, and she still hadn't come to visit me. Each time we chatted she would tell me that she knew she had to come and visit, but in the next breath had an excuse for why it wasn't possible at that moment. She had classes, her mother was ill, or she was working on her dissertation. I know she was in school and working on her master's, but it would have only been an hour-long flight from Tehran to Ankara. She could have come for a weekend, but I didn't press the point.

For refugees whose cases are accepted by the United States, there are two more interviews before the person is admitted into the country.

There were several people in the congregation who had been through those interviews as well. They told me all about their experience. I listened to what they said, and I wanted to make a good impression, but ultimately I put my trust in God.

These interviews weren't held in the UN building; they were held in the United States Citizenship and Immigration Services offices in Istanbul. It was staffed only by Americans, and I was curious to see what they would be like. As soon as I arrived, they smiled and asked if I needed water or anything else. I felt welcomed, as if they wanted to help and make me comfortable.

After I got back to Kayseri, Baris came over to see how it went. As we often did, we walked through the fruit trees in the grounds while I told him about it.

"So that means you're getting closer to leaving," he said.

I shrugged. "Closer, but there are some refugees who wait for months or years even after the interviews are over."

"What about Sahar? When is she coming here to see you?" he asked.

This wasn't the first time he'd asked. Over the course of those months, I had given him all the excuses she'd given me. Looking back, most of them didn't make sense. She said she was afraid to fly, but then told me about traveling by plane with her sister. She said she couldn't get a passport, but there were Iranian girls Sahar's age who traveled from Iran to come to our church every few months who had passports. I was running out of things to say to Baris when he asked. I fell back on the problem we'd always had. "It's her family."

He'd offered to pay for her ticket, to pick her up at the airport, to allow us to use his apartment in the city if she would prefer that. Each time I relayed the excuses she gave me. If he didn't believe it, he didn't say anything. This time, he didn't let it drop.

He was silent for a moment. "I have daughters. I don't know if I'd want to let my daughter go to a different country on her own, especially if I didn't know who she was going to see. What if I went to see her family? Let them know she'd be safe and staying with me."

"You would do that?" I asked. He had done so much already.

"Of course. You two have been apart for a long time. If you aren't married by the time you leave, it'll be even harder to bring her to America. If me visiting will make her family feel more comfortable about letting her come here, I'll do it."

CHAPTER SEVENTEEN

I nodded. "Thank you. Let me talk to Sahar. I'll let her know you want to come and find the best time."

That night I called her.

We'd been talking and laughing, and I thought it was the perfect time to tell her about Baris's offer. Her eyes widened and she sat back just a fraction. It was enough.

"My family doesn't even know you that well. What do you think some perfect stranger from another country can say to change their minds, especially when that stranger can't speak a word of the language?"

"So, you don't even want to let him try?" I asked.

"I didn't say that, but you know how they are. They never listen to me, so why should they listen to him?"

"He cares about both of us and he wants to help," I said, but couldn't keep the anger out of my voice anymore. Not when she was so insulting to such a generous man. "You want me to throw that offer back in his face?"

"I'm trying to explain that it's not as simple as just coming here. Besides, I'm in school and my mother hasn't been well and Zohre has been really busy with work—"

I shook my head. "You don't want to come here; you don't want him to go there. I don't know what you want, but I'm done with this. If you refuse to meet with him, we're finished." I closed the chat and blocked her on Skype.

Saying those words saddened me, but hearing all the excuses hurt more. There was nothing else to do. I turned out the lights and went to bed.

Chapter Eighteen

FOR THREE LONG days I didn't respond to her messages.

All I wanted was for Sahar and me to be together but talking and patience hadn't done any good. Many times, I went to unblock her, but I always pulled my hand away. I tried to keep myself busy at the church, but even that didn't really take my mind off it. After Bible study, Mozhde asked what was wrong. I couldn't tell her; it was too embarrassing. I might be able to convince myself that Sahar had too much going on with school to visit, but I could see no reason why she would refuse to even meet Baris. How could I explain to someone else what I didn't understand myself?

I mumbled some excuse about being busy to Mozhde. She didn't believe it, but she didn't press me. And things went on as badly as before.

On the third night, I was startled awake by an urgent knocking on the front door. It was after two in the morning, a shocking hour to have a visitor, especially an insistent one. Tik wasn't barking though. That limited the number of people it could be. I opened the door to find Baris standing there in rumpled sweats. I needed a moment to reassure myself that it was him. I had only seen him neatly dressed.

I stepped aside so he could enter. "What happened? What's wrong?"

"What happened between you and Sahar?" he asked as soon as he crossed the threshold.

He deserved the truth, but it was so hard to form the words. I

CHAPTER EIGHTEEN

couldn't look at him. "I told her you wanted to come and meet her family. She didn't like the idea and we argued."

"She's texted me fifty times in the past twenty-four hours. Tonight, she called and said that if you didn't get in touch with her, she would kill herself."

I had given Sahar Baris's number in case of an emergency, and now, standing in the dim entry facing the man who had been so generous to me, I regretted it. "When did she call you?" I asked.

"Just before I left to come here. I couldn't live with it if she actually did something to herself."

"I'm so sorry she disturbed you. I never thought she would do that."

He shook his head and started up the stairs. "Just get in touch with her. I'm going to sleep."

I picked up the laptop and stretched out in bed, the computer on my stomach. It only took a few keystrokes to unblock her and send a message. Sahar answered immediately. She was sitting on her bed in her dim room, her hair a mess, face streaked with tears. I didn't let her speak. "What do you think you're doing?"

"I just—"

"You just what? You thought you would try and get me kicked out into the street? You thought you'd upset Baris and his family in the middle of the night? Do you realize that it's only because of him that I'm not still sleeping in a park?"

"You weren't answering me. What was I supposed to do?" Her voice was strained under the pressure of keeping quiet.

"Well, it would have been very simple. You could have spent an hour on a plane to come here."

"I told you why—"

"You've given me nothing but excuses for months now. When I first got here and didn't know where I was going to be sleeping from one night to the next, I didn't want you to have to deal with that kind of uncertainty. But as soon as he brought me to the villa, Baris made it clear that you were welcome, and every time he asks, I still have to keep making excuses for why my wife doesn't want to be with me."

"It's not an excuse. You know I'm in school—"

"And why don't you want Baris to go there?"

She looked away, swiping at her tears.

"Well? I'm waiting."

"It's not as simple as that," she said. I'd heard it all before.

"No? When I came to Turkey, you told me you'd follow in a few weeks and we'd get married. Even before that, you told your mother that you didn't care what anyone said, you'd marry me anyway. Now you won't even let someone who's done nothing but help me for months, without asking anything in return, visit you for an afternoon?"

"I didn't say he never could."

"Good, because if Baris still wants to have anything to do with either one of us, he's going to go to Iran and you're going to talk to him."

"I've been trying to get in touch with you to tell you that he could come. You had me blocked. What else was I supposed to do?" She pulled a blanket around her shoulders. "Was he angry?"

The tension in my shoulders began to ease. "I know he wasn't happy." I took a deep, settling breath. "Alright. You got back in touch with me, and I'm not going anywhere. We'll get the rest worked out. Get some sleep now and we'll talk about it again later today."

She agreed and we said good night. I closed the laptop, set it on the nightstand, and rubbed my eyes. This should not have been so difficult.

It took three weeks for Baris to make arrangements for his five-day-long visit to Iran. In that time Sahar seemed excited about the prospect of meeting him. She asked what she should wear and what kind of a gift she should give him to welcome him. She wanted to make a good impression.

Baris and I talked about the things he should see when he visited,

CHAPTER EIGHTEEN

including King Cyrus's palace in the south of Iran. We'd talked about it before, and I told Baris that if he ever went to Iran, it was one of the places he shouldn't miss. Now was the time to see it, and he and Sahar made plans to go to the National Museum of Iran in Tehran.

In the three weeks that led up to his departure, the Yale leadership attempted to poison Baris' mind against me. Even though our church was not the only alternative, Yale blamed us for their shrinking membership. Baris told me that representatives of Yale had shown up at his office. He didn't tell me exactly what they said, but he assured me he didn't believe a word of it. I wish I could say that I was surprised, but I wasn't. I was still working with Yale when one of their pastors offered to introduce Sahar to someone else. Someone who was not a refugee. If my relationship was a target, why not the home I had found and the community I had helped build?

I couldn't dwell on it. My second interview with the USCIS was scheduled, and I began to think about what I could do for him. He had given me so much. I wanted to give him something more than flowerbeds in return. He and I had spent hours each day in conversation. I had told him so many things about myself and my life, but I left out any information about the company. I didn't want him to think that I was trying to take advantage of his kindness, or that I was making comparisons between what he had and what I had left behind.

When I told him I wanted to build him another, smaller villa on the property, he was suspicious. I went online and showed him photos of some of the domes and other projects I had designed and built in Iran.

"You did this?" he asked, pointing to the screen.

"Yes," I said and brought up a series of images that showed step-by-step progress.

He scrolled through each one, his appreciation of my skill growing with each new photo. "When I get back, we'll talk more about this."

I'm not sure when he did it, but Baris told his friends about my company. They had always treated me well, but their attitude shifted.

They began to ask my opinions on their building projects and offer me work. I gave my opinion, but I wouldn't be in the country long enough to complete the projects, so I had to decline.

The last time I saw Baris before the trip was the day before he left. He knew where he was going to stay, where he was going to visit, and he had meetings arranged with Sahar on her own so that she could get to know him. Later he would meet with Sahar, her mother, and sister, so that the family could get to know him. He had an interpreter lined up because while I was managing well enough in Turkish, he hadn't learned any Farsi. There was nothing more to discuss. It was still foremost in my mind though, even as the conversation wandered through all the more ordinary things that we usually talked about.

All I could think about was Baris coming back to Turkey with plans for Sahar's arrival and everything that would mean.

After Baris left, I did my best to keep myself busy. Whenever worry seduced me away from one project or another, I reminded myself that if anyone could convince Sahar's family to let her come to Turkey, it was Baris. Before I left, I could have asked Behram or one of the others if they had heard anything from Sahar about how it was going, but she'd stopped all contact with them soon after I left for Turkey. I resolved to wait until she or Baris contacted me.

Two days into the visit, Sahar and I talked. Things seemed to be going well. Baris had offered to bring the entire family to Turkey if that's what they wanted. One of his friends had a large house they could use for as long as they needed it. She didn't tell me how they answered. I don't know why I didn't ask, but I didn't. I thought she would be excited to tell me.

When Baris got back, I was anxious to know how his meeting with Sahar's family went. The day after he got back, we took a walk through the fruit trees in the garden. I waited as long as I could for him to bring it up, but finally I asked how the trip had gone.

CHAPTER EIGHTEEN

"Well, Tehran is a beautiful city, but getting through customs at the airport was a nightmare. They treated me like a criminal, barking question after question at me. Once I got through all that, the rest of the trip was good."

He told me about meeting Sahar on her own and about meeting Yalda and Zohre. "It's hard to believe that Sahar is Yalda's daughter. They don't look anything alike."

I laughed. "What did you think of Sahar?" I asked.

"She's a nice girl," he said and fell silent for a moment, pausing to examine the slowly ripening fruit. "But are you sure that she's the one for you?"

"Yes. I know she is," I said with a confidence I didn't feel. He nodded and let the matter drop.

When I spoke with Sahar, it seemed like she had enjoyed getting to know Baris, but she never mentioned the real purpose of his visit. If I brought it up, she would change the subject, saying that she couldn't make plans because it would distract her from her dissertation.

His visit hadn't changed anything.

Soon after he got back, I gave him a list of materials to build the brick fireplace that would be central to the new villa. Baris had them delivered to the garden. I built it against the surrounding wall, creating an arched space for a barbecue grill on top. I carved the stone mantel and decorative elements myself. It took three days to go from a pile of bricks and unworked stone to a fully formed central element to a kitchen, complete with chimney. When Baris saw it, he readily gave me permission to start building the rest of the house.

I was excited to get started, but the work on the barbecue had aggravated my back injury. The next day Baris came over, he found me leaning to the left and walking gingerly.

"What's wrong?" he asked.

I could see the surprise on his face. "It's an old injury. I just need to rest it a day or two."

I don't think he believed me, but he didn't push for more.

After a few days of rest, I was ready to get started. Baris's cousins, Gurkan, Emrah, and half a dozen laborers began to build the structure based on the plans I had drawn. I was at the USCIS offices being interviewed for the second time while they were building the walls. When I got back it was already taking shape.

There were many tasks that required more than one person, but I wanted to do as much of the work myself as I could. Once the roof was on and the kitchen cabinets installed, I began the tilework in there and in the bathroom. The kitchen tile began halfway up the wall, but the bathroom was tiled from the floor to the ceiling as well as the floors in both rooms and the hallway. The long days of bending and stretching brought on agony worse than anything I'd endured since coming to Turkey.

I couldn't stand up straight, couldn't walk without holding onto something. When Baris came by that evening, he found me around the back of the villa near the door, shuffling slowly along the wall. He rushed over to me, worry etched around his eyes.

"Are you alright?"

He could see the state I was in. It was no good denying it. "No."

"You need a doctor."

"No, I just need to rest for three or four days."

"You can't even stand up straight. I'm not leaving you in this condition."

I could have coped, but he wasn't going to take no for an answer. I nodded and leaned heavily on the wall as I started toward the car.

"It's not that far. I'll carry you."

"No," I said firmly. "Just let me lean on you and I can make it."

He put my arm around his shoulders and helped me around the house and into the car.

He was silent through most of the ride to the hospital, but I know he was wondering what was really going on. I already knew. When I was in Urmia, I had seen a doctor and been told that I would

CHAPTER EIGHTEEN

eventually need surgery on the damaged disc in my back. I hoped I could avoid it for a while longer.

Fifteen minutes later we arrived at a private hospital. He could have taken me to the public hospital where care would have been free, but I think he felt guilty that the project I was doing for him had put me in this state. A doctor saw me almost immediately. Again, surgery was recommended, but the recovery period would have delayed my departure for America. I opted for a cortisone shot and a few days of rest.

Baris stopped by like he always did, but he never asked what had caused a thirty-year-old man to be in so much pain. When I was feeling better, we sat on the balcony looking at the new house.

"The villa's looking good," he said. "I can always hire someone to finish it."

"No," I said. "I can finish it. Besides, there's the pond and the landscaping to do yet."

"I have the plans you drew and the fireplace—"

I shook my head. "It wouldn't be the same."

He could see how determined I was. He let it drop.

Weeks passed and the shell became a house. Then we began the landscaping outside the new villa, taking out the old, patchy lawn and reseeding it. I added a pond with bright goldfish and a wrought-iron fence along the driveway, as well as a gate into the orchard.

Our church had grown large enough to have three services. We'd replaced music from a laptop with live music provided by our members. I didn't preach. I left that to a different member of the congregation at each service. If someone wasn't confident enough to prepare and give the lesson on their own, I had them work with a partner. We held Bible study several times a week for anyone who wanted to attend, and other events, like backgammon tournaments, so that people could enjoy each other's company and further strengthen their sense of community.

There was another, handpicked group who had expressed interest in being pastors. For them there would be intense study based on the model that I had experienced in Istanbul arranged slightly differently. Instead of setting aside weeks, there would be three to five days each month devoted solely to intensive classes. Because their days began at six thirty and didn't end until ten at night, participants stayed overnight at the church. We even provided meals so that nothing would distract them.

Behram, Saba, and others came from Iran on a regular basis to teach. Only the people who were in this select group knew who they were. Everyone else was accustomed to people visiting our services. They were seen as nothing more than welcome guests who came back every few months.

During this time, I began thinking about where in America I should go. I knew people in several different states, but I didn't want to plan for myself. This had started out as God's journey, and I knew I had to follow his plan, whatever that plan happened to be. I knew many refugees had faced that same question. Sometimes, they asked the entire church to pray for them. I didn't want to do that. I asked a few people, including Aziz. He was the first one who told me that I should go to Michigan.

I had never even heard of Michigan, but when I looked it up online, the weather was the first thing I noticed. I couldn't imagine living in a place that cold for so much of the year. When I saw Aziz again, I told him that he'd made a mistake.

He nodded. "Maybe," he said. "I've never heard of Michigan. It just came to me while I was praying, and I thought I'd tell you about it." He smiled. "You'll find the right place for you."

A week or so later I happened to be on Facebook when I saw a photo of Hesam's friend Jeffrey come across my newsfeed. I saw that he was in America, so I sent him a private message congratulating him on getting out of Turkey. He messaged me back and asked where I was in the process. He and I hadn't spoken in months, but I learned that he was in Michigan and he described it as green and beautiful.

CHAPTER EIGHTEEN

He also told me that he'd be my sponsor. That meant I'd be able to tell the USCIS that I had a friend in the state. I asked for his information and said I would think about it.

The next thing I did was message Sahar. She started to research schools in Michigan and thought that she could probably get accepted to Michigan State University.

"Just get accepted to one of the schools you're looking at," I said. "I'm pretty sure that I'm going to Michigan. Jeffrey even knows a PhD candidate who can give advice about getting a student visa with MSU."

I emailed the USCIS that I wanted to go to Michigan and sent the phone number and address Jeffrey had given me. A week later, I had my acceptance.

Chapter Nineteen

MY TIME IN Turkey grew shorter. A medical appointment at the USCIS offices created a medical record and history that would follow me to America. After that, I had three months before my departure.

Usually refugees use this time to wrap up their affairs in the country, prepare to leave, and clear any outstanding debts. I had things to take care of too, but for me it wasn't as simple as paying bills or deciding what to take and what to leave behind. I had to think of the church we had built.

Our entire membership were refugees. Eventually they would all leave to go to other countries. When they left, they would be replaced by others who were newly arrived. There were many who were leaders, who could have taken over, but they, too, would leave. At best, I would be transferring my problem to them.

During that time, I learned that my younger brother Parsa's pastor had been arrested in Iran. Parsa had converted when I was living in Urmia. He'd come to visit me, and we spent a couple of days visiting and talking about John and the other Gospels. After that I had put him in touch with another pastor, Babak. I had been in Turkey for two and a half years when I learned that Babak had been arrested. There was a tacit agreement among Christians. Those who were arrested and tortured would hold their silence for as long as possible to give the members of their house churches time to make their own decisions about what to do next. Babak's picture and story were already posted on the Yale website. Publicity like that can sometimes make

CHAPTER NINETEEN

the situation worse for everyone. The day after Babak's arrest, I invited Parsa to come to Turkey.

Since I hadn't found anyone to lead our church after I left, passing things on to him seemed like an idea. But he wasn't an experienced leader, especially not to so many people who were also under such pressure. There were others who were willing to assist him. I trusted that he would turn to them when he needed help.

And he would be safe.

To fly would draw too much scrutiny, so Parsa took the train from Tehran to Van and then another train to Kayseri. The entire journey would take nearly twenty-four hours. There was nothing I could do but wait. Questions scratched and dug with insidious thorns the whole time he was in Iran. Was it already too late? Would he be stopped at the border? Would someone notice that his last name was the same as mine and detain him on the chance we were related?

He texted me after he crossed the border safely, and keen worries gave way to anticipation. My brother would be back with me for the three weeks before I left for America.

Baris and I arrived at Kayseri's tiny train station fifteen minutes before the train was due to arrive. Despite the late hour, there were members of our church there to greet the train as part of our outreach plan for newly arrived refugees who needed directions around the city, a place to stay, or any other assistance we could offer regardless of religion. They tried to keep me distracted in conversation as we waited on the single platform. I looked down the track, searching for the train every few minutes. I tried to think of the time that we would have together and not how quickly it would be over.

The train's horn sounded before it came into view. I was on my feet, taking a few strides back and forth. Those few minutes seemed stretched and contorted until at last the train rumbled into the station with squealing brakes and the smell of diesel.

Moments later, the doors to the carriages opened, and travel-weary people stepped out with baggage or family or both in tow. I didn't know where he'd been on the train, so I walked further along. Then there he stepped out of one of the last carriages. I could see the weight of exhaustion on his shoulders and around his red-rimmed eyes. He looked older than the last time I'd seen him. The beard he wore contributed to that.

As soon as Parsa saw me, he dropped the bags he was carrying and for a moment we just held onto each other, my fingers wrapped in a handful of his shirt and his fingers wrapped in mine. Nothing else mattered. My brother was back with me. He was crying and I felt the pressure of incipient tears in my throat. Maybe, if Baris had stayed back for another minute or two, those tears would have become more than a possibility.

The platform was beginning to empty when I made the introductions. Baris shook Parsa's hand and then hugged him. "You're his brother." Baris said to Parsa in Turkish. "To me, you're like him."

I translated. Baris and I both picked up Parsa's bags and took him back to the villa. Baris stayed long enough to make sure that we had everything we needed; then he left us alone to get reacquainted in our own way.

---∞---

I was happy to have my brother with me and to see him settling into our church, but I had given up on seeing Sahar again until after she was able to get a student visa to join me in America. Two weeks before I was scheduled to leave Turkey, Sahar said she wanted to come and see me. At first, I laughed.

"What?" she asked. "I'm serious. I haven't booked anything yet because I wanted to ask about dates."

"I'm set to leave for America in two weeks. You've had two and a half years to come and see me."

She gave a little shrug. "I told you why I couldn't."

After all the discussions, arguments, and disappointments, now she treated coming to see me like such a simple thing? It was insulting. "You gave me excuse after excuse, even after Baris came to see you and offered to bring your whole family here. So, suddenly, after all this time, your mother isn't sick anymore, you can get a passport, you're not afraid to fly. Everything is finally perfect? No. Seeing you now will only make leaving harder. Don't come."

She sat back a little. "I was in school, and it's not my fault that things were happening."

I shook my head. "It's too late for you to come here. Focus on getting into a PhD program in Michigan and getting a student visa."

Sahar studied me through narrowed eyes. "Maybe there's another reason you don't want me to come. Maybe you're seeing someone else."

It was an obvious attempt to play on my emotions. I sighed. "I'm not seeing anyone else. It's just the wrong time."

The last few weeks leading up to my departure were stressful. I had my ticket, I had a plan for the church, but what would I do after I got to America?

Baris knew how stressed I would be before I left. Months before, he told me he'd arranged a trip to Cappadocia for the two of us. Since Parsa was staying with me, he was invited too.

Located less than an hour southwest of Kayseri, the valleys of Cappadocia look as though they belong to another world. Over the eons, nature sculpted the towering cones of golden stone that huddle next to each other as the land rises and falls. The human beings who made their homes there literally carved their lives out of the stone itself, creating chambers and tunnels through the rock and refining their endeavors to include ventilation and natural light. As time went on, the local stone was used to link and augment the conical fairy chimneys and cliffside dwellings to create terraces and buildings that looked as though they were formed by the earth itself. The wind chased around these natural formations as well as the man-made ones, reminding me of the constant whisper of the wind on Ali's plain.

Because it was so close to Kayseri, I had visited Cappadocia on day trips with other refugees, especially those who were visiting our church from other cities. We'd share the cost of renting a van, pack food and water, and enjoy a day in one of the most magically beautiful places in Turkey for very little money.

This time the three of us stayed in one of the hotels created from the myriad of caves. Modern luxuries in neutral tones were seamlessly combined with traditional floral relief carvings and friezes on the hewn stone walls. At night the air moving through the ventilation shafts and windows tugged at the edges of my mind as I tried to discern the secrets the eddying air was carrying.

It was Parsa's first visit to the region, so he spent the warm days exploring on quad bike tours and balloon rides. Baris and I did some exploring, but much of our time was spent on the terraces with our tea, looking out over the valley. Manicured pockets of emerald-green gardens stood out against the rock and dusty soil. Colorful hot air balloons rose and descended back to the valley floor again while we tried to fit a lifetime of conversations into those final, short days.

"You don't have to leave, you know. You've been here long enough; you can get citizenship. I'll support you," Baris said one afternoon, his eyes on the vista before him.

I shook my head. "Baris—"

He turned to me. "I know the others offered you work. I've known them a long time and I know their offers are sincere, but if you aren't sure about working with any of them, I can understand that. You don't really know them very well. Work with me. The garden is so big, even if I divide it, there will still be plenty of space. I want to build apartments at the end opposite the house. Be my partner."

He wouldn't have made the offer if he weren't serious. If I stayed, I could find the same kind of success I'd had in Tehran. His friends had already proved that they were more than willing to hire me, and their influence would lead to more, larger projects. It would have been so easy, but it wasn't right. I knew I couldn't stay. "I only came to Turkey because I was forced to leave Iran. This isn't where I'm destined to be."

He took a sip of his tea, contemplating my answer. "I suppose I knew you would say that. What happened in the park that day, well, I still don't know what happened, but I know I can never repeat it. I

CHAPTER NINETEEN

just had to make sure you knew there were other options."

Conversation drifted on the air from people around us on the terrace, but Baris and I fell into silence again.

Even if Parsa was on his own adventures during the day, at sunset we were always together on one of the stone terraces. We watched the silhouettes of the balloons rising against the pinks and golds painted against the clouds and reflected on the steep sides of the rock formations. No matter what the rest of the evening held, we savored these moments of quiet.

Later, we'd go on to dinner and take in one of the shows of traditional Turkish dancing in a restaurant built into a cave. Tables were arranged around the performance area. While we ate, we watched groups of men and women in traditional costumes perform synchronized dances that had been performed the same way for centuries. Music and rhythm filled the air around us while color whirled before our eyes, filling our senses with the moment and creating bright memories of the three of us there, smiling, and eating together.

Sahar and I only talked a couple of times when I was in Cappadocia. She hadn't said anything more about her offer to come to Turkey, but there was a coolness in the way she spoke that magnified the distance between us.

On the last night we were there, I sat watching the last intense rays of the sun gilding the valley below. The sun dipped below the horizon, leaving behind ribbons of pink and orange that would soon fade into deep darkness and stars.

Baris took a deep breath and then let it out. "That's our last sunset together here," he said.

Silence enfolded us again. Wonderful as Baris and his family had been to me, I wondered why I couldn't watch the sunset in my own country.

That night, Sahar and I had our final Skype conversation before I left for America. There was so much I wanted to say, so much she wanted to say, and all of it was too big, too broad, and too deep for words. We were already so far apart, and it wouldn't be long before I was going to be even farther away. We both avoided the obvious.

"How is Cappadocia?" she asked.

"It was nice. It was good to have a little time with Baris and Parsa," I said and fell silent for a thoughtful moment. "Did I send you the pictures I took of the sunset the other day?"

She sat up a little straighter. "No."

I sent them to her and then showed her the view from my hotel balcony. The lights of the valley stretched out below.

It was all surface, there were no true feelings or deep intimacies, but it was all either of us could manage at the time.

The day we left we spent long hours exploring the valley before heading back home in the late afternoon. When we arrived at the villa, Laila, Ofugh, and their two daughters, Ausan and Aynur, were waiting for us. We sat on the balcony in the soft summer evening, and all enjoyed the delicious meal that Laila had prepared. When I thought of the way my sojourn in Turkey had begun—completely alone on a seemingly endless bus journey into an unknown future surrounded by strangers—I couldn't have imagined that it would end in this beautiful place surrounded by the love of a family who had welcomed me as one of their own.

After hugs, tears, and well wishes, Laila and the others left late that evening. Baris stayed. My flight left Kayseri at seven thirty in the morning, and he was going to take me to the airport. I went to the far end of the garden to say goodbye to my dog, Tok, then went back to the house to check that I had everything packed that I wanted to take with me. There was nothing more to do other than go to bed and try to sleep. I lay there, studying the ceiling in the dark. In the next twenty-four hours, I would be seven thousand miles away from everyone I knew, from everything I was familiar with. A different culture, a different language, a different people. All in the space of a few short hours. A couple of hours before I had to be up, I finally drifted into an uneasy sleep.

We moved silently through the house at four in the morning. It was too early for conversation. There was nothing more to say anyway. Hints

CHAPTER NINETEEN

of dawn were just beginning to tease at the dark sky when we stepped outside. Tik, who was lying in front of his house, raised his head, studying all the unaccustomed early morning activity. He could see that something was wrong. The rottweiler mix danced around and between Baris and me, whining and looking for reassurance as we walked to the car parked just outside the large gate. He'd seen me come and go since he was a puppy, but he could tell this was different. This was forever.

We got halfway to the car before he ran forward howling, putting himself between us and the car. I'd never heard him make that sound before. The quiet tension that had been simmering in the air around us broke. All three of us started to cry. Tik looked from Baris to Parsa and then at me. I led him back into the garden and held him there while I came out the smaller door next to the gate. He scrabbled at the ground under the gate, trying to squeeze his whole body through a tiny gap that was barely big enough for his muzzle. His desperate whining was only barely muffled. I couldn't stand it. I got in the car. Parsa and Baris would take good care of him.

The sun rose on a gray, overcast day as Baris drove the three of us to the airport. Silence had collected around us again. Every so often, someone made a comment to try to dispel it, but the weight of the atmosphere made conversation impossible.

The silence remained once we got to the airport. Baris bought us breakfast at the café. None of us could eat. Our table was a singular island of quiet surrounded by people and conversation and laughter. Baris toyed with a bit of bread, turning it slowly in his hand, his eyes fixed on it. I don't know how long we had been sitting there when tears began to slide down his cheeks. He wiped them away and took a deep breath before he got up.

"I'll be back," Baris said.

I didn't watch where he went. When he got back, he handed me a small box. Inside was a small gold medallion on a piece of red ribbon. Stars and flowers surrounded the profile of Ataturk, the founder of the Republic of Turkey.

I looked at him. "You shouldn't do that."

"I want you to have it," he said firmly.

I nodded and put the box into my carry-on bag. Baris' generosity never ceased to amaze me. This moment stretched on until it was broken by the announcement calling my flight. The three of us looked at each other. They walked with me as far as they could to the gate. Parsa hugged me first. I'd only had three weeks with him in the last four years, and now I was leaving. Baris hugged me next, tears flowing again.

I know the people around us wondered what was going on. The Kayseri airport was small and regional. Scenes of long-term loss were an unaccustomed sight, especially between a Turkish man and a foreigner. That didn't matter to us. Parsa hugged me one last time.

Baris put a hand on my shoulder and one hand on Parsa's. "Don't worry," he said to me. "I'll take care of him."

I knew he would. As I walked down the jetway to board the plane, I looked back to see my brother and Baris at the wide window, waving until I was out of sight.

Once I got on the plane, I texted Sahar. I wanted her to know that I was on my way.

---∞---

In Istanbul, I took the subway to Ataturk International Airport and was directed to an area of the airport set aside for refugees on their way to their destination country.

I went to the desk for those bound for the United States and presented the Turkish ID I'd been issued as a refugee. I was given a blue and white bag with all of my paperwork inside it and told to keep it with me at all times. It would act as my identification and passport to get into the country.

There were a few other refugees waiting by the same desk. One was a man from Somalia who had his two wives and ten children with him along with a mountain of luggage. There was one other Iranian man in our group.

I was glad to have someone to talk to for the nearly three-hour

CHAPTER NINETEEN

wait. He introduced himself as Kambiz. I soon found out that he was not someone I wanted to spend a great deal of time with. A sailor would have blushed at the foul language that salted his conversation. I hoped that we weren't going to be seated together on the plane. Thankfully, we were placed several rows apart. The Somali family was toward the back. I was seated next to a stranger.

I took out my phone. I didn't know when I would be able to contact Sahar again. I couldn't let this opportunity go to waste.

I'm on the plane in Istanbul, I typed. *My phone is probably going to stop working soon.* I hit "Send."

This time she responded. *Good luck in the USA!*

I smiled a little and put my phone away. I looked around the steadily filling plane and wondered how I was going to pass the twelve hours until we got to Chicago. Then I met my seatmate. She was an American girl from Wisconsin. Through pantomime and her few words of Turkish, she told me that she'd been vacationing and was headed home.

Most of the time we played backgammon while I watched my Iranian acquaintance make numerous trips to the bar, becoming progressively more drunk until we were a few hours away from Chicago. By the time we got off the plane, I had learned a couple of words in English, the first of which was "backgammon." Kambiz had given himself time to sober up enough to be allowed onto the connecting flight.

In Chicago we were met by an older woman who represented the USCIS. She welcomed us to the country and led us to our next plane bound for Michigan. I was expecting a jet, but we were put on a much smaller plane. The inside was so cramped that the person in the window seat had to tilt their head with the curve of the wall. All the way to Michigan, the plan shook and fluttered and bumped along. More than once I wondered if we were going to get there at all. I didn't relax until we were on the ground again.

On June 17, 2014, Jeffrey, Kambiz's friend Ahmad, and George, our case manager from the refugee office, met my flight at the tiny Lansing airport.

It was another new beginning.

Part III
America

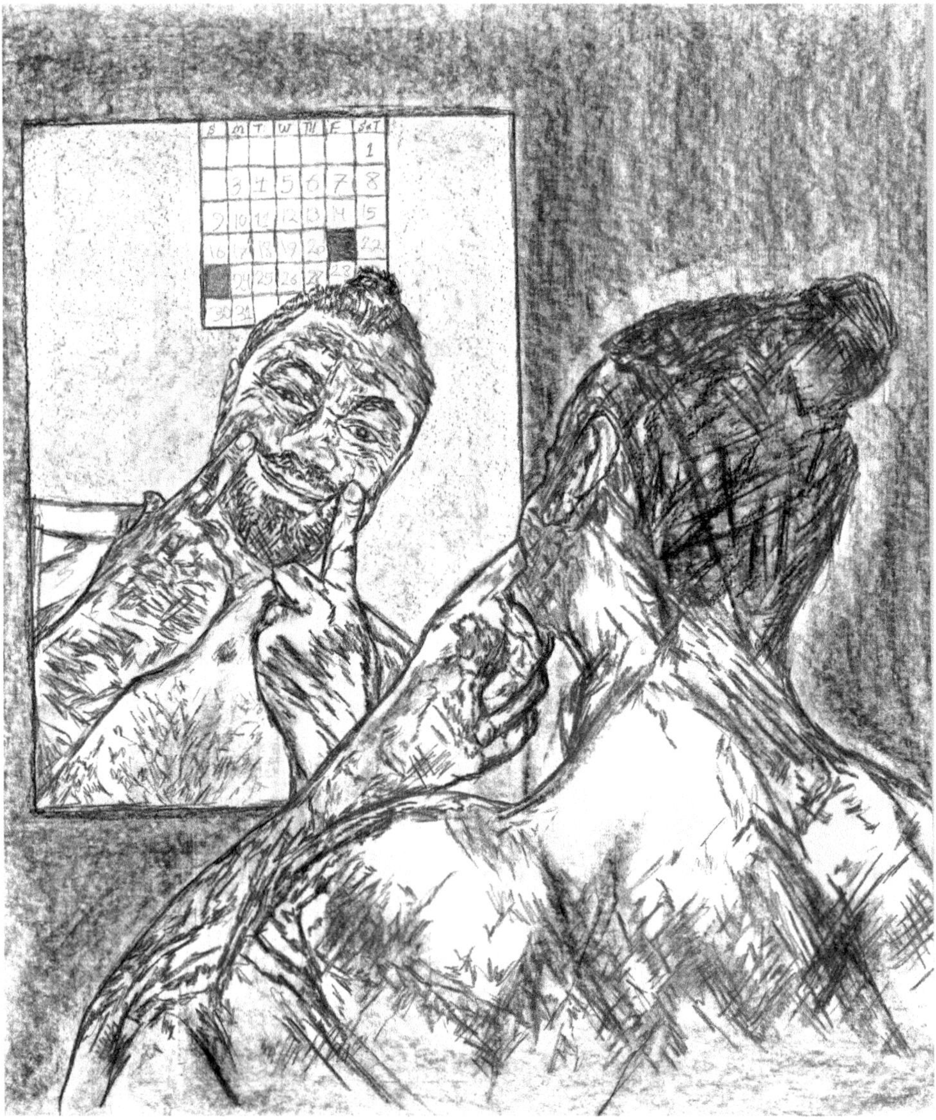

Chapter Twenty

GEORGE TOOK KAMBIZ, our friends, and me into the city of Lansing. To me, calling it a city seemed like an overstatement. The streets George took were narrower than the streets in Tehran and they were dark. Even in the villages in Iran, darkness was held at bay with streetlights and outdoor bulbs on houses and buildings. This sort of darkness reminded me of Ali's plain; a place in the middle of nowhere.

While we drove, I looked for the city skyline. There wasn't one. I looked at Jeffrey. He just smiled a little and then looked away. He'd only arrived a few months ago, but he knew the questions that were tumbling around in my head. This was America? I had waited for months and gone through multiple interviews to come to a dark, flat little place.

For miles the world was illuminated largely by our headlights. Finally, we turned onto a larger road with evenly spaced streetlights. There were businesses and houses lining either side. Every so often, I caught a glimpse of something else that surprised me—everyone seemed to have a lawn.

In the Middle East, water is scarce. Manicured gardens and lawns were reserved for the wealthy. These lawns stood in stark contrast to the look of the small, simple houses that lined the streets. These couldn't be the houses of the wealthy. There were no apartment buildings that I could see, just more houses.

"Here we are," George said as we pulled up before one house. He motioned for us to follow him. He led us down a set of outdoor stairs into the living room of a basement apartment. A wooden table and two chairs sat near one of the high windows, and a worn brown couch sat against the opposite wall. The musty tinge in the air struck me immediately. "You have a living room and kitchen out here. On the right is the bedroom, and the door on the left is the bathroom. Beautiful, isn't it?" He was smiling when he said it.

At that time Jeffrey still didn't know English very well, so Ahmad translated for us without editorial commentary.

The threadbare brown carpet and white walls didn't rise to the level of utilitarian. Nothing about it was beautiful.

"There's some food in the fridge, so if you're hungry feel free to eat," George said. We were still looking around the spartan little apartment when he took some paperwork out of a folder and placed it on the table. "Just sign here."

It was all written in English, but we signed where we were told to. He put it back in the folder again.

"I'll be back tomorrow morning at ten to bring you to the refugee center," George said and there was little to do but wish him good night.

I didn't want to share a one-bedroom apartment with a stranger, but I thought that it would be temporary. I tried to sort through the tangle of questions and exhaustion that settled around me, but the day had been too long and too emotional. I'd try to work it out after some rest.

I got a few hours of sleep, but I was still tired when I woke up. Once the fog of exhaustion and travel had begun to clear, I realized I was waking up on another continent for the first time. I had traveled to other countries for many different reasons, but another continent was something new and exciting. It was a blank page on which I could write the lines of my new life.

Before I could do that, I had to deal with the reality of my new

CHAPTER TWENTY

housing situation. Kambiz and I were both itching as if insects had been crawling on us while we slept. I went to shower and found cockroaches in the bathroom. Not only was the place ugly and inappropriate for housing two strangers, but it was also infested with vermin. In less than twenty-four hours, I had gone from living in a spacious villa surrounded by fruit trees in one of the best parts of Kayseri to sharing a bug-infested one-bedroom apartment with a man I didn't know. Was this where I was supposed to be?

It was rainy and overcast when George arrived to take us to the refugee center. It wasn't far, but it was my first good look at the city. My first impression had been right—it was small with squat, unattractive buildings. This was the capital of the state? We passed several buses, but there weren't as many as I would have expected from a city with a good public transportation system. I didn't see anything that looked like the entrance to the subway. To live here I'd have to have a car.

As we drove into the parking lot, I saw St. Joseph's Catholic Cemetery through the gaps in the trees. I was immediately transported back to when I was a child and my family would drive past the Armenian cemetery. This time I didn't have to stretch and turn to catch a glimpse of the crosses on the graves. There were no high walls or solid gates to keep people out. No one to question why someone would want to enter. It was just a quiet expanse of green where everyone was welcome.

For hours we were kept busy with paperwork and then had to sit through a class to introduce us to the basics of everyday life in America. We were given bus passes and told how to use them. We were told that Americans were most comfortable with a conversational distance of arm's length to a bit more. Some store brands were cheaper. Landlords had basic responsibilities which included pest control. Then we were told that after we'd been in America for six months, we'd be able to apply for financial aid to attend college.

I'd talked about colleges and universities in the United States with

Sahar for years, and I often practiced writing the names of the different schools so that I could begin to learn to write English words. When our instructor, a Somali man who had been here for close to ten years, spelled "college" as "collage," I had to speak up.

"Shouldn't that be e-g-e?" I asked.

He turned and looked at the whiteboard, studying the word. "I think you're right." He erased the "a" and changed it to an "e."

Kambiz leaned over to me. "He's supposed to be teaching us and he can't even spell?" He shook his head. "God help us."

It would become a familiar refrain over the next few days.

When we finished there was about an hour before George was going to take us back to the apartment. The rain had faded to gentle, intermittent showers, so I walked through the tree line and down the road that wound through the graveyard. The stones were all shapes and sizes, some figural, some plain. Most bore carved crosses. I walked down the rows and trailed my fingertips over the wet tops of the markers. Every so often the clouds would part and shafts of bright sunlight would touch the stones or the trees before it faded and disappeared again. As fraught and uncertain as my arrival in America had been, a feeling of peace washed over me.

I'm not sure how long I had been wandering through the graves, but George came out to find me.

He pointed toward the city outside the cemetery, then spread his hands and raised his shoulders in a questioning way. I guessed that he wondered what I was doing walking in here with the dead when there were so many other places to see.

I wanted to tell him that I'd waited for so long to walk through a cemetery like this. To see the crosses and touch the stones, free to come and go as I wished. I wanted to tell him that, to me, it was a beautiful place. I didn't know how to begin. I put my hand over my heart instead and hoped he understood.

CHAPTER TWENTY

For the next few days we attended classes at the refugee center, taking the bus from the apartment. Even that was different from what I was accustomed to. When I needed to use public transportation in Iran or Turkey, I usually chose to use the subways. The few times I rode the bus, there was a button mounted to a pole in the middle of the bus to indicate to the driver that a stop was needed. In Lansing, there is no subway, and the first time Kambiz and I got on the bus, I didn't see a button either. At first, we rode and watched the other passengers. The bus stopped at the next few stops, and I thought that maybe there wasn't a way to indicate, they stopped everywhere along the route. That couldn't be it because the driver passed the next couple of stops. Eventually we saw another passenger pull the cord that ran along the tops of the windows on both sides of the bus. It was alright if you were sitting in the seat next to the window, but if you were in an aisle seat or standing, you'd have to reach over someone to pull the cord. I didn't like disturbing other people when I didn't know how to ask them to forgive me.

My favorite parts of the day were the breaks in the classes. Whenever I had a bit of time, I wandered through the cemetery. I walked the different paths and absorbed the peace of the place.

One thing I wanted but hadn't managed yet was to talk with Sahar. The laptop I had been using belonged to Baris. We didn't have Wi-Fi at the apartment anyway. Kambiz had an iPad mini, and we were close enough to a local restaurant that we could connect to their Wi-Fi. He let me use it to contact Sahar.

I set up the iPad so that the camera would show me against one of the bare white walls.

"So, what's it like? Where are you living?" she asked. Even through Skype I could see the excited curiosity sparkling in her eyes.

I didn't want to tell her. I gave a little shrug. "It's just temporary."

"So? I want to see," she said.

"I'm trying to change it," I said. I picked up the tablet and showed her the small, mostly empty space.

"There's only one bedroom?" she asked. "They're making you live

BECOMING JOSHUA

in the same room with someone you don't even know?"

"I was shocked too, but maybe that's just how they do it at first." I wasn't sure that was true, but I hoped it was.

A thoughtful silence grew between us, and then she asked. "So how was the trip?"

It was a more comfortable topic. I sat down again and started to describe it.

I wanted to explore this new city. I had to locate the practical things everyone needs, like grocery stores, but I also wanted to find a church. Sunday was only a few days away, and even though the refugee center had given me a list, I didn't know which one to choose. Since my arrival the weather had been gray and rainy. I took the bus into the center of the city anyway.

Despite the weather, I'd expected to find people walking from place to place. This was the capital city in the middle of the week. There were buildings and shops lining both sides of the streets, but the sidewalks were surprisingly empty. It was strange. I tried the imposing doors of each church I passed. Each time, I found them locked. Even when I knocked, no one answered. How could these enormous buildings be completely empty?

Our church in Turkey was never empty. Even when there wasn't an event going on, someone always lived there to make sure that if anyone knocked, they could be welcomed. Over there, people were coming and going all the time. These buildings could have been put to so many uses. Why were they standing empty? I shook my head. America was a very different place than anywhere I had lived before. It was going to take time, probably years, before I got used to it. Standing before yet another set of locked doors, I asked to be guided to the right place and the right people.

Eventually I came across an older couple sitting on a bench outside a sandwich shop. They were holding a large piece of white

CHAPTER TWENTY

cardboard with something written on it in thick black marker. They had two young boys with them. Both boys looked like they were less than ten. The older couple sat close to each other and tilted their heads closer as they spoke. Smiles came easily to their lips and brightened their eyes. The pair watched people pass by, but the children were watching me. They looked like nice people. I used Google to translate the sign.

"Free Pray" came up on the screen.

Free pray? Did they charge people for praying here? It didn't matter if they did; this prayer was offered for free. I walked over to them. I wanted to talk with other Christians, but my word or two of English didn't fit the situation.

I pointed to the sign and said, "Pray."

They understood I didn't know English, but they didn't care. They only cared that I wanted to pray with them. We joined hands and closed our eyes. They began to pray out loud. It reminded me of when I distributed Bibles in Istanbul. Many times, when we gave someone a Bible, they asked for a prayer as well. We'd stand with them on the sidewalk and pray much like this.

After the prayer ended, they asked what church I attended and where I lived. It took time to understand what they were saying and then to find a way to answer, but they didn't rush me, and they didn't give up trying to make themselves understood. They invited me to their church on Sunday. I accepted and tried to express my gratitude.

He introduced himself as Mike and his wife as Mary. The boys were their grandchildren.

The rain began again, and they offered to give me a ride home. I accepted and showed Mike my address written on a piece of paper. They came back on Sunday morning to give me a ride to church.

I'm not sure what I was expecting, but we pulled into a sprawling parking lot in front of an enormous building. We walked into a rounded space that looked more like a movie theater with comfortable seats and a large screen over the semicircular dais. There was a Bible in a holder behind every chair, and I found myself calculating how much it would cost to smuggle so many. Mike and Mary introduced me to several people. They all smiled and welcomed me.

As the band got ready at the front, the room filled with sounds of people talking and laughing with each other. I couldn't understand what they were saying, but there was no hesitation in the way they spoke to each other. There were no forbidden topics and no questions that couldn't be asked. They didn't have to hide. They didn't need security stationed along the road or guarding entrances. Why couldn't my community have the same freedom?

The service began with electric guitars and drums. People all around me had their eyes on the band. They listened to and enjoyed the music as if they were at a concert. No one that I could see had their eyes closed, listening to God. When the music ended the pastor ran down the aisle and leapt up onto the wide platform as if he were a superhero. He turned on his heel to face the congregation and shouted, "Hallelujah!"

I knew the word, but it seemed like he was using it as an exclamation of his own excitement rather than an offering of praise to God.

When he began to speak, he moved back and forth in front of his audience wearing shoes that must have cost several hundred dollars and in a suit that was probably worth five times that. I wondered how he could talk to the poor when he was dressed like that. I listened to the inflection in his voice and watched the way he gestured as he spoke. He was an actor. Every inflection perfect, every gesture polished.

I could see the power of money, of the building, of the belief that this strutting man had some special knowledge they couldn't have. I had no doubt that this would be the most difficult place I had ever talked about Jesus.

Mike leaned over to me. "Are you okay?" His voice was quiet.

I couldn't answer. I didn't have the words then and I still don't have them now for what I was feeling, watching a brash and gaudy show of grand religious gestures. That day inspired me to move away from religion and focus on the message, the real message, behind the words.

Chapter Twenty-One

LEARNING ENGLISH BECAME a priority. The refugee center had taught us the basics of American culture and daily survival, but to learn the language, they directed us to English classes held at the public library. Jeffrey had gone to the same classes and knew the instructor, Emma. The first day at the refugee office, he'd also told me that she was Christian.

We went to classes several times a week to learn basic conversation and common slang like "What's up?" It was a common greeting that seemed strange. *Up where?* I wondered. I knew several languages, but they had nothing in common with English. I spent hours each day studying.

As Emma got to know more about me, she began to tell me that I needed to meet her pastor. I wasn't sure why she would especially want the two of us to meet, but I thought she might be inviting me to their church. I was still attending services with Mike and Mary, even though it seemed more like a show.

One of the best parts of being at the library was that I had access to computers. Each day I could Skype Sahar for an hour at a time. I couldn't speak out loud in the library, but I could watch her image on the screen as we typed messages back and forth.

The chill that had existed between us before I left Turkey had abated, and we spoke easily again. No matter where we started, our conversation always turned back to her coming here for her PhD.

"MSU has a good program, but there are a few other schools I've been looking at too," she said.

I knew she was only interested in MSU in the first place because it was close to me. I didn't care what school she chose or what state we lived in. If we were together, it didn't matter. "Just get accepted to one of them. Once you're here, I can keep you here."

Mike and Mary helped me so much in those early days. When they found out that we had only one pan, two plates, two forks, and a single spoon in our kitchen, they took me to Meijer and showed me around the store. They even bought a set of dishes for me. They gave me rides to church every week and were very patient when my poor English made communication difficult. Their many small kindnesses might have seemed insignificant to them, but they meant so much to me.

Independence Day was my first holiday in America. I'd been here for a little more than two weeks when we first heard what sounded like gunfire. It went on for too long though, and rapid popping, occasional whistling sounds, and deep booms were too varied to be someone shooting.

We went outside in front of the apartment in time to see a red chrysanthemum-shaped firework burst in the distance. It was a celebration of some kind, but we didn't know where to go to get a good view of the display. Instead we sat outside and listened to the township's display and the bangs and pops from people celebrating in the neighborhood around us. Occasionally we would see showers of red, blue, or gold sparks glittering high over our heads.

I'm not sure how long we'd been watching when Jeffrey and Ahmad drove into the parking lot.

"Do you know what they're celebrating?" Jeffrey asked after we greeted them.

CHAPTER TWENTY-ONE

I grinned. "Someone told them I'm finally here. They wanted to welcome me."

Everyone laughed but Jeffrey shook his head. "It's Independence Day. The day America declared themselves separate from Britain."

Rebellion, revolution, celebration. We sat together in the warm evening, surrounded by the sounds and sights of a country celebrating its autonomy.

Kambiz and I were not suited as roommates. We just lived too differently. I'd been in the basement apartment for three weeks when Jeffrey called and said he'd found an apartment and wanted a roommate. I went with him to look at it. The three-bedroom apartment was bright and airy with more than enough space for the two of us. Three weeks after my arrival, I moved in with Jeffrey.

Jeffrey was a bit older than I was, but living with him was so much better than living with Kambiz. He'd told me he'd gotten a new job, but I didn't know the whole story until one evening soon after we moved in. We were sitting on the floor in the mostly empty living room on beige carpeting. I'd been telling him how I'd ended up living with Kambiz in the first place.

"You were lucky," he said. "When I first came here, they put me in an apartment with a Somali man. We didn't even speak the same language. Try living with someone you can't communicate with."

"I thought you were living with a PhD student," I said.

"Eventually. Before that I was homeless."

"Wait, when you told me I should come here—"

He nodded. "I'd lost my job and lost my apartment. When I went to my caseworker for help, he took me to the homeless shelter. I was there a few days before some friends invited me to stay with them. Otherwise, I would have stayed at the shelter or been forced into the street. A week after you got here, I got a job. Besides, when I messaged you, I was lonely here."

As soon as I moved in with him, I got on Jeffrey's phone plan and bought a smartphone. The next time I messaged Sahar at the library, I showed her the phone.

"You should download this app." She gave me an unfamiliar name. Even though I couldn't hear her voice, I could see the excitement on her face.

"Why? What's it for?" I asked. I'd had apps on my phone that were related to the work I did, but never for entertainment. Between work and the group, I didn't have time.

"We can video chat anywhere for free. No more going to a library and typing."

I downloaded the app immediately and glanced through its capabilities. I didn't really care what it did, as long as it worked the way she said it did. It felt so good to be able to talk to Sahar whenever I wanted to again, and to be able to hear her voice instead of just seeing her words on the screen. There were still thousands of miles between us, but it felt as though some of the emotional distance between us had shrunk.

Learning English was still difficult, and so was making sense of the cultural differences. Being immersed in the language helped, but it was so different from any other language I knew.

I'd only been in America for a few weeks when I woke up one morning in agony. I couldn't even stand up. Every other time the pain in my back had flared up, it had been brought on by work. I hadn't done anything recently; I didn't even have a job yet. The time might have come where I'd need to have surgery, like the doctor in Urmia had said, but I didn't know how to make an appointment with a specialist.

Mike and Mary stopped by just about every day. We never kept the door locked, and they always let themselves in. I was crawling on

CHAPTER TWENTY-ONE

the living room floor when they arrived.

Mike took me to the emergency room. I wasn't sure how I was going to communicate. Pantomime would only take me so far in ordinary conversation. Thankfully there was access to a competent translator by phone. Through him, the doctor recommended that I see a specialist the next day for a steroid injection. He prescribed pain medication in the meantime.

Mike also made an appointment for me with a chiropractor. I'd never been to one and wasn't even sure what one did. When I looked it up online, the description sounded like massage.

I realized how wrong I'd been at the first appointment. It was more like a wrestling match than medical treatment. I walked out of the treatment room in more pain. I thought I had to keep going because I had been given a schedule of weekly appointments. The chiropractor did his best to help, but after the fourth appointment, the pain was worse than ever. When I got home that day, I stood in the shower and let the hot spray hit my back. Sometimes that would help me relax. It didn't help. I managed to get out of the shower, but I'd only taken a couple of steps when my legs buckled. I fell and lay there, half in the bathroom and half out, trying to figure out how to get up again.

Jeffrey heard me fall. He knew that I was in pain, but he hadn't realized how bad it was until he came into the room and saw me lying on the floor, unable to stand. He called 911.

I was in the hospital for a week while they controlled my pain with morphine, gave me steroids, and prescribed rest. Many people from the church came to see me. I didn't know any of them, but we all knew Jesus, and that was enough. Emma, my English teacher from the library, visited me too. I couldn't speak to Sahar by video. I couldn't let her see me like that. I told her that I was busy or about to go somewhere, anything to keep the conversation by text so that I could hide what was really going on.

Before they agreed to release me, the doctors were concerned that I would be alone. Emma and her husband came to sit with me

229

while Jeffrey was at work. The hospital brought me back to the apartment at a little after nine in the morning. I lay on the floor because it was more comfortable. They sat next to me, kept me company, and made sure that I had what I needed. They left an hour or so before Jeffrey was due to get home. Everything I needed was within reach. I thought I would be fine and so did they.

I closed my eyes and relaxed in the quiet apartment. A wave of nausea hit. I tried to take deep breaths, but my chest felt tight. It felt like my throat was closing. I thought it was an allergic reaction. I couldn't wait for Jeffrey to get back. I called 911 myself. I could hear the operator asking me questions, but I couldn't speak, not even in my own language. The paramedics found me within a few minutes.

The first time I had been admitted into the hospital, the only translator I had was over the phone. Unlike the translator for my emergency room visit, the person couldn't speak Farsi well enough to have a conversation. Translating the medical terminology was beyond him. This time there was one of the medical staff who spoke Farsi. She told me that I had appendicitis and needed immediate surgery. All the pain medication I'd been given had masked the early symptoms.

Between the pain in my back and the pain from the surgery, I was unable to move much at all. They kept me in the hospital, controlling the pain with heavy doses of medication every few hours. The pain was still there, but the drugs made me sleep most of the time.

Even in the state I was in, I knew that I had to keep learning English. The translators they provided were only by phone, and they weren't available all the time. The PhD students Jeffrey had introduced me to weren't always able to visit. I wanted to be able to communicate on a basic level. Jeffrey brought vocabulary books for me. When I was awake enough, I'd study, and write the words and their definitions, committing them to memory as best I could under the circumstances.

Mike and Mary came to see me often in the beginning. When Jeffrey went to class at the library, he let Emma know that I was hospitalized. She began coming with her pastor, Richard. After that I saw

CHAPTER TWENTY-ONE

Mike and Mary less frequently, even though I didn't know why at the time.

For weeks I just lay there, unable to move much, sleeping most of the time, lying to the woman I loved because I couldn't bring myself to tell her that I couldn't even walk. What had I done coming here? With every day that passed, my dignity eroded a little more, leaving me raw and withdrawn from everything. When I looked at myself, I wasn't even a shadow of the man I had been only a few months before. I couldn't do the simplest things the way I wanted, not even bathe or wash my hair. My long hair had always been a part of me, but I wasn't myself anymore, not really. The hair had to go.

The next time Jeffrey came in to see me, I asked him to bring me the clippers.

"Why?" he asked.

I gestured to my head. "It's too hard to take care of here." I couldn't meet his eyes as I said it.

He stroked his own bald head. "I knew eventually you'd try to look as good as me."

We both smiled, but he knew it wasn't fashion or practicality. He did his best to keep my spirits up.

The next time he came to see me, he brought the clippers. I held them in my hand, my finger moving over the smooth surface. I didn't have a choice. I turned it on. This was just another loss. I drew the blades down the middle of my scalp to the crown of my head. Now there was no turning back. I drew the clippers in neat lines as far back as I was able to reach. Jeffrey finished the back of my head, then handed me a mirror. I beheld a stranger, but he was my new reality.

Time passed in a medicated haze. There was nothing more the doctors could do for me, but they didn't think I would be able to manage well enough on my own to be released. After conferences with the doctors and my caseworker, it was decided that I would be sent to a rehabilitation facility until I was able to function without assistance. I could barely move, so I knew I wasn't able to cope on my own, but I wasn't sure what they meant by rehab. I thought it might be another hospital specifically for recovery. The place I was sent to was full of elderly people. I struggled more than some of them. It was a constant reminder that I wasn't getting any better.

I couldn't keep the truth from Sahar any longer, but I couldn't bring myself to tell her the whole story either.

When I texted her, I gave her morsels of truth beginning with the fact that I was in the hospital. I couldn't tell her everything by text. It wasn't fair to her. Holding the phone for as long as it would take to have a conversation by video would be uncomfortable. I gave Jeffrey some of the welcome money provided by the refugee center and asked him to buy me an inexpensive laptop. I couldn't make myself contact her right away, so I lay there staring at the laptop for days until I couldn't put it off any longer.

As soon as she answered, I could see the shock pass over her face.

"What happened to you? Why did you cut your hair?"

I shook my head as much as I dared. "It was too hard to take care of in the hospital. It'll grow back." I tried to sound positive. I didn't manage it.

"You said you had appendicitis. You'd only be in a few days."

"I wasn't in the hospital just because of appendicitis." I opened my mouth and closed it again. "It was back pain too."

She was silent. "I knew it had to be more. I can see the pain on your face and see it in the way you move. How bad is it?"

There were enough doctors in her family that no matter what I told her, she would investigate it. "Not bad," I said. "Just a herniated disc." I wasn't quite able to look into her eyes as I said it.

"But you're all alone there," she noted, and her eyebrows drew together.

"Not really. There are a lot of other Christians who come to visit me every day."

"I wish I was there with you."

There was an incendiary burst behind my eyes. "You wish—whose fault is it that you're not here? How many times did we talk about you coming to Turkey? How many times did we talk about getting married? Even if we'd just been living together, you could have been under my case. We could have come here together. Don't tell me now that you wish you were here. You had plenty of chances to be here. You didn't take any of them." I ended the chat.

I stayed there almost two weeks. They weren't really doing anything for me, just telling me to rest while they tried to manage the pain. I couldn't get around without using a walker. Things that I used to do without thinking had become tasks that required planning and time. There was no reason to stay. I signed myself out against the advice of the doctors.

My caseworker arranged to get a hospital bed sent to my home and have a physical therapist come to see me every day. I'd had physical therapy before for wrestling injuries, but I wasn't sure what they'd be able to do in my home when I could barely move. But it was something other than drugs and rest.

The therapist the hospital sent to me, Lory, was an older woman with a bright smile and a warm manner. The first time she came in, she looked at my books stacked up near the bed and noticed that my Bible was one of the things I had within easy reach.

"You're Christian?" she asked.

"Yes," I said.

She smiled. "Me too."

Lory spent an hour with me each day. She helped me move my limbs when I couldn't, but she also taught me how to do everyday tasks while using a walker. A few new strategies kept me from hurting myself more. Sometimes she filled the space between us with bright conversation. Sometimes she listened while I tried to answer her questions with my limited English. Each day before she left, she prayed with me.

When I was still in the hospital, Richard had come to visit often. After I got out, I began attending his church. At that time his small congregation met in a basement a tenth of the size of Mike and Mary's church. In that way it reminded me of some of the services we'd had in Iran. Usually we'd meet in the host's living room, but we had to make sure we spoke quietly. When we wanted to have music or to do other things that might draw attention, we met in the host's basement.

Mike and Mary had stopped dropping by, but most days members of Richard's church came to visit. I'm certain he suggested that they come and probably even helped them work out a schedule. He may have even suggested what their topics of conversation should be. Whatever the source, the visits always followed a similar pattern.

They brought food, usually only enough for me. In the beginning they would make small talk, but from the hungry curiosity in their eyes, I could see that they were only waiting until they could ask the questions they really wanted the answers to.

They wanted to know about prison. They wanted all the details, every indignity, all the things I had tried so hard to forget. The loss of my health had been difficult enough to take, but now I felt like I was nothing more than the story of the darkest months in my life. Like an animal in a zoo, and the food they brought was the price of admission. All the loss, the time in prison, none of that hurt as much as that realization.

Jeffrey could see how it was affecting me. "You can't take it so seriously," he said to me one evening after the latest group had left. "They're trying to be nice, to show interest. They're just making a mess of it."

If they'd wanted to show interest, they could have asked if there was anything I needed, or if they could do anything to help Sahar come here. They could have even offered to help me improve my English. No one did. Not once.

I just nodded at Jeffrey. He was trying to help. It was not his fault he couldn't.

Sahar was worried about me too. She could see the changes in me. Things that were irritating before now sparked my anger. Whenever we talked, she tried to stick to positive things. She already

CHAPTER TWENTY-ONE

knew English, so when we talked, she helped me learn the language. She would tell me how well I was doing and that I probably knew more than she did because I was learning all the slang terms that she hadn't learned. Like saying the hamster is dead but the wheel is still spinning was a way to say someone isn't so smart.

I know she was trying, but in my heart, I blamed her more than ever. When she would ask how I was, or when I would see that worried look on her face, I knew she could have been with me. Except for her excuses. I was done rationalizing all that. When my anger flared, she listened without arguing. What could she have said? For all the uncertainty and struggle for the past four years, she had chosen not to be here with me.

Chapter Twenty-Two

MY MONTHLY VISITS to the doctor left me frustrated. To be able to lurch along using a walker and brace was a slow and painful process, but to go through all that and receive no help was almost more than I could stand. The appointments always went the same way. I would be told to take the pain medication and rest. Every few months I was given another steroid injection. It felt like this was going to be my life.

Sahar had asked for the CD of the MRI they did while I was in the hospital. My laptop didn't have a CD drive, so I had Dana, one of the PhD students Jeffrey introduced me to, help me convert it into a form I could send. I was sure that now had to be the time for surgery, but my doctor thought otherwise. Maybe with other medical opinions I could convince him.

When Sahar got back to me, five prominent neurosurgeons with worldwide reputations agreed that surgery was the best option.

The next time I went to the doctor, I tried to convey that through the inadequate translator the doctor's office provided. The doctor stood across the room with his arms folded. He was as far away as he could get without being outside the room. He shook his head when I mentioned the other doctors.

His eyes narrowed. "Where are these doctors?"

"Iran," I said.

He shook his head. "You're too young for surgery. We'll schedule another cortisone injection." He didn't wait for my agreement; he left.

CHAPTER TWENTY-TWO

He'd never even examined me. I wondered how many years I would lose before I would be allowed to get my life back.

When I was still able to go to classes at the library, Emma had told us about more opportunities to learn English at the local community college. We'd gone on a tour of the campus, and I'd met with Sharon, an advisor who helped me enroll. To me, it was more than learning English. All my accomplishments in Iran had been erased by the government. My name had been taken off buildings my company designed and built. My accomplishments in wrestling had been expunged. I wanted something that couldn't be taken away. A degree from an American university would be that something.

To qualify for financial aid, I needed to have been in America for six months, but Emma had told all of us that we would have to take a placement test first, and that could be done at any time. Any time became now. It had become too easy to just stay home. I took the bus to the campus. Even with all Lory had taught me, getting around was still slow. I stood at the bus stop and looked up at the building I needed to go to.

I'd have to walk through crowds of students to get there. They'd stare at the brace and the walker and wonder what was wrong with me. Even if I got through all of that, there were the people at the testing center.

What if they asked me what I wanted and I couldn't tell them? What if I tried to tell them and they didn't understand me? What if that upset them and I wouldn't be allowed to come back? I stood there, leaning on my walker as my heart pounded and breath came hard.

I couldn't do it. I couldn't go in.

There were tables outside of a coffee shop across the street. I crossed the street, but when I got there, I was afraid to sit down. I had to go inside and check that it would be alright first. I had been a wrestler, I had fought with machetes in the street, I had looked into the eyes of the men who tortured me. Now the pain, the uncertainty, and the medication had changed me. My confidence and my self-esteem had been replaced with anxiety and timidity.

I didn't go inside that day. I didn't go inside the next time I went either. Each time I would sit in front of the coffee shop and watch the students walking easily between the buildings in the bright autumn sunshine. Some were alone, looking at phones. Others walked in groups, laughing together, deep in animated conversation that made the rest of the world seem unimportant. Where would I fit into all that? I didn't have an answer. If I wanted to learn English, if I wanted to get a degree, I would have to figure it out.

Near the end of November, I decided I couldn't let the pain rule my life. I found my courage and went inside to take the test. My heart was pounding as I walked toward the building. To me, it felt like everyone was staring at me and my back brace and wondering why I was moving so slowly. Sitting in the silent testing center and looking at the test didn't do anything to allay my anxieties.

The test went on for a slice of forever. When the results came back, my breath caught; I was placed into English Level 1. It was the lowest level, but there were people who had been here longer than I had who didn't even get that. I went to find Sharon. She smiled when she saw me, but that smile brought a glow to her whole face when she looked at the results.

"Good for you!" she said and gestured for me to sit. "Let's get you signed up for some classes." She tapped her keyboard and turned the monitor around so that I could see it. "There are two classes that are part of Level 1. One for reading and writing and one for grammar. Right now, there are openings in all of them. What does your schedule look like now?"

I wasn't doing anything, but I still used the bus to get around. An 8 a.m. class would mean I'd have to catch the 7 a.m. bus, and even the smallest delay would make me late. I chose classes starting at 10 a.m. Mondays and Wednesdays.

In the spring semester of 2015, I would be a student again.

CHAPTER TWENTY-TWO

That day, Sharon introduced me to an on-campus group for international students. I attended a few of their social events before their fall semester ended. Everyone welcomed me and I began to feel more comfortable on campus.

The first day of classes was an overcast day in January. There was no snow on the ground, but it was cold enough that another snow wouldn't be far off. I walked with labored steps through unfamiliar halls, searching for the reading class. I wove between students who all seemed to know where they were going and checked the room numbers against the printout of my schedule. Nothing matched up. Panic began to flutter against my ribcage. I could find rooms with numbers that were similar but not the right one.

The students who had filled the halls when I began looking had all walked into their classrooms. The building grew quiet and the edges of the panic sharpened. I gave up and went to Sharon's office in the StarZone.

She smiled when I walked in. "How's your first day going?"

"Not good," I said. "I can't find the class."

Sharon looked at my schedule. "Oh, that room," she said. "It's not where you'd expect. Come on. I'll walk you over."

As we walked, she pointed out other places on campus that I might find useful, like the Learning Commons.

We reached the oddly placed classroom. I saw that the class had already started through the narrow windows next to the closed door. I leaned against the wall. "I'm so late."

Sharon gave me a reassuring smile. "It's the first day. Everyone is trying to figure out schedules and parking and where their classes are. Instructors expect it. If you want, stop in at the end of the day and let me know how it went."

I didn't like the idea of walking into class late. It would have been so easy to just walk away, go back to the coffee shop or even go back home. But I wouldn't learn anything that way. I went in, ready to apologize. The instructor welcomed me and invited me to sit wherever I liked.

She couldn't pronounce my name at first, but that didn't matter. In fact, it was a good thing. There were many articles about me online, posted by Christian groups. Searching my name would have brought up a whole list of results. I didn't want my classmates or instructors to get to know me that way.

When I got home that evening, I emailed those websites where articles about me were posted. I asked politely that they be taken down. Some removed the articles within a few days. Others removed my name and photo.

All I'd wanted was to have a normal life. This would be a fresh start.

I'd only been back to school for a few days when Richard came over to the apartment with his laptop. He often came to visit, but this time it was with an unusual request.

"You know I have a website," he said. "I'd like to write an article about Islam and Christianity. You're the only person I know who has an accurate view of both."

I had written about and posted my opinions online before. The article would be in English on a website that was visited mostly by members of Richard's small congregation. He was a pastor. I trusted that he would know how to maintain my privacy and safety. I spent a few hours using my limited English trying to tell him my experiences, my opinions, and my beliefs supported by verses from the Qur'an and the Bible.

Richard asked questions and prompted me when he needed to; his fingers created a constant, bright tapping on the keys of the laptop.

After we finished, I didn't think much about it. I was in America; I should be able to share my opinions freely.

CHAPTER TWENTY-TWO

I was at school when the article was posted. Jeffrey was a member of Richard's website, so he saw it as soon as it came out. At the time, his English was only a little better than mine, so he had Dana help with the translation.

"Do you know what he wrote?" Jeffrey asked when I got home.

"He asked about Islam and Christianity. I gave him some verses from the Qur'an. Why?" I asked.

"He posted your picture and your name." There was a brittle edge to his voice.

"What?" I couldn't believe Richard would do that to me. "Send me the link."

Jeffrey emailed it. I brought the article up on my laptop.

The first thing I saw was my photo. At the time, my English wasn't good enough to read most of the text, but I saw my name and location. How could he have been so thoughtless? So stupid?

"Do you know how insulting this is?" Jeffrey asked. "The students who helped me when I was homeless are all Muslim."

"It's just what the verses say, isn't it?" I looked at the screen again and tried to discern meaning from the unfamiliar words.

"No. It's a lot more than that."

Having my name and picture out there was bad enough. If there was more, I had to know what it was. Jeffrey couldn't explain it well enough. I called Dana and asked him to come over.

He went through it paragraph by paragraph. The further he went, the harder it was to look at Dana. The verses were right, but the venom injected into the commentary and attributed to me was entirely Richard's creation. The language he had used wasn't meant to inform; it was designed to anger and inflame.

"I haven't known you long, but I never thought you would say those things," Dana said when we got to the end. All I could do was shake my head in disbelief.

"I didn't," I insisted. "I told him about some verses so that he could look them up himself." I pointed at the screen. "Obviously he couldn't get anything else I said right because he couldn't even get

241

my pastor's name right. You think I would insult my friends, my family, by calling them barbarians? He took everything and twisted it."

"He knows his audience," Dana said. "Have you seen how many comments he has on this post?"

"I didn't look at that," I said.

A seemingly endless list scrolled by on the screen. I didn't even try to read them all. The article itself was poisonous enough. The comments must be worse.

"This is more than he usually gets?" I asked, already knowing the answer.

Dana nodded. "A lot more. He's using you to grow his audience."

I handed him my phone. "Will you write a text in English for me? I want to tell him to take it down, and I don't want him to use the excuse that he didn't understand what I was saying."

He composed a text to Richard that made it perfectly clear that I wanted the article taken down immediately. I Skyped Sahar after Dana left. She was always searching online for anything about me. I knew she would find the article and I wanted a chance to explain. I sent her the link.

I watched on Skype while she read. I could see the surprise on her face when she saw my photo and then watched her cover her mouth as the shock deepened. When she reached the end, she shook her head, then looked up at the camera again.

She looked at me as if I was a stranger. Seeing that expression on her face was more painful than Richard's betrayal.

"I don't know what's happened to you, but you've changed," she said. "The man I knew would never have said those things."

"I promise you; I had no idea how he was going to use what I gave him. I've already told him to take it down."

"What difference is that going to make? It's out there. Anyone could have shared it or copied it or reposted it to their own site. Did you even think about how this would affect me? My family could be in danger. I could be in danger. Did that even cross your mind before you gave your interview?"

CHAPTER TWENTY-TWO

"I just wanted to share, like I always have," I said and kept my voice deliberately calm.

"That's just my point. Why can't you just stop all this? Why can't we just live a normal life like everyone else?"

"You know I want that too. I've decided I'm not going to go to his church or any other from now on. I'll get him to take the article down. It's the best I can do."

She took a deep breath and studied me before she shook her head and looked away. "I need some time to think. Just give me a few days." She ended the chat.

The silence that followed was fathomless, and I was drowning in it. I grabbed my phone and called Richard again.

All my calls went to his voice mail. It took until the next day for him to get back to me, and then it was a text.

I'm out of town right now and I don't have internet access.

Where could he be that there was no Internet access? There was no coffee shop with Wi-Fi? There was no library that would let him use a computer for a few minutes? Obviously, he could still use his phone. If he was truly so isolated, he could have called someone to take the article down for him. I believe he was consulting with others about what to do. The article was clearly garnering him a lot of attention.

The article had only been posted for two days when the repercussions began. The small community of students and others I'd met through Jeffrey disappeared. I knew I had offended all of them and I didn't blame them for being upset. For them it wasn't just an insult. That might be forgiven. They all had families in Iran and still went home to visit. Being associated with me could bring them under the scrutiny of the government and all the consequences that would come along with that.

Then I got a phone call from a man who threatened my life. In the article, Richard had used my name, my location, and my photo. It had been easy to find me.

I deactivated all my social media accounts. Then I called Richard again. Once he heard about the threat, he was at my house within three hours.

"Someone threatened you?" he asked.

"Of course they did. I converted other Muslims to Christianity. I told you what the verses said. You published my name, my address—what did you expect would happen? Anyone could find me. Sahar is afraid. Anything could happen to her or her family in Iran. You have to take it down before something worse happens."

He looked down at his hands. "It's a popular piece. Seems like everyone is interested in what you have to say."

"I'm not the one who said it, you did," I insisted. "If it destroys my life, if it gets someone killed, that's alright as long as it's popular?"

He hesitated. "Of course not, I'll take care of it," he said and laughed a little. "Though, if you had been killed, just think how far the story would spread." He might have been trying to make a joke to ease my mind, but there was a greedy truth in the words.

As long as he got what he wanted, it wouldn't matter who got hurt.

He didn't take down the article, but he did remove my photo, my name, and anything else that could identify me, referring to me only as "my friend." It made me wonder why he chose that phrase. We were both Christian. He should have referred to me as "my brother." It showed me where I stood in his eyes.

I couldn't stand the silence with Sahar. One of the things we often used on the phone app were the bear and bunny emojis. After a few days, I drew a picture using them, took a photo, and sent it to her. She responded with a laugh, and we began to talk again. After the changes in the article, I knew she still wasn't comfortable, but we were able to communicate about practical things.

Chapter Twenty-Three

AFTER MONTHS OF steroids, therapy, and a lot of rest, I was able to limp along without aid. I couldn't sit for more than thirty minutes at a stretch, so I would spend some of the class time lying on the floor. My instructors never told me not to. They just helped me learn. They treated the work I turned in as if it were important to them, using it to show me not only what I did wrong, but how I could improve.

Their support became one of the few constants in my life.

Near the end of that first semester, other pastors began to call and message that they wanted to see me. I agreed, but I didn't know what to expect. They might have wanted to write about me like Richard had, or they might have wanted to treat my life like an evening's entertainment. Those who came didn't want either. They asked how I was and if I needed anything. I think they knew what Richard had done and were trying to show that they weren't all like that.

―――∞―――

The summer semester at the community college was only half as long as the spring and fall semesters, but it covered the same amount of material. The heavier workload meant that there were far fewer students on campus in the summer. I didn't want to have a three-month gap between my studies, so I took a Level 2 English course in the summer.

I'd been in America for almost a year when the semester started that June. I was still in pain and using medication that robbed me of my focus. Getting to and from campus was still a challenge, and the buses didn't run as often in the summer. I began to arrive early in the morning and stay in the library until it closed late in the evening.

The campus, which had been a hive of activity only a few weeks before, was quiet. The library felt especially empty during the summer semester. Most students who were still taking classes preferred to access resources online. That meant that I had those sprawling silent spaces mostly to myself. I could sit in the bright sunshine flooding in through one of the tall windows while I studied. I could nap in one of the private study rooms or behind one of the long shelves whenever I needed to. The librarians were always happy to see me, always ready to help when I needed it. The college I had been so anxious about entering became one of the places I always felt welcome.

Sahar was working toward getting into MSU. She sent me her resume to show to Dana. He and I had become roommates soon after Richard's article was posted. At the time he was working toward his second PhD in computer science. We both knew he'd be able to offer good advice. And we needed that.

Sahar and I had been apart for so long, longer than we'd spent together. She was the one person I had left, and I needed to have her with me. I was still in contact with Behram and Samad and the others, but that wasn't the same. Sahar was my wife and had been since that evening in the garden when we made our promises to each other, but I wanted to marry as everyone else did. I wanted to have a home and children. I wanted to live without hiding or running or the constant threat of discovery. She was the key to the normal life I'd wanted for so long.

I thought she wanted the same things.

Each time Sahar and I talked, it seemed like there was some further development in her plan. She talked not only about the programs she was interested in, but also about the areas where schools were located, and opinions expressed by people who were students there. As far as I knew, Sahar didn't know anyone in America. Dana suggested

CHAPTER TWENTY-THREE

to me that she might have joined student groups on Facebook or other social networking sites. I didn't question it at the time. Sahar always researched things that interested her. In the middle of a conversation she would stop and search online for information if a topic made her curious. I told myself that these new connections were just a part of her penchant for thorough research.

It was a humid day in August, and we'd been talking for a while when she said, "When I get there, we should just live together for a while."

It wasn't a question; it was a statement. An odd one too, coming after talking of states and schools. I wasn't sure I had really heard her correctly. I stared at the screen.

"What do you mean? We both promised and God was our witness. We're already married in the ways that matter."

"Right, so why should we rush to marry in the eyes of the law when that doesn't matter?"

There was a cold practicality in her words. "You want me to help you come here. You want to use my friends to help you, and then when you get here, you just want to leave whenever you want?"

I ended the call. If I'd waited for her to respond, I knew I would have said something insulting in return.

How could she even make that suggestion? We'd already lived together because, in Iran, we didn't have any other choice. Now, after all the sacrifices I'd made, she didn't want to change that. I couldn't understand. I texted her and told her I needed some time.

The silence between us lasted a day; then we began to talk again. There was no discussion of living together, no apologies or explanations—we just moved on as if nothing had happened. The question lay buried under a shallow layer of small talk and sketched plans of the future.

The medication, disability, and isolation had changed me. There were changes in her too. All those conversations we had, all those plans we were making, there used to be such certainty in her voice. She used to look at the screen and meet my eyes and talk as if she could see our future before her. Now, there was an air of "wait and see" that hovered around all those plans. As if tomorrow might change everything. Meanwhile, we still talked, still planned, smiled, and laughed about the ordinary things. As if this chasm between us were normal.

I missed the Sahar I knew before.

Then, a month later, everything did change.

The conversation had been no different than a thousand others. She told me she had narrowed down her school choices and that she was planning to meet some friends for coffee soon. It was almost as warm and pleasant as things used to be. When we said goodbye, I wanted that closeness I was feeling to continue. I remembered reading that the app we used had the ability to give GPS coordinates for a phone if the person had their location enabled. I'd thought it was interesting at the time, but I'd never used it. After tapping several menus, I found the location of Sahar's phone. She'd told me she was at home, in the north, but the location was clearly in Tehran. The background of our chat was nondescript enough that she could have been anywhere.

I stared at the screen and considered what that meant. For months there had been things in our conversations that hadn't seemed to fit. They were little things that were so easy to ignore and rationalize at the time, but now they all came back. There was the carefully curated view she showed me on video chat and the practiced answers she had to explain differences I noticed in her location. There were the questions she didn't quite answer and the questions she avoided altogether. There were all those excuses when I was in Turkey and then this idea of just living together in America. I had ignored so many things. I couldn't ignore this.

I didn't care where she was. I'd never tried to tell her where she could or couldn't go. I had never tried to monitor where she was or what she was doing. The location wasn't important. The lie was.

I texted her. *Where did you say you were?* Part of me hoped that I had just misunderstood the app, or that the location was off, or anything that made it all make sense.

Home, she texted back.

What are you doing? I typed.

Nothing, just reading.

I'd given her every opportunity, but she wasn't going to tell me the truth. *You're not at home.*

I stared at the screen, watching for the message to arrive. The ten minutes it took seemed like forever.

What do you mean? In those four written words, I could feel the caution in her voice.

You're in Tehran. I sent a video chat request.

She refused the request. She was not at home. *What makes you think I'm in Tehran?*

You know the app we use to video chat? The one you wanted me to download? It lets me see the GPS location of your phone, I texted. Sahar researched everything she did. She would have known all the features of the app, including how to disable them if she wanted to. I sent another request.

She ignored it. *You were checking up on me?*

I missed you. All you had to do was tell me the truth.

You believe GPS on some stupid app before you believe me?

This isn't a matter of a few blocks, Sahar. We both know that you don't go to Tehran without a reason. What could you be doing that you can't tell me about?

It took over an hour for her to answer the chat request. When her image appeared on the screen, there was a blank wall behind her.

"I was telling you the truth," she said. "You just misunderstood." There were cracks in the edges of her calm. Her face flushed red.

"Prove it. Show me the view."

She hesitated, then moved over to the window. Sunlight danced along the familiar rooflines of the city.

I couldn't ignore this or rationalize it away. "You don't think I recognize the city I lived in for years?"

She looked like she was about to start crying, but she was trying so hard to keep it together. "We moved. I just didn't have a chance to tell you yet." The artificial calm that permeated her voice was calculated to make the words sound honest and reasonable. For me, knowing her so well, it had the opposite effect.

"You're lying. I don't know why you're lying, but I know you are, and you won't even admit it." I felt sick to my stomach. I ended the chat and blocked her, but the lie loomed over me. I couldn't stay in that room any longer. I went for a walk around the quiet complex. I couldn't move fast enough to get away from the memories and questions that were tangled up in my head. When had she started lying? Had anything she'd said to me been real?

In the weeks that followed I went through the motions of my life as if I were sleepwalking. I sat in class and let the instructor's words wash over me. I went to the library and stared at the computer. I opened my books to study, and the letters tied themselves in knots in front of me. I deleted dozens of overwrought messages from Sahar without opening them. There was nothing she could say that I hadn't already heard a thousand times.

We had been so happy in the beginning. The situation wasn't what we had wanted, but there wasn't conflict, argument, and doubt. The distance between us had created all those things. I was the one who had borne the weight of that distance since the beginning. I had left my business, my friends, and my city. Each of those things created a jagged edge that began to fray the ties that bound Sahar and me together. I had left my country with little more than the clothes I wore. She gave me empty promises.

I left the community in Turkey. I gave up more friends and new opportunities to come to America. She gave me obvious lies. Maybe she found my current silence painful, but I wanted her to have some sense of what I had been going through during those years while she had been comfortable at home with her family, pursuing the education she wanted.

CHAPTER TWENTY-THREE

I didn't respond to anything she sent for several weeks. At the end of October, the messages stopped coming. Maybe she was finally beginning to think about why she'd lied in the first place. That silence between us lengthened and deepened, but it did nothing to change how I felt about her. She was my wife and I wanted her with me. I texted and asked how her applications were going.

She didn't respond.

I could wait. She'd come around eventually.

My birthday came and went at the end of November, but Sahar didn't contact me. No text had arrived when I was distracted, no voice mail when I stepped away. By eight in the evening, five in the morning in Tehran, I couldn't deny it any longer. She wasn't going to call. No matter how angry either of us was, she wouldn't have let a special day pass in cold silence. Not if she was still my wife.

The frayed threads between us snapped one by one; the pain of each one crested and ebbed to be followed by another. Everything was gone. I could have found a way to begin again as long as I had her. But now, what did I have? My pain? My losses? My disability? Everything good, everything solid, everything I had held onto for the months in prison, the years I'd spent exiled from my home, everything was gone.

The air left my body, and all my strength went with it. Just standing was too much. I sank down into the corner next to my bed, my knees drawn up to my chest. It was an effort just to breathe. She was gone and I was completely alone.

My life stopped.

I didn't sleep.

I didn't eat.

I didn't speak. Not with anyone here, not with anyone one in Iran. What could I say? The woman I'd called my wife, the woman I'd lived with and made plans with, the one who'd been there at the inception of the group that had been central to my life for so long didn't want to be my wife anymore. It was too humiliating.

Memories of her were everywhere, and every one dug in and drew blood.

When I felt anything, it was anger. It suffused every muscle of my body. Not anger at her. I was angry at God. He had put her into my path at a time when I hadn't known I needed her. Now he'd taken her from me when I needed her the most.

Dana did his best. He'd knock on my door and tell me that there was coffee in the kitchen or that he'd left me some dinner. He didn't ask what was wrong; he just tried to be a bridge back to the world.

I spent weeks in that room, enmeshed in that loss. What was I now? What would my life be? What could it be? Those four walls became my world. Even sleep was no escape because I didn't sleep. Powerful sleeping pills only gave me a few hours of oblivion.

The classes I had enrolled in were still in session, but I didn't go. My instructor had always been so supportive, so I felt I owed her something. I forced myself to write an email, telling my instructor that I'd had some problems in the last few weeks. I couldn't be specific. If I had to repeat the class, so be it. I hit "send."

Her generosity surprised me.

I'm sorry to hear you're having such a difficult time. Just turn in your final paper, she wrote back. *You had most of the work done, and the paper is the only major part of your grade that's missing. As long as you email it to me by the due date, it'll be like you turned it in with the rest of the class.*

She'd given me an opportunity. Despite the fatigue, despite the hours of emptiness, despite the bouts of rage, I didn't want to waste that.

I had the bones of the paper already written. I could only focus for a few minutes at a time. I made slow progress, but it would never be good enough to turn in unless I got some help. I couldn't get that sitting alone in my room. I left the house for the first time in weeks.

CHAPTER TWENTY-THREE

—⚭—

I had been to the Learning Commons a couple of times, but I never felt comfortable there. The large space was designed to be collaborative and multifunctional. Students could meet and study or just socialize with friends. They could get the help of a tutor or relax in the sunshine in front of the floor-to-ceiling windows. For me, the noise and constant motion made it almost impossible to work there.

The last thing I wanted was to be anywhere near people. Exhaustion only made my anxiety worse, and the ever-present pain throbbed below all of it. I thought everyone was looking at my back brace, that they were too loud and standing too close. I reminded myself that I had to finish the paper.

I had met with a tutor once before, but she wasn't available this time. Someone at the front desk made an appointment for me with Michelle. She was an older lady with a welcoming smile that, for just a heartbeat, made me think she was glad to see me. She tried to put me at ease while she read my paper, but we were sitting at one of the tables in the middle of the common area. People were coming and going all around us, and each time someone passed too close, I'd flinch.

Michelle saw what I needed. "You know, it's really busy here today. Why don't I see if one of the group study rooms is available?"

We continued our meeting in the quiet of one of the three glass-fronted cubicles. I'd chosen a topic that I knew well, Islam and Christianity. I was questioning both. I'd included verses from the Bible, and Michelle knew them. She was able to talk about the verses, but she was repeating what she'd been taught. To make matters worse, she tried to change my words. I thought she was trying to change my opinion to bring it more in line with what she had learned about Christianity. I needed help with my grammar, but this felt like changing the essence of the paper. It was as if she were telling me that just because she had been born into Christianity, she must know more than I did. I didn't want to meet with her again.

I went back to my room again and stayed there until my next appointment.

It was the last week of the semester, and anxious students were clustered around the front desk when I arrived in the Learning Commons. While I waited, Michelle came out and welcomed me.

I could have told her that I wanted to meet with someone else, but I couldn't make myself say it when she looked so glad to see me. She already had the room reserved, so we walked back and began to work again. This time, I was determined to get her to listen to me. One of the verses in my paper was John 1:1, the one that had drawn me to the Gospel of John. I began to explain the meaning of the "word" the verse mentions was not as a word, but as the breath that gave Adam life. As I talked, I watched Michelle sit back in the chair and really listen to me. When I fell silent, she leaned forward a little.

"Tell me more," she said.

She listened and helped me put my ideas into the right words that expressed what I wanted to say.

When I left the Learning Commons that day, I felt better about the paper. But I still didn't want to see anyone. I went home again and stayed there.

In those isolated days, my diary was my constant companion. I'd written and drawn my thoughts and ideas since I was a child, but now that small brown book became the only place that I could put words to my anger without fear of judgment. Not my anger at Sahar, but my anger at the one who had truly deceived me—God.

God was the one who brought us together all those years ago when everything was just beginning. He had witnessed our promise to each other in the place where so many lives had begun again. How could God bring us together like that, keep us together for so many years, through prison, the time in Turkey, and now, when I had nothing else but her, he took her away? Was He that jealous? How could I think of myself as free if I were subject to the whims of a possessive

CHAPTER TWENTY-THREE

and greedy God?

My pen tore into the creamy paper. The angry questions impressed deep enough to scar several pages at a time. This was another prison. Not as silent, not as dark, but I was completely alone. Completely empty. I began to draw those feelings onto scraps of paper. Then I refined them, transferred them to the diary. The only one I could trust with all my secrets was the trash can. It devoured my imperfectly rendered images of isolation and pain. It accepted my anger and loss without flinching or judgment.

Dana knew I was struggling, but it was too humiliating to tell him why. He never pushed the point. He just tried to be there for me as best he could as he had before.

My phone was set to silent, and I ignored all messages. I felt like I was living with a second-degree burn. Everything was too much to bear. Even if I did answer, what would I say? How could I tell Behram or any of the others that Sahar had left me? They'd watched us grow close. They'd been there the night we made our promise. They'd commemorated the event when they turned the garden into a wedding venue. How could I admit to them that it was over? How could I say that my wife didn't want me anymore?

Chapter Twenty-Four

I HADN'T REALIZED how much I had lost until I'd come to America. Maybe I didn't have time to think about it before, but now I struggled under the weight of the emptiness. On Christmas day, the loneliness reached an unbearable peak. I needed to talk to someone, someone who knew me. Who did I have? No family. No childhood friends.

Even though I usually waited for others to contact me, I sent Ali a video chat request.

He answered immediately. I caught a glimpse of the wide-open space of the empty warehouse where he conducted business. A few members of his gang were there with him. There was an air of tension around them.

Ali turned his phone so that they couldn't see my image. "What's going on?" he asked.

I'd always prided myself on my strength, but strength wasn't working anymore. "I'm upset. I need to talk."

He looked past the screen. "Out," he said to the others. I could hear them shuffle away. Once they were gone, he looked back to the screen. "Now, what's going on?"

I shrugged. "I'm alone."

"Alone? Man, you're an army."

"Maybe I was, but not here. Nothing's what I thought it would be." I told him about my loss of mobility, my frustration about doctors who wouldn't listen and didn't try to help. I couldn't bring myself to tell him anything else.

CHAPTER TWENTY-FOUR

He listened without interrupting and then fell silent. "And losing someone isn't easy."

I nodded. I don't know how he found out, but it didn't surprise me that he knew.

"So how can I help? Money? Help with getting started in business?"

"No. I don't need money and it's not the right time to start a business. I'm still learning how things work here."

"Then what can I do?"

"Just listen," I said.

And he did listen. When I stopped talking, he started. He reminded me of those days we had spent on his plain. Hearing about the sheep got me thinking again about Christianity and the Good Shepherd. That time seemed wasted now.

"Hey, did I tell you what happened to Nazy?" Ali asked me. Nazy was his favorite donkey. Ali and I were the only two people who'd been able to ride her. Just the mention of the donkey's name brought back memories of the plain, the sheep and the secrets whispered by the wind.

"No, what happened?" I asked, finally able to smile at something. He told me, and it felt good to be lost in conversation.

By the time we said goodbye, we were both laughing. I turned away from the computer and looked around at my empty room.

The quiet pressed in tighter than it had before. I was a long way from home. A long way from everything.

A new semester was set to begin. I didn't want to be around people, but not going back to school wasn't an option. I wanted to speak English as smoothly as Farsi. Dana was always encouraging me, as was our other friend Majid, who explained math in Farsi and then translated it to English.

When it was time to go back to school, I had looked forward to my writing class. Even though I had only completed Level 3, my

BECOMING JOSHUA

instructor had so much confidence in me that she signed for me to begin taking academic classes as well. I chose Psychology and American History.

A week or two after the semester started, I went back to the Learning Commons. I had been progressing through my English classes, but I didn't have anyone to consistently practice speaking and listening with. I began to spend more time with Michelle. Sometimes I brought paragraphs with me, but much of the time it was just conversation. Michelle would let me talk about whatever I wanted to talk about and correct me when it was necessary. I needed that. Immersion was the only way I was going to improve.

As the weeks passed, I found myself building a rapport with Michelle. We talked about what I was working on for the class, but often we talked about the Bible. In many ways we were teaching each other, and I enjoyed it. Michelle and I met often, not just in the Learning Commons, but other places on campus as well. After several weeks, Michelle asked if I would like to meet her husband. She talked about him most times we met, and since she and I were spending so much time together, I agreed.

We planned to meet a few days later. I was looking forward to it. I left campus with Michelle that evening, and we went out for pizza. I still wouldn't go to a restaurant alone, but now I wasn't alone. Cameron came directly from work, so Michelle introduced me to him in the parking lot. Right away I felt at ease with him. I was glad the restaurant wasn't crowded that evening. At the time, I had very few opportunities to practice my English outside of school. Being able to focus on the two of them made it easier to have a conversation.

The waitress left us with menus.

"What do you like on your pizza?" Michelle asked after a bit.

"Whatever Cameron wants," I said. "Maybe something with chicken."

He ordered a pizza with chicken and vegetables, then turned to me. "Michelle has told me a little about you. Has she told you anything about me?"

CHAPTER TWENTY-FOUR

"No, nothing."

"I work at MSU now, but I produce podcasts too," he began.

Cameron's English sounded different from Michelle's. I had to listen closely to understand him, and there were times when he didn't understand me at all. Michelle was more accustomed to how I spoke by then, so she became the interpreter for both of us.

"Tell me about yourself?" he asked.

I wasn't sure where to start. "I came here a couple of years ago with a few clothes and about twenty dollars."

"Oh," he said. "Well, when I came here, I didn't have any money, I couldn't speak the language, and I was naked. Thirty seconds after coming to this country, I was yanked upside down and smacked on the butt."

I could see the humor sparkling in his eyes. I laughed.

When dinner arrived, we talked a little more about Christianity. I learned that Cameron's views were less religious than Michelle's. He liked to listen, read, and make his own decisions based on his own understanding.

The more we talked, the more I enjoyed his company.

Michelle gave me a ride back home that evening. Unlike some meals I'd shared with others, I didn't feel like I was simply there to talk about myself. They shared as much as I did.

The three of us began to meet often. We'd go out for coffee, to the movies, to lunch or dinner. The more time I spent with them, the more confident I was becoming among other English-speaking people. They also always respected my privacy. Instead of asking about my past, they asked what movie I wanted to see or where I wanted to eat. They let me feel more comfortable with the myriad of daily interactions many take for granted, like choosing and ordering food in a restaurant. Even though I had been here for a little more than a year and a half at that point, Michelle and Cameron helped me adjust to life in America without expecting anything in return. As time went on, I began to tell them a little more about myself. Not because they asked me to, but because I trusted them. And they saw me. They saw the most important pain I carried, the loss of my family.

The other connections I had ignored for so many months made a reappearance in my life. I received a text from Cyrus. Just as I rarely called others, Cyrus almost never contacted anyone, and he rarely responded when anyone contacted him. *How is the weather in Michigan?*

We'd been through so much; I couldn't disrespect him by not answering. *It's alright. How is Florida?*

It's good. Do you have time to talk?

I agreed and sent him a video chat request. We started with the relatively safe topic of the overcast skies of Michigan and the sunshine and warmth of Florida until we exhausted the topic. He paused. "Are you alright?" he asked. "No one has heard from you in months. You haven't been responding to messages. Everyone is worried."

I searched for something to say. "Life in America is different. I've been busy with school and trying to learn English. My back has gotten worse. My doctor doesn't seem to want to help me, not really. They just give me pain medication. I don't have a community anymore." I began to pour out every loss, every pain since I arrived in America. I couldn't bring myself to tell him about the loss of Sahar. From the way he looked at me, I could tell I didn't have to.

Cyrus was silent, his eyes fixed on mine. "You've been through a lot, but you should be thankful. Even if you don't have her, you know she's all right."

He was right. Sahar could have been arrested and gone through the same trauma that his wife Deborah had. She may not have been with me, but she was safe. I flushed with embarrassment.

"Cyrus—"

"Coming to America is a big change," he said. "You have to find a balance. The others can't be the center of your life anymore, but you can't just cut everyone off."

After we hung up, I thought about what Cyrus had said, and about what it had taken for him to reach out and say it. Even if he never responded, he was still reading at least some of the messages. He was

CHAPTER TWENTY-FOUR

right. I couldn't just abandon everyone.

A couple of days later, Cyrus texted that Deborah was home.

I hadn't talked to Deborah in years. So, I called.

"Cyrus told me about Sahar," she said after a few minutes of catching up.

I didn't know what to say. She didn't wait for an answer.

"You have to move forward. Find someone else, but don't choose someone religious. If you do, you'll make yourself into a slave to religion all over again. You already broke with tradition by living with Sahar. You promised before God and lived up to that promise, even when the two of you were apart for all those years. Find someone who understands the value of a promise and live together. Have children and let them choose for themselves what way they want to follow. Do what you taught all of us to do."

"What I taught you?" I asked.

"How long has it been since you've been in Iran?" she asked.

"Six or seven years," I said.

"And yet they all look to you. Haven't you ever thought about why?"

I was silent searching for something to say. "Well—"

"They look to you because you're the one who showed them the true God. If you had only brought them religion, why would they need you? They would know the religious view and that would be all they need. Is it in the book, yes or no. You always wanted them to think deeply about who Jesus is and then trusted them to do it. That's why they love you. That's why they want you to be involved, no matter how long you've been away."

I had never thought of it in that way before.

"Now. How long has it been since you've seen the children?" she asked.

That was a question I could answer. "Too long," I said and sent a video chat request.

On March 20th, Michelle accompanied me to the Nowruz celebrations at MSU. We arrived in the parking lot at the same time as Dana and Majid, so we all went in together.

Bright, rhythmic music wove with the murmur of people gathering, and the scent of saffron from the buffet mingled with perfume of spring flowers placed around the room. The sound of laughter and conversation surrounded us. I wanted to show Michelle the haft-sin display, so we made our way to the tables covered in white cloths and adorned with hyacinths and daffodils. Bright orange goldfish swam in a round bowl in front of a mirror while dishes of colored eggs, garlic, sprouted grass, coins, a sweet wheat germ pudding called samanu, sumac berries, the dried fruit of the oleaster tree, and other representations of spring and renewal were arrayed among glowing candles.

"This is beautiful," Michelle said, drawn to the fish dancing with their reflections in the mirror. "So, are each of the objects traditional or are they chosen more by the taste of the person setting up the display?"

"Both," I said. "Some people add things that have meaning for them, but some go back thousands of years. Like the fish. They represent life without limits."

"The eggs represent fertility," Majid said.

"The candles are energy or creativity," Dana added.

Others contributed their perspective as well, eager to share their own take on tradition with someone eager to learn. The welcome that had been extended to all of us didn't last though. People began to look at me. Those who had been friendly turned away and went to talk to others, and there were looks thrown in my direction. It was a small community. They had all heard about the article, if not read it.

Dana and Majid looked at each other. "We should get a table," Majid said.

We sat near the dance floor at a table decorated with fruit and flowers. I was reminded of the wedding where I met Farhan for the first time. That seemed like a lifetime ago. Now there was an undercurrent of tension in the air. I couldn't hear what was being said, but

CHAPTER TWENTY-FOUR

sometimes I would catch someone looking in my direction. As soon as I met their eyes, they looked away.

"Ignore it," Dana said. "They just like having something to talk about."

Maybe he was right, but that article had left a trail of destruction through my life.

The looks were bad enough, but when we went through the buffet line, I could hear what people were saying. They were speaking in Farsi, so Michelle didn't understand. I did. I tried to focus on her and the questions she was asking about the food. There are no dishes that are served exclusively on Nowruz, but Michelle was eager to try a bit of everything. I filled my own plate while people around us made a point not to look at me.

"These events should really be for MSU students only," the woman behind me said pointedly.

"Or we should at least have more control over who gets in," her friend replied.

I knew they were referring to me. We got our meal and went back to the table. A few minutes later they turned up the music. I was grateful. I wouldn't have to listen to what they were saying.

———∞———

The fact that Michelle and Cameron had never asked about my past made it easier for me to choose what I wanted to share with them. One weekend, we were sitting in my living room and I decided to tell them how I converted to Christianity.

"I would draw the cross all the time when I was little. I didn't know why, but it was the first tattoo I got when I was still a teenager. After that I didn't really think about any religion until I met someone who gave me a copy of the Bible. I spent the day reading it. That night, when I went to bed, I had a dream." I didn't want to give any more details about the wedding or Farhan. That wasn't necessary. The dream wasn't something I could hold back. From the beginning it was something meant to be shared with others.

There was growing wonder around them when I told them about the colors and the sword. Their eyes widened when I described how the blade sliced so easily through my throat, and the lack of fear that accompanied the rush of blood that followed. I shared the moment of healing and the sensation of the bread in my mouth.

Cameron was the first to speak. "When he changed your blood, he changed you. That means you have authority."

Authority? I wasn't sure how to respond to such a declaration. No one did. At last Michelle spoke.

"So, what did you do then?" she asked.

"I went to a house church for a while and then I had a house church of my own for a while." Not the whole truth, but it was enough.

"Do you still have a connection with those people?" Cameron asked.

I was silent for a moment. "Not for a while because of a lot of different things, but, yes."

"I thought you did," Michelle said. "So how does that work? Is it just a service in the pastor's home?"

"We don't have pastors. Everyone is a leader, and they're trusted to define their own way of being a leader. Different people share the message every week and then everyone discusses what they heard and how they understood it. Then if anyone has a problem or a need, anything from needing a job to a spiritual question, they can talk about it after that the meeting and the group does their best to help. If money is contributed, it stays within the group, and they choose how to spend it. Because it's held in someone's home, there is no cost to maintain the building, and there is no pastor to pay."

From the looks on their faces, I could tell that the idea appealed to them. After that, I felt as if I could share more about my life.

Chapter Twenty-Five

I HAD TOLD Cyrus I would get back in touch with the others, but I hadn't done it. It was time to make good on my promise.

I texted Behram. *How are things going?*

How are you? We were worried. We need you.

I stared at the text. They needed me? What could they need me for? Our group wasn't supposed to have a central leadership. Things should have been going on as usual with or without me or any of the other leaders. It upset me to think that they had been so anxious to get back in touch, not out of concern for me, but because they wanted something from me. We set a meeting for the next day; then I did my best to ignore what was coming.

The next day, twenty people were gathered in Samad's spacious living room. Some were sitting on the sofas; others were on the floor so that they could be seen. It didn't take long for the greetings to end and the arguments to start. I lay there and listened to a debate about two of the leaders who wanted to use their knowledge of visual media to reach out to East Asia. The others disagreed. They thought splitting the group in two would draw too much attention from the government.

This was the problem they needed me to solve?

I listened to them for as long as I could. Then I had to say something.

"You're all leaders. You have to do what you think is right. Set up house churches and share the message, but don't share the internal structure of what we do."

The two agreed and the meeting began to wrap up. People had begun to relax, and I could see that some were relieved to have the topic closed. Quiet conversations started.

"Thank you," Samad said to me. "We've been talking about this for weeks and we haven't gotten anywhere. I know you're getting accustomed to life in America, but you can't just disappear like that." He was smiling and I could hear the humor in his voice, but it upset me. They didn't miss me. They wanted me to solve their problems.

"I am getting settled," I said. "And my wife left me." The words came out in a rush.

Silence fell and people who had looked away were facing the camera again.

"We should pray," someone at the back said.

"What do you want to pray for? Did I ask you for prayer?"

I could see the shock on their faces. They didn't understand. They couldn't help.

Such deeply emotional topics were almost never addressed. I wasn't surprised when Samad changed the subject. "So, what is life in America like?"

I started by telling them about school and learning English. It was all surface, but it was a topic that kept everyone comfortable.

―∞―

As that semester progressed, I still struggled with the physical pain. Dana made sure that I got to my doctor's appointments and helped with translation. Michelle and Cameron knew I was in pain, but they also knew I was seeing a doctor. I'm sure they thought I was getting good care. I was convinced otherwise. I had been an athlete since I was a child and I could barely walk. I still had to lie on the floor halfway through class. I hadn't been able to go to the gym in years. I didn't know if I'd ever be able to go again.

Everything I had been was slipping away.

Maybe I could have coped with the physical symptoms, but I was

CHAPTER TWENTY-FIVE

alone. I had no community around me, not after the article. No truly close friends, and no wife. Everything that my life was tethered to was gone. The medication only intensified that unmoored feeling, and the sea around me was vast. I retreated to my room again. For a week I didn't see or speak to anyone, not even Michelle or Cameron.

They showed up at my apartment and sat next to my door for hours. It made me angry, knowing that they were out there, just waiting. Then I thought more about it. They cared. Even if everyone else had forgotten about me, they hadn't.

I went back to the hospital again for a week that June because I couldn't move. The last time I'd been hospitalized, I'd had many visitors from Richard's church, but they were all strangers to me. While I appreciated that they took time to visit me, it wasn't always comfortable to be surrounded by them. This time, Dana, Majid, Michelle, and Cameron were my only visitors. They came in at different times during the day and spent evenings with me. I was still in pain, but I was much more comfortable being with people who were there because they cared about me.

Majid told me that Cameron even stayed with me one day while I slept. I'm sure he was surprised. So was I, but it reinforced the idea that he and Michelle cared about me in ways I could never have expected.

Cameron and Michelle didn't ask why I was in so much pain, but they were concerned about whether I was getting the right treatment. I was working on my classes online, and Michelle had come over to help if she could.

"How many doctors have you seen?" Michelle asked during a break in our classwork.

"Only one," I said.

"And there's no surgery they can do or anything?" Her brow was creased.

"There is, but he says I'm too young and he won't do it."

"Have you thought about getting a second opinion?" she asked.

"I'm not sure how to find someone else. Besides, wouldn't this doctor have referred me to someone else if he couldn't help me?" In Iran, that's how it would have happened.

"Not necessarily. I hate to see you in so much pain. Would it be alright if I found someone for you?" she asked.

"Of course," I said.

"Do you have a diagnosis? I need to be able to tell the doctor's office something when I make the appointment."

"I'll get my records together and bring them to you," I said.

I gathered a stack of paperwork several inches thick from hospitalizations, doctor's visits, and tests and brought it all to Michelle. She made an appointment for me with a doctor at the University of Michigan. I had to wait more than a month, and there was no guarantee I'd hear anything different, but after so much frustration I had to at least try.

Cameron and Michelle had both been deeply involved with the church for many years, but now they attended the small church in their hometown. If they were comfortable there, I thought I might be too. I called and asked if I could go with them the next Sunday. They were happy to have me come along. I walked in just before the service began. I had planned to leave just before the end, but then I saw a familiar face among the congregation. The name escaped me, but she recognized me and came over to where I was sitting.

"I thought that was you! It's good to see you again."

"Lory," I greeted the physical therapist who had helped me so much in the beginning. "It's good seeing you too."

I felt more at ease when I saw Lory. I felt like I belonged when I heard Pastor Mike speak. In all the other churches I had been to, the pastor seemed like no more than a storytelling showman. Pastor

CHAPTER TWENTY-FIVE

Mike's lesson came entirely from the Bible, not a story about something that happened to his family during the week or a vacation they'd taken.

I stayed to meet him after the service. He was humble, and not someone playing at being humble because that's what he was supposed to be. I looked forward to the next Sunday.

A few weeks after I began attending the church, Pastor Mike invited us to lunch. Dana and Majid came with Cameron, Michelle, and me. We spent the afternoon in pleasant conversation. Michelle and Cameron had told him about the house churches in Turkey because they'd asked if they could. I'd expected questions, but all Pastor Mike said was "Tell me about that, if you want to."

I didn't feel comfortable telling anyone about all the details, so I gave them an overview.

They wanted to help however they could. I had offered to sponsor several refugees from Turkey, and now the entire congregation wanted to become involved. They donated furniture, clothing, money, and even a car so that when the refugees arrived, they'd have what they needed to begin their lives.

Others offered to show them around the city, to take them to the grocery store and help with shopping. Those things and a myriad of others were essential to ordinary life in America. They were also things that the Refugee Center expected us to figure out on our own.

I was overwhelmed by their generosity. They didn't want to write articles or take credit for this. They just wanted to do what they could to welcome refugees to the area.

Michelle and Cameron both took the day off to bring me to Ann Arbor for my appointment. Dana and Majid had told me that the University of Michigan was the best place to go, but I wasn't expecting a different opinion than the one I'd already gotten. It was a chance at a solution, and I had to take it. Michelle and Cameron came into the office with me. I didn't want my limited English to keep me from understanding something important that the doctor said to me.

Dr. Bansal didn't stand across the room and look at me with suspicion. He knelt in front of me and took off my shoes so that he could better assess the numbness in my feet. He took his time to make sure he understood what I was feeling. When he was finished, he helped me put my shoes back on again.

After he got back to his feet, he scrolled through the information on his computer. "Give me a minute to take another look at your MRI." He left the room.

"That was completely different than seeing the doctor in Lansing," I said to Cameron and Michelle.

"How?" Michelle asked.

"The doctor in Lansing never even touched me. He just stood across the room and told me to take more pills or get another cortisone shot."

Dr Bansal came back a few minutes later.

"Anyone with a medical degree should be able to look at this MRI and know that you need surgery. Why didn't your doctor want to do it?" he asked.

"He said I'm too young."

He looked at me. "You tell him I'll do it because you're young. You can't waste years waiting. The office will call you to schedule the surgery."

In October of 2016, a little more than two years after the pain had disabled me, I had spinal fusion surgery scheduled. It was major surgery and there was a risk I could be paralyzed after. I had no other options. I spent the intervening weeks tangled in nervous anticipation and unstable hope. Some days crept by while others flew. The nights were the same.

I lay awake the night before the surgery. What would happen if the surgery went wrong and I were paralyzed? How would my life change? I'd already gone through so much, and I didn't think I could handle any more. Christianity talked about freedom, but I hadn't seen

CHAPTER TWENTY-FIVE

much of that freedom since my conversion. I'd be even more limited if I lost the use of my legs. There was no choice. It was either surgery or debilitating pain. I'd had enough pain. It was late when I fell into an uneasy sleep.

The next day Michelle and Cameron took me back to Ann Arbor. I felt hopeful. In Iran I had been told that I would need surgery in a few years. In Turkey, surgery had been recommended, but I had been too close to leaving for America. Now I was finally getting the treatment for the underlying problem and not just temporary pain relief. On the way there we talked and laughed. While we were waiting in the hospital, we passed the time the same way until it was nearly time for me to be taken into the operating room. Then they took my hands and we prayed together. Ten minutes before I was scheduled to go into surgery, I was moved to a space just across from one of the operating rooms. I saw Dr. Bansal come out of the operating room, take off his mask, and rub his eyes. His shoulders slumped as he walked past me without saying a word.

"Something's wrong," I said.

Michelle and Cameron did their best to assure me that everything was fine, but I could tell from the way they were looking at each other that they didn't believe that any more than I did.

A few minutes later, Dr. Bansal's assistant came in. "I'm sorry, but Dr. Bansal isn't able to do your surgery today. We'll call you to reschedule."

I had waited so long to find someone who would help me. Now, I'd have to wait even longer. The ride home passed in silence.

"It's a good thing that Dr. Bansal was brave enough to say he couldn't do it today," Cameron said.

I agreed, but as the miles rolled past, I became increasingly sure that the whole thing was a lie. No one wanted to help me. No one could help me. They just wanted to play with me. To give me hope and then snatch it away.

The surgery was rescheduled for November, but I didn't believe that it was going to happen. It was just another lie, just another false hope. I wanted to go back to Turkey. I had prospects there. Baris would help me with that. I would also be closer to the people I cared about. I could use my skills and build a successful business. What did I have here? Disability and loss? Why would I want to stay? The way I saw it, God had taken away my chance at a normal life. I couldn't go back to church. It would have been a lie to stand there and worship with those people.

Cameron and Michelle spent hours with me every day leading up to the second appointment. They tried to convince me to stay. "What are you going to do when you get there?" they'd ask. "You'll still need surgery. You'll need help before and after, and then there's the trip to get there." I still didn't think the surgery was going to happen, but I knew they were right about the rest.

"This isn't going to happen today either," I said to Cameron on the way there.

"Last time was a fluke. You'll see." He at least sounded confident.

I shook my head. "You watch, just before I'm supposed to go in, something will change again."

I know they didn't believe me. I went through the now familiar routine of getting checked in and changed and was waiting when Doctor Bansal came in.

"I want to give you a chance to consider your options. We could do the fusion, or we could do surgery to remove the part of the disc that's causing you pain."

"Which one would you recommend?" I asked.

"Today, I think removing the disc is the best option. Think about it and I'll come back in a little bit." He walked out of the room. It didn't sound like a choice to me.

Cameron and Michelle watched the doctor leave and then turned to me.

"I don't think he wants to do the fusion," I said.

"He said the choice was yours," Cameron said.

"Let's see. I'll do whatever he recommends because I trust him, but I'm going to tell him I want the fusion. We'll see if he wants to do it."

CHAPTER TWENTY-FIVE

"Okay, you were right about something happening, but let's not push it," Michelle said.

"I'm just going to see if he's really giving me a choice," I said.

Ten minutes later, the doctor came back in. I told him I wanted the fusion.

"I don't want to do that," he said, although he didn't share his reasons.

I looked knowingly at Michelle and Cameron and told the doctor to do the other surgery.

Chapter Twenty-Six

THAT OPERATION CHANGED my life. The pain that had been my constant companion for years steadily faded and then disappeared. By the end of December, I didn't need medication. I could walk for hours, but I still had little confidence on the Michigan ice.

My writing class had been frozen, and I'd been allowed to drop the other without penalty. I worked on finishing my classwork while I waited and recovered.

When the new semester started, I was able to walk without pain and I had people around me who cared about me. Those years of disability and medication had isolated me. I went back ready to focus on school, but I was also able to see how much my instructors cared. They took me seriously and listened to what I had to say. They fostered my love of writing and were always trying to help me improve by making time for me. They didn't tell me they were too busy, or that sitting with a student who was still struggling with English was not their job.

With my new clarity, I understood that they had always treated me as though I was important. They were interested in my goals and dreams and wanted to help me reach them. They wanted me to be who I was and helped me to heal my wounded dignity so that I could. I had expected that they would teach me English, but I never expected that they would teach me the meaning of love.

I began to work with one of my instructors on a project to tell the stories of people who were homeless in the Lansing area. My

CHAPTER TWENTY-SIX

professor, Martina, several other students, and I went to the Volunteers of America shelter to listen to the people who were staying there.

When we first arrived, I thought that the shelter was part of a good plan to assist people who needed it. In Iran there were no shelters. There is no one to help people who have lost everything. I thought that here, they were given a way to start again. I was wrong. Yes, people had a place to sleep for a short time, but the issues that led to their being homeless in the first place were never addressed. It was no more than a holding pen, a hopeless place.

I'd been told that the person I had come to see wasn't there, but I went up to the second floor anyway. This was no home. It wasn't even a comfortable place to stay. Men made old by their hardship, trauma, and loss sat around on furniture that belonged in an office. Military insignia was everywhere on the walls. Most of the men wore camouflage jackets. It was a room full of veterans. How could that be? They'd served their country. How could they end up homeless, forgotten by everyone?

The next time I went, I brought extra coffee. A small knot of men was standing by the door in the cold February air. I noticed one of the younger men in a desert camouflage jacket and a knit hat sitting on the curb. I handed out most of the coffee and then offered him the last cup.

"Did you serve?" I asked.

"Yeah," he said and then hesitated a moment. He looked at me warily, but he took the coffee. "I was in Iraq."

"Which city?" I asked.

He turned his head as he looked at me. "You know Iraq?"

I nodded and sat next to him. "I've been to a few places. Where were you stationed?"

There was a US base just outside Sulaymaniyah. As we talked, I remembered the American service members I had seen in my visits to Iraq. I remembered the pride I saw in their eyes and in the way they held their shoulders. Every day they faced danger, but they did it in the service of their country. I couldn't reconcile that memory with the

BECOMING JOSHUA

hollow man who sat on the cold pavement beside me.

He began by telling me about his platoon and their comradeship. He talked about the places they'd been and some of the good times they'd shared together. We were both smiling at his stories, but then other memories bit and his smile faded. He looked away. His head twitched as if he were hearing something I could not.

"There was a bomb," he said. "On the side of the road."

The story was etched on fragments of shrapnel buried in his head and his heart. There were times when he became overwhelmed and fell silent. All the while his eyes focused on a place long ago and far away. His past was still incised by those terrible memories, bloodied and raw.

He'd turned to alcohol to soften the sharp edges. The people who'd known him before said that he wasn't the same, but he didn't think he could ever be the man they had known. That had driven him further into the bottle, further away from friends, family and society. Little by little, everything slipped away, leaving him with nothing but the unyielding judgments of others and a hopelessness in place of departed pride.

This man's life, his potential, was being wasted. I looked around and realized he wasn't the only one. All these men who spent their days here, none had the prospect of moving on.

"Aren't you entitled to help from the government?" I asked.

He shrugged. "Little bit of money, maybe. What good's that going to do me? The government used me for what they could get, and when I was too damaged to be useful, they threw me away. Besides," he said and got to his feet, "I'm lucky."

I stood too. "Lucky?"

He nodded. "I'm young. Maybe something will change. For a lot of the guys here, their time's up. They're just waiting for the end."

I had listened to so many people who had lost everything, so many who thought that they had nothing to offer. None of that had prepared me for his certainty. I left the shelter upset. I spent hours talking to Martina, trying to understand how this could happen. There

CHAPTER TWENTY-SIX

was nothing she could say to reassure me. But that gave me a renewed passion for the project and the people we were meeting.

———⦻———

That semester I began to live again. The confidence I'd lost when disability ruled my life came back with the help of Cameron and Michelle. I'd spent many happy hours having lunch, having dinner, or drinking coffee with them. They had always ordered for me. Now, because of their encouragement, I was beginning to speak for myself in those situations.

I was still healing, but the pain was gone. Every action was not a series of carefully planned and executed movements. I could go out shopping or stand and cook a meal. I could walk to class or visit the men at the shelter, all without thinking about anything other than the task at hand. Everything was beginning to feel wonderfully ordinary.

One evening I was cooking chicken and rice when I heard the ping of an arriving email. In between stirring my dinner, I glanced over at my laptop.

"Forgive and forget us" was the title of the email. It was from Sahar's sister, Zohre. The spoon slipped and stopped as I stared at the words. An anxious chill chased over my skin. Forget? How could I forget how Sahar looked that night in the garden? The way I'd watched her smiling all evening as we celebrated others and the way her eyes had shone in the starlight as we made our promise. How could I forget even one moment of that night or the years that followed? The scent of burning rice drew me out of the past. I moved the pan off the burner and turned the stove off.

I looked back at the screen again. The message was still there, still taunting me. I couldn't open it. I didn't know if I even wanted to open it. I needed time to think. I went outside and walked through the small park next to my apartment.

I didn't have to open the email. I could just delete it. Put the whole thing out of my mind and go on as if it had been lost somewhere in

BECOMING JOSHUA

the electronic ether. Nothing could change what had happened. I should just forget the message had ever arrived. This didn't need to displace the normalcy that I'd been enjoying.

Why would she email after all this time anyway? One terrible possibility kept tickling at the back of my unsettled mind. What if something had happened to Sahar?

When I returned home, the terrible possibilities began to grow and multiply in my mind. They pushed everything else out and made it impossible for me to focus. I gave up and opened my email. Staring at the title of the message again made a thousand terrible images flash before my eyes. My heart pounded as I clicked on the message.

I hope this email gives you peace and calms your mind.

I know you are a faithful man, and forgiveness is part of what you believe. So, I hope after reading my email you can forgive me and my family for what we did to you and your life. We knew how much you and my sister loved each other, but we didn't want you to marry because you are a Christian. No one in the family could face losing Sahar, and that's what would have happened if you and she had married.

But how could we stop the wedding? Sahar was living with you nearly as much as she was living with us. She made no secret of the fact that she wanted to be with you, and the family insisting that this was wrong for her had no effect. My sister was torn between the man she loved and her family. We put her under constant pressure and convinced her that this marriage would destroy our family. We were afraid our old mother and father probably could not have tolerated the pain of losing her. We made it clear that if something would have happened to them, Sahar would have been responsible, and then no one could have forgiven her. We knew she couldn't stand the idea of being made into an outcast.

It was hard for us to make this decision, but we thought the only way to keep you away from our family and Sahar was to force you to leave the country. We knew the power of your love, but we also knew the power of distance. So, we decided to call the police and explain to them who you were and what you were doing exactly.

CHAPTER TWENTY-SIX

Sahar gave all the information to the police. She told them where your house was and that there were Bibles stored there. We knew you weren't at home because she had contact with you. We didn't want you to go to jail; we just wanted you to disappear from our lives forever. We knew you would not be able to come back to Iran, so it was the best way to keep you far away from our family and my sister.

She was supposed to talk to you for a while and then make some excuse to break up with you. After you left, she couldn't stop blaming herself. She wanted to leave Iran to join you. But you were a refugee and homeless; you couldn't even take care of yourself. She couldn't leave you alone in such a difficult situation, so she decided to Skype with you and keep your hopes up. She didn't want you to feel like you had lost everything all at once.

I knew it was wrong, but I hope you understand the situation. She used many medications to calm herself, but she lost control. We couldn't bear to see how she tortured herself every day; she really wanted to come and be your wife. After you went to the US and you told her you had been threatened, it seemed like the perfect time to make her end the relationship with you forever. Every day she cried because she couldn't do that.

To commit suicide, she overdosed on her medications, but we saved her. Finally, we admitted her into the psychiatric hospital. She was there for two months. During that time, she didn't have access to the internet or phone. We helped her to forget you. Now she is better and has someone in her life.

Please forgive and forget us.

I was shaking as I read the words. Sahar's tears were never far from my mind. I read it several times, searching for the phrase that would tell me something terrible had happened to her. Finally, I began to understand the betrayal, the worry, the hope, and the despair.

I recalled the night before I left for Turkey. All the uncertainty spun around me again, and her voice came back to me. *I'll join you in Turkey in a few months. We can get married there and start our lives with all of this behind us.*

I thought it had been God's journey, but it wasn't. God may have been there, but my traveling had begun with the deception of people.

Forgive and forget? No. I read the words again and felt the guilt I had been holding since that final argument slid away. I had been released. The rest—Sahar, Zohre, Yalda, all the lies from so many directions—I wouldn't forget, but I would close the chapter and move on.

The email went into the archives.

Even though I had stopped going to church, I still read the Bible. It was one such evening when that powerfully quiet voice came to me again and said, *It's time to call him Dad.*

After the last argument with my family, I swore I would never again call anyone "father." As close as Baris and I had been, I hadn't considered referring to him that way. Something about Cameron was different. The voice that had guided me in the right direction for so long had given permission. This was the right time.

The next time I saw Cameron and Michelle, we were at a minor league baseball game.

"I'm going to go get some hot dogs," Cameron said. "You can't watch baseball without a hot dog. It's tradition." He got up, leaving Michelle and me.

The stands around us erupted into a cheer for something that happened on the field, but I wasn't following the game well enough to know what it was.

"I was wondering if it would be alright if I called the two of you Dad and Mom," I said to her. In all the time I'd known them, I hadn't referred to them in any way. Even though they had both introduced themselves by their first names, using them had always seemed disrespectful.

Michelle smiled. "Well, it's about time you called us something."

We could see Cameron coming back with hot dogs and drinks. "Will you let me tell him?" I asked.

CHAPTER TWENTY-SIX

"Sure."

Another cheer went up as Cameron made his way down the row toward us. He was the right person, but this wasn't the right time.

A few days later I went to Cameron's office with coffee. We sat down and talked a little about the baseball game.

We were halfway through our coffee when the conversation quieted. I looked at him. "You know that I don't call anyone Dad and haven't for a long time."

"Yes," he said.

"I want to call you Dad."

"If you'll let me call you my son," he replied without pause. Tears filled his eyes and he hugged me.

A few days later we went out to an early dinner. It was a beautiful August evening with fluffy white clouds drifting through the bright blue sky with a practiced indolence. We walked through the park next to my apartment, following the winding concrete path. At first, we were silent, just enjoying the perfect evening and each other's company.

"We think of you as our son. You think of us as Dad and Mom. How would you feel about legally being our son?" Mom asked.

I hadn't thought about it, but the idea came from God, and I knew it was good. "I'd like that. What do we have to do?"

"I've been looking into it," Mom said. "We'll have to find a lawyer and go through the courts, but since you're an adult, it should be a fairly straightforward process. From what I read, it should take anywhere from a few months to close to a year, depending on how quickly we can get onto the judge's calendar."

"Find the lawyer," I said.

BECOMING JOSHUA

Things moved quickly from that point on. I began to get to know their son, their daughter, Mom's parents, and Dad's mom. They welcomed me into their homes for meals and celebrations and into their family with a generous spirit.

Mom and Dad had found a lawyer to handle the legal part of the process. She hadn't handled the adoption of an adult before, and I think she was a little amused by the idea at first. But amusement was no bar to things. She got the paperwork started.

My new family and I were walking through the same park after lunch on one of those rare fall days when the air is warm, and the bright sunshine sparkled in the yellows and golds in the trees.

"The adoption is going to be official in a few months. Did you want to choose a new name?" Mom asked.

I thought for a minute. "Judas," I said.

Mom and Dad stopped and looked at me.

"That's not a name that's usually given to people," Mom said. "Why do you want it?"

"Judas betrayed Jesus because he had to. I probably betray Jesus ten times a day without thinking about it."

They looked at each other. I could see they were trying to find something to say.

"But the parents always name the child, so you choose," I said.

They began to walk with me again. "Is there any other name from the Bible that you especially like?"

I shook my head. "I believe you'll choose the right name."

"Let us think about it for a bit. We'll find something that fits your character," Dad said.

They called me up, weeks later, and told me they had found a name. We met for dinner on the MSU campus. The dining area at Brody Hall was crowded with students eating together and studying

CHAPTER TWENTY-SIX

alone. We split up and chose different meals and then found a table together. The reason we were there was more important than the food. They placed a small gift bag on the table. Inside was a scroll in soft, sunset colors. The name they chose and its meaning printed on it.

"Why did you choose it?" I asked after I had read the scroll.

"Because you converted so many people," Mom said.

"Is it a name you'd want?" Dad asked.

I nodded, my eyes still drinking in the letters. It all made sense. "Yes, it is."

We began to use the name and variants of it immediately, trying to see which one fit best.

A few weeks after they gave me my new name, Mom and Dad were in my living room after lunch.

"I know you don't want to go to church, and that's fine, but why not start a house church?" Dad said.

A house church? Here? Why would a place where there were different churches on every corner need a house church? The more I thought about it though, the more sense it made. I knew from bitter experience how those buildings were only filled when the pastor was putting on his show. People sat and watched without any real involvement in what was going on during the service. It was impersonal and had little to do with the real message. Maybe a house church made sense. Maybe it's just what Christianity in America needed.

"I'll do it," I said to him. "But I'll only be the host. You'll be the one who gives the lesson to start with."

I began a group text and included anyone who might be interested. At our first meeting there were six people, and not all of them Christian. Everyone stood in my living room, unsure of what to expect or what they were supposed to do.

"Please, everyone, sit," I said, waiting for them to make themselves comfortable. Then I made a short announcement about the way the day would go: a few minutes of music, then the lesson and discussion to follow, and finally lunch.

It took a few weeks for everyone to become comfortable, but they kept coming back. We grew closer as a group, and more people joined. They began to look to Dad for answers when they were struggling. It was beautiful to see that group of relative strangers turn toward each other and grow together. Through their discussions and the questions they asked, I could see they were thinking deeply about the lesson and how to bring it into their lives. It was the beginning of a community. It didn't matter if they called themselves Christian or not.

In the spring semester of 2018, I began my first job in America. I had been hired by the college as a Supplemental Instruction Leader. I wasn't even sure what that was at first, but it meant that even though I was still a student myself, I would be allowed to help other people who are just beginning to learn English.

The instructors who had helped me so much now trusted me to assist their students. Sitting in on those classes gave me greater perspective this time and made me a more confident writer. Instead of only receiving the kindness of my instructors, I passed that kindness along to the students who trusted me enough to ask for my help. I had become a part of the fabric of the place that had helped me to heal.

On a sunny Friday a couple of weeks after I began my new job, Majid, Mom, Dad, and the extended family that had welcomed me so warmly met me at the courthouse to make my adoption official.

"There's our grandson," Grandma said when I walked in. It was the first time they'd referred to me that way. We posed for photos, laughed, and enjoyed each other's company in the few minutes we

CHAPTER TWENTY-SIX

had to wait for our turn in court. The judge had never presided over the adoption of an adult before. The lawyer told us to expect questions, but there were none.

With an official declaration, he made me Michelle and Cameron's son.

On February 2, 2018, thirteen years to the day after my baptism in Iran, I became Joshua and another new chapter began.

CPSIA information can be obtained
at www.ICGtesting.com
Printed in the USA
JSHW060847280722
28481JS00002B/8